GURU

GURU

A LONG WALK TO SUCCESS

AN AUTOBIOGRAPHY

Narendra Raval with Kailash Mota

BLOOMSBURY
NEW DELHI • LONDON • OXFORD • NEW YORK • SYDNEY

BLOOMSBURY INDIA
Bloomsbury Publishing India Pvt. Ltd
Second Floor, LSC Building No. 4, DDA Complex, Pocket C – 6 & 7,
Vasant Kunj, New Delhi 110070

BLOOMSBURY, BLOOMSBURY INDIA and the Diana logo are trademarks of
Bloomsbury Publishing Plc

First published in India 2018
This edition published 2018

ISBN: HB: 978-9-3871-4687-7; eBook: 978-9-3871-4688-4

2 4 6 8 10 9 7 5 3 1

Typeset by Manipal Digital
Printed and bound in India by Thomson Press India Ltd.

My soulmate, best friend and wife, Neeta,
for sharing my life and supporting me in each of my endeavours

Our children, Devang, Tulsi and Devrath, and our
daughter-in-law, Prakurti, for bringing sunshine in
our lives and joy to our souls

Our two lovely little grandchildren, Aaryan and Ananya,
for making my world a softer, kinder and warmer place to live in

All the people of Kenya
for making me the person that I am today

Narendra Raval's (Guru's) share of proceeds from this book will be utilized for charitable, medical and educational purposes for the needy children in Africa.

CONTENTS

Prologue: Dreams Come True xiii

Part I: My Early Years (1961–1978)

1. The Beginning 3
2. Happy Days Are Here 16
3. Generosity and Philanthropy: First Lessons Learnt 22
4. Surendranagar: First Taste of an Outside World 25
5. Necessity is the Mother of Invention: My Business Instincts 33
6. The First Turning Point: Bhuj 39

Part II: Priesthood (1978–1981)

7. Karibu Kenya 63
8. A Priest's Life: Challenges and Victories 67
9. Love for Family 83
10. Bolt from the Blue 88

Part III: A New Beginning (1981–1985)

11. Back to Kenya 97
12. Kisumu: Family Love and Affection 101
13. Guru: A Priest and An Astrologer 105
14. A Date with Destiny: Meeting President Daniel Arap Moi 112
15. Practise What You Preach 116
16. Saint to Steel: The Journey Begins 119
17. My First UK Visit: Experience of A Life Time 124
18. Status Regularised and Back to Square One 130

19. Steel and Hardware Business: A Solid Foundation 135
20. Love and Marriage 144

Part IV: The Birth and Rise of My Business Empire (1986–Present)

21. My First Step: Steel Centre Limited 157
22. An Accounting Nightmare 169
23. This Telephone Rings 173
24. My Astral Travel: A Spiritual Experience 176
25. Birth of Devki Steel Mills Limited 179
26. A Landmark: Trader to Manufacturer 187
27. There is no Religion Greater than Truth 192
28. Expansion and Growth of Devki Steel Mills Limited 195
29. Testing Times: The Furnace Blast Episode 208
30. Success and Jealousy 214
31. Our First Major Diversification: Maisha Mabati Mills Limited 218
32. The Biggest Milestone: National Cement Company Limited 224
33. Other Business Ventures 233
34. Flying High: A Dream Comes True 238
35. Business, Politics and Astrology 243
36. Our Contributions to the Kenyan Economy 248
37. My Business Vision: The Way Forward 253

Part V: Charity And Philanthropy

38. Giving Back to Society 261
39. Corporate Social Responsibility 265
40. Bhuj Earthquake 274
41. Awards And Accolades 278

Part VI: Family

42. My Family 287
43. Guru is God's Blessing to Me 290
44. Next to God, Thy Parents 296

Conclusion

My Legacy 303

सत्यमेव जयते

प्रधान मंत्री

Prime Minister

MESSAGE

I am delighted to know that a book is being published on the life journey of Shri Narendra Raval.

I have known Shri Narendra Raval for years. His life journey is very interesting and deeply inspiring. He devoted himself to spiritual pursuits and then distinguished himself as an entrepreneur. Shri Narendra Raval is at the peak of success yet retains his humility that has endeared him to a cross section of society.

Shri Narendra Raval has done commendable work in brining India and Kenya closer. He is a successful Kenyan and someone who is proud of his Indian roots.

A book on the life of Shri Narendra Raval will teach the younger generation about the power of hardwork and determination. Fascinating nuggets from his life will make the book a pleasant read.

Congratulations for the effort to chronicle the life of Shri Narendra Raval.

(Narendra Modi)

New Delhi
25 September, 2017

FOREWORD BY PRESIDENT UHURU KENYATTA

I am delighted to dedicate this message to the memoirs of Shri Narendra Raval "Guru". All those who know Shri Narendra have long looked forward to the day when he would finally publish his memoirs. Few of us have lived as interesting or examples in our lives.

Throughout the time I have known him — as a friend, as an entrepreneur, as a proud Kenyan — I have thought that his story ought to be set down, both to remind the younger generation of Kenyans what life was like, and to inspire them to follow the example Shri Narendra has set.

I am delighted that Shri Narendra has finally shared his story with the world. To read it is to learn the power of persistence. To read it is to see how effectively a man can unite success in business with service to his community. The final crucial lesson we can learn, I believe, is the ease with which Shri Narendra combined respect for his roots in India with devotion and patriotism to Kenya.

May his example inspire his readers, and may he continue to serve and to prosper.

UHURU KENYATTA, C.G.H.,
PRESIDENT OF THE REPUBLIC OF KENYA

THE LORD LOOMBA OF MOOR PARK, CBE

HOUSE OF LORDS, LONDON SW1A 0PW
Mobile: 077 4030 5362, Email: raj@loomba.com

FOREWORD

*It has been my pleasure to have been associated with Narendra Raval, "**Guru**", for the more than a decade now. When we first met in London many years ago, I was amazed at his simplicity, straightforwardness and down to earth attitude despite being the kingpin of the East African steel, cement and infrastructure industry. What amazed me most was his journey from a priest in the Swaminarayan temple in Bhuj India to a business tycoon in Africa, with a net-worth of more than US$ 450 Million. I was moved by his struggle and inspired by his devotion, dedication, vision, foresight, hard-work and his "**Never Give Up**" attitude towards life, which is why he is at the peak of the African business and industry.*

*More than a 'man of steel', **Guru** is a man with a golden heart and a great philanthropist in the truest sense. Apart from the families of his 4,000 plus work-force who directly depend on him for their livelihood, there are millions of Kenyan families, who have largely benefitted by his generous contributions to the society. His Corporate Social Responsibility (CSR) programmes of promoting education by setting up schools in remote places like Mukatana, Emali and Ruiru is highly commendable. What touches my heart is his selfless support to the society through the orphanage he financially assists in Athi River near Nairobi, where more than 70-75 orphans are taken care of. My association with **Guru** the "Philantrophist" began through **The Loomba Foundation,** for which I am Founder and Chairman Trustee. The foundation was primarily founded to support the widows in India, whose lives are affected after the death of the husband to the extent that they are often ostracised from their societies. Gradually, we have spread the wings of our foundation across Europe and Africa. When I explained the concept of our foundation, **Guru** immediately expressed his interest in supporting widows in Kenya and agreed to become the Trustee of the Loomba Foundation for Kenya. With his vision and efforts, he has supported widows in rural places in Kenya by assisting them financially to set up small businesses, supplying them with equipment so that they can be self-reliant and in some cases provided employment. Recognising his altruistic services to widows, **Guru** was presented with an award at 10, Downing Street, in London, on 23rd June, 2012, felicitated by the then Deputy Prime Minister, The Rt Hon Nick Clegg MP.*

Flanked by British Deputy Prime Minister Rt. Hon. Nick Clegg MP and The Lord Raj Loomba CBE "Guru" is receiving an award in recognition of his support for widows in Kenya at No. 10 Downing Street in London on 23rd June, 2012

*Recently, when **Guru** met me in London, he shared his thoughts about publishing his autobiography, so that he could show to the world that, nothing is impossible in this world with a willing heart and determined mind. I endorse his views and agree that, if **Guru** who served as a priest in a temple at the age of 16 -17 years, can carve a niche for himself in Africa and be ranked as 41st richest person in Africa, by The Forbes Magazine for the year 2015, then anybody out there can succeed through sheer hard-work, dedication, vision and rising up to all the challenges life throws. I am confident that this autobiography will inspire you to succeed in life.*

*My Best Wishes to **Guru** on publishing his autobiography and also all his future endeavours.*

The Lord Loomba CBE
House of Lords
London, SW1A OPW

31st March, 2017

PROLOGUE
DREAMS COME TRUE

Yes, dreams do come true. I have seen dreams becoming a reality in my life...

I have always dreamt big, no matter what the circumstance. Even the toughest of times at the boarding school in Surendranagar, Gujarat, could not keep me from my day dreams. There was one particular dream that I had seen at Surendranagar with my eyes open, however, which I went on to fulfil many years later. It had to do with riding a helicopter.

It so happened that the then Prime Minister of India, Smt. Indira Gandhi, had visited Surendranagar on one of her election campaigns. She had addressed an enormous public gathering at a prominent ground, and being an orator par excellence, thousands had flocked to listen to her. I was one among the many. I was accompanied by my grandfather. They said Indira Gandhi was to arrive in a helicopter, and I had never seen one in my life! As the crowd cheered wildly on her arrival by a helicopter, all I could see was the aircraft.

That was the day I started dreaming of riding a helicopter someday. It was the dream of an impoverished twelve-year-old, without proper clothes on his back or shoes on his feet, studying at a charitable boarding school on a free scholarship. Today, I own an aviation company; I have my own commercial pilot's licence; and most importantly, I have my own helicopter!

In 2014, after we received our first commercial helicopter, I decided to take my 'dream' ride with children just like myself – albeit, forty-four years ago. In Athi River, Kenya, our business group runs an orphanage, where more than seventy children are sheltered and cared for. They were among the first to accompany me on my maiden helicopter ride. Turn by turn, I ensured that all the children got an opportunity to ride up into the clouds with me for I could see myself among them.

I remember blinking back tears of joy. My heart could hardly hold all my happiness that day...

There was another desire of mine that I had the good fortune to realise in my lifetime. This one had to do with the innumerable days of hunger and privation I had to go through in my childhood, which gave birth to my desire to feed hungry children when I gained that ability later in life.

During my boarding school days in Gujarat, we had to take turns in carrying heavy sacks of flour on the way back from school for the day's meals. This was the toughest of all our routines, because we had to walk bare feet for 6 km on each side of the journey, saddled with a 7 kg weight on an empty belly. At three in the afternoon under a glaring sun, returning with the sacks from the flour mill was a pitiful task for young children. The hunger would often drive me wild, and I would grab handfuls of the flour and gobble it up.

Today, I am one of the trustees of the ISKCON foundation in Kenya. The 'Food for Life' programme is one of the most important activities of this foundation, undertaken across sixty countries. Through this programme, children are given free mid-day meals. I often participate in serving the children personally, and I invariably become overwhelmed with emotions, recognising myself among the young children, eagerly waiting for their turn to be served!

Today, at the pinnacle of my career, I am constantly quizzed about my life and my business achievements.

How could an ordinary priest become a successful industrialist?

How do you manage your business empire of more than US$ 400 million?

How do you control your workforce of over 4,000?

How did you feature among Forbes Top 50 richest in Africa?

What is the secret of your success?

It was when I met Kailash Mota that he suggested I pen down my autobiography. He convinced me that this would be the best way to answer all the questions I am constantly asked about the trials and successes I have faced in life. He willingly agreed to pen down my journey.

Through this book, I would like to inspire youth around the world, who aspire to see their dreams turning into reality. Just as I have seen them happening. To them I say:

Dare to dream with your eyes open,

Put all the sweat, hard work and determination to achieve them,

Have the courage to face all adversities,

Never give up on your dreams even if it means to stand alone,

Your dreams will come true.

Even if I manage to inspire a few to dream and succeed, I would consider my efforts rewarded.

Let me share my life's journey with you.

Narendra Raval

PART I

MY EARLY YEARS
1961-1978

• CHAPTER 1 •

THE BEGINNING

My life began from the tiny village of Mathak, at Halvad Taluka in the Surendranagar district of Gujarat, India. Mathak had a population of around 4,000 (which remains more or less the same to this day). While the nearest railway station of Halvad is about 25 km from our village, the major towns and cities of Morbi, Surendranagar and Rajkot are at a distance of about 60–90 km.

Back in those days, Mathak did not have any proper roads, electricity or even telephone connections. There were hardly any cars or private vehicles in our village and state-owned buses were our main mode of transport. Our village school was a small building with a couple of rooms. Farming, cattle rearing and trading in farm produce were the main sources of livelihood. Farmers were heavily dependent on the monsoons and the village landlords (zamindars). They were dependent on the latter for loans to buy fertilisers and equipment, and on the rains for a good crop. Both being uncertain, the village farmers lived most of their lives in debt. The traders too lived in similar circumstances, depending on neighbouring villages and towns for their business.

Some time ago, on a visit to one of our plants in Emali (near Nairobi in Kenya), we had to make an unscheduled stop at a small village, since our car had broken down. Sitting outside the garage, I felt nostalgic in that rural ambience as I recalled my village, Mathak, in faraway India. This village, too, had small hutments and houses, dusty and muddy roads, with no electricity or power. As the car was being fixed, I took a leisurely walk around the little hamlet. I saw hawkers vending their wares along the roadside, cattle ambling along the roads, a few small shops, people drawing water from a nearby well, children studying under a tree, while some youngsters loafed about. This seemingly idyllic picture spoke of lack of growth and development in the region, with illiteracy and under employment for its people. I could relate to this scenario and draw conclusions, because I had also begun my journey from a similar tiny village.

There are those who are born with a silver spoon and blessed with good fortune throughout their lives. Unfortunately, most of us, including myself, cannot boast of such privileged beginnings. I was born into a family of dire circumstances, where struggle was the order of the day. Enough food and decent clothing were luxuries and footwear was unthinkable! In those days, even the Gram Panchayat School (local village school) that I studied in, had facilities to teach up to grade 5 only. Recently, I managed to get a photograph of what used to be my primary school. It sent me reminiscing about my childhood.

My school as it stands today.

My school is now a place where cattle stay.

What I want to drive home with this book is that it isn't only the circumstances that make a man, but the strength of character with which we face and overcome these circumstances that shapes us. Swami Vivekananda had famously said, 'Every soul is potentially divine.' Our inherent strengths and hidden possibilities are endless, but it is up to us to realise our true potential within a lifetime.

My circumstances through life reflect Swami Vivekananda's beautiful words, and I quote, 'All the power is within you, you can do anything and everything, believe in that; don't believe that you are weak. Stand up and express that divinity within you.'

As I said earlier, not all of us get a level playing field. We are shaped into our unique selves by the manner in which we choose to use the resources we have. Remember that people may block your path with stones. What you choose to do with the stones is up to you. Whether you build bridges or a wall, the choice is your's. It is said that whenever life throws challenges at you, it also brings opportunities with it. I firmly believe that if we focus on the opportunities hidden within each challenge, it will always culminate in success. In the words of the famous American educator, Stephen Richard Covey, 'Success is when you realize obstacles you face are challenges to help you become better and your response equals the challenge.'

My first opportunities came parcelled with the initial challenges of life in a village and family disputes. I was born on 18 August 1961, in a Gujarati–Brahmin family. It is a tradition in most communities in India that the first child is always born at his mother's parental home, and accordingly, I was born in my mother's village, Bodka. It is yet another tiny village with a population close to that of Mathak, in Jodiya Tehsil of Jamnagar district in Gujarat. I stayed there for almost a year in my infancy, before arriving at Mathak.

At my father's home, we were all part of my Dadaji's (paternal grandfather) enormous joint family. My father, Rameshchandra Chunilal Raval, and my mother, Muktaben Rameschandra Raval, lovingly called me Batuk, as did other extended family and friends. Our family was soon joined by my younger brother, Bhavesh (who is now settled in Kisumu, Kenya) and my younger sister, Sangeeta (Sangeeta Sureshkumar Vyas, settled in Rajkot, Gujarat).

I was a particularly naughty and mischievous child, whose sole purpose in life was to pull pranks on family, friends, teachers, neighbours and just about anyone I came across! On a lighter note, I guess the beatings my father gave me as a child, must have outweighed the food that my mother provided! That was how troublesome a child I was.

My Dadaji, Chunilal Tribhuvan Raval, was a teacher. He headed the Mathak Taluka Panchayat School, the local village school that we all attended initially. Being a strict disciplinarian, he was respected by the entire village and was lovingly known as 'Masterji' (honourable teacher). After his retirement, he bought a shop and started to trade in local agriculture-commodities including cotton, groundnuts and wheat. My father automatically became part of my grandfather's business, as an integral male member of the family. We used to purchase the commodities directly from farmers of neighbouring villages before selling them in the wholesale markets of the bigger towns and cities near our village. Sometimes, farmers would also come to our shop to sell their produce. In those days, my grandfather was the second richest person in our village; and hence many farmers took small loans from him, often selling their crops to settle their dues. Dadaji owned two farms as well, whose crops were sold too.

The world over, Gujaratis are known for their business acumen and innovative money-making skills. True to the blood that ran in my veins, I, too, was born with innate business skills. From my childhood to this day, setting up my own business and making money have been my primary focus in life. I learnt my first lessons of business, trading and making profits from my grandfather. As part of his work, my father had to travel to neighbouring villages to source commodities. He used to meet farmers; bargain and negotiate with them; and buy the produce at a good price. After weighing it, he would transport the produce in bullock carts to our village to store them. At the right time, he would sell the produce in wholesale markets at higher prices and earn profits.

As a child, I was never keen on my studies in school. So right from an early age, I would sit at my grandfather's shop and observe him. I also accompanied my father on his village rounds and witnessed the sourcing of crops and the hard negotiations. I also watched them selling the produce in wholesale markets at higher prices to make huge profits.

Profit is what fascinated me, and I guess that was how the foundation of a future businessman was laid.

Our's was a large and traditional joint family with numerous cousins, aunts and uncles. They are always the best thing for children, with no dearth of playmates or adults to supervise them; but our happiness of staying together in a joint family and business was short lived. My Dadaji had three sons and eight daughters. Love and differences of opinion, often go hand in hand in all joint families, and especially in the businesses run by families. Dadaji and my father were different personalities with their own styles of conducting business. While my grandfather adopted a traditional business approach, my father had more liberal and humane ways of doing things, which sometimes resulted in loss, but that was his way. Differences of opinion were common among them. Since all of us lived under a common roof, these differences spilled over into our family life too. With each day's passing, tempers shot up, arguments increased and tensions mounted. This continued for more than a year and the writing was on the wall. Finally, in 1971, when I was barely ten years old, the inevitable happened.

One day it so happened that a particular mortgage case brought the two of them at complete loggerheads. Things went out of control and my grandfather ordered my father to leave the house immediately. It was late in the night, but my father did not hesitate for a moment. He asked my mother to bring along my brother, Bhavesh, and me (Sangeeta was yet to come). Amid a tearful farewell from all the women of the household, and with the entire village watching the high drama, we stepped out of Dadaji's house never to return. With that, not only had we said goodbye to the family, but also to the good life. We moved to a small house in the village with a bedroom, a living room, a kitchen and a veranda. I felt as if we had been stripped off of all our luxuries and stayed awake that entire night, unable to sleep. I remember that my brother and I were very upset about why we had to leave our home, and could not stop bawling and howling, as is the way with children. As a child, it had taken me a very long time to come to terms with what had happened to us overnight. Even today, painful memories of that fateful day are still fresh in my mind.

Our home in Mathak as it stands now (photographed in 2016).

Life gave us a nasty shock when we separated from our joint family. Though we had a separate home to live in, my father hardly had any resources or savings to make the ends meet. To add to our woes, it took nearly six months for the family to reach a settlement as to what my father was entitled to. Those six months were the longest and darkest of our lives and only God knows how we managed to tide them over. Even today, thinking about those days brings me great pain. This was my first experience of what it meant to struggle for survival. I hardly had two pair of dresses to wear and walked bare feet. Food was a luxury and we often went to bed hungry. I remember very well that at one point of time, all that my father could afford to buy as food for the family was karthi (a kind of bean). It was considered to be poor men's food, and hence cheap, but was healthy and would fill our bellies for longer. A kilogram of karthi lasted the family for almost three weeks; but even this, my father used to buy on credit from a couple of shopkeepers, who had known us all our lives. My mother used to cook a curry from the grain and we would gratefully wolf it down with bajrarotlas (flat bread made from pearl millet flour). Even today, whenever I eat karthi, I am reminded of those tough times and pray that no one goes through such an ordeal in their lives.

As a ten-year-old, it was difficult for me to come to terms with such a difficult life. I was both angry and frustrated at the state of affairs that we were in. While we were struggling to survive, my cousins, uncles and aunts had the best of everything that life could offer. The relationship between the families had simply come to a grinding halt. We were not even allowed to step into either of Dadaji's houses in Mathak or in Morbi. Though years later Bhavesh did stay at my grandfather's house in Morbi for his studies, I was entirely banned from his threshold, especially because I was a rebellious and 'disobedient' child who could not accept the injustice meted out to us. From the minute we were thrown out, unjust discrimination was all that we faced everywhere we went in the village.

As a practice, I used to go to my grandfather's farm every day. When I walked into the farm the day after my father left the big house, I could clearly see the change in the eyes of the farm workers. It was a reality check, when I realised that we were no longer welcome either at Dadaji's house or at his farm. My uncle, who was my age, also changed his attitude towards me. Similarly, my other uncle and aunts also changed their behaviour. All this made me hate the village. I lost my child-like joy and happiness all at once. One day I was a proud millionaire's grandchild and on the next, nobody wanted to know me. I think it made me stronger. I loved my parents dearly and couldn't bear to see their daily struggle. So much so that even at that tender age, I felt the need to work hard and help them change their lives for the better. I lost my childhood and my education. All I could focus on was how to earn money. On many days, I would bunk school and go off to sit by the village lake, contemplating our sudden fall from grace. I thought I understood that it was money that made all the difference in this world. I vowed to earn a lot of money in my life; and this thought was the first turning point in my life.

During this period, my grandfather persuaded me to work in his shop and take up all that my father used to do. Trusting my business skills, I was tempted to accept his offer. This would not only be of help to my family, but would also improve my business skills. However, my conscience told me to consult my father before taking any hasty decisions. On hearing Dadaji's offer, my father dragged me into the house before landing a sound slap across my face. 'Batuk, don't you realise why I quit my father's house and his business? If you start working at your grandfather's shop, do you realise that you will be nothing but a slave in that house? That by the time you turn twenty-five, you will be left good for nothing but to polish the shoes of your uncles?' He added in anguish, 'Always think of working for yourself and not for anyone else.' Even to this day, the sound of that slap reverberates in my ears and sends a chill down my spine; but more than the physical hurt, it was his words that left a lasting impression on my young mind. I am thankful for my father's wisdom today.

After six months of negotiation and deliberation, my grandfather agreed to pay INR 6,000 as final settlement of my father's claim to his inheritance for separating from his business and his family. Considering my grandfather's status and wealth, I felt that gross injustice had been done to our family; but I still remember that sigh of relief on my father's face. There was something that we could look forward to now. With this amount, my father started trading in spare parts for new as well as second-hand oil engines, which included bearings, grease, oil, nuts, bolts and machinery spares, etc. He set up his shop right next to Dadaji's. We used to source the spares from cities like Rajkot and Ahmedabad. Somehow, he managed to provide for his family now.

Present state of the shops from where my father used to run his business.
(The two shops in depleted condition were my father's shops;
the other two shops in good condition belonged to my grandather.)

Every circumstance in life teaches us something new. The time I spent with my father in his business also helped me a lot. He was not only intelligent, but also hard working, and by assisting him in his business, the foundation for my future was being laid. To illustrate how hard working he was, let me share an anecdote with you.

Among the many items, we used to deal in engine oil too, which would be delivered in oil tankers to the village. Since our village roads were too narrow for trucks to get to our shop, they used be parked near the edge of the village. Oil used to be filled in 200 litre barrels from the truck; and there would be at least fifty of them delivered at a time. Since we could not afford a shop assistant, my father used to single-handedly, push all those barrels with his hands and feet, all the way to our shop. He was never short of ideas and would never shy away from working hard. Working with him taught me many valuable lessons in life.

Life has been my school, and life's circumstances my teachers. I was never interested in studying in a real classroom. There are certain people in this world, who are not meant to excel academically, and, I guess, I was one of them! I had innate business skills. I was an animal lover and a mischievous lad too. always held firm beliefs, listened to my heart and could never stand injustice of any kind. An encyclopaedia may not do justice to all the colourful incident and experiences I've had as a child, but let me share the ones that I still remember.

My close friends and I used to skip classes most of the time and loaf about the village. Every day, I used to get a beating from my father for some mischief or the other. I loved riding bicycles. But we never could buy one, so I always used to borrow my friends' bikes. I was always on the lookout for a quick ride, so whenever anybody parked a bicycle without locking it, I would take it out for a good ride. More often than not, I used to get beaten up by the cycle owner, but the pleasure of the ride compensated for the beatings!

I have always trusted my instincts to guide me through life. Once it so happened that a self-styled 'god-man' (sadhu) had stationed himself at a temple in our village. Impressed by his religious discourses, the villagers began sending their children to attend his sermons, as did my father. This phoney saint taught youngsters morally incorrect lessons. He wanted to take me with him to Junagadh (another city in Gujarat). Oblivious of his ill intentions, my father pressurised me to go with the man and beat me up for refusing to do so. I stood my ground, however, and refused to go. In the end, when the villagers discovered the saint's true colours, they threw him out of the village. My father never brought up the subject with me again.

As an animal lover, I would be attracted to birds and animals of all kinds. Back in those days, mahouts would bring their elephants to our village. The elephants used to parade around the entire village, as householders offered them food and money. At the end of the day, the mahout would take his elephant to the village outskirts to rest for the night. I was fascinated by them and followed them wherever they went. Even at night, I would quietly sit by as the elephants rested. Whenever I would not return home at night, my father would ask for where the elephants were rested in the village. He knew where to find me. It goes without saying that the journey back home would never be easy and I could always expect a thrashing!

Despite being naughty, I could never tolerate injustice of any kind. In our school, children of an affluent community, the Darbars, also studied with us. They had superior airs and were extremely arrogant. Though they ill-treated and beat other students, nobody ever complained. I was indifferent to their arrogance, because as a Brahmin boy, the boys respected me. On one occasion, the boys beat up my uncle, who was of my age and studied in my village school. Furious at their audacity, I beat them up fair and square. When the complains reached my father's ears, I was given a beating of my life.

Meanwhile, our family finally had something to be thankful for, as my father slowly settled down in his business. However, complaints of my mischief-making and indifference towards my studies kept them anxious. Not a single day passed without any complaint. If there were any awards for mischief-making, I would probably have won a gold medal! Even my father was tired of beating me up every day. One day, I finally told my father that I was not interested in studying, but wanted to earn and support our family.

I remember my father put his hand around my shoulders and took me for a walk. He told me that this was my time to study in school and not to earn money. I tried to convince him that school was not my cup of tea, but he explained the role of education in life and I agreed to continue going to school. In hindsight, I guess, my life would have been very different had I attained a college education. However, our village school, Mathak Taluka Panchayat School, only had facilities to teach up to grade 5, and it was inevitable that I move to another town or village to continue my education. It was decided that I would go to my Nanaji's home (maternal grandfather) in Jodiya for further studies.

Life was about to change and throw a major challenge at me. At ten, I was to leave my family, friends and my village behind to pursue my education. I accepted the decision, knowing that the path ahead would be a tough one. After almost forty-five years, I know that it was this trial that brought out my inner strength and my hidden abilities to the fore, which I never knew existed.

• CHAPTER 2 •

HAPPY DAYS ARE HERE

As I looked out the window of my bus headed for Jodiya, I could see birds flying high in the blue skies. I realised that they reflected my sense of freedom and joy at having stepped out of my disturbed family nest. Disturbed with my every day mischief, disinterest in school and the constant barrage of complaints against me, my family had sent to me to Jodiya. They fondly hoped that I would turn into a new leaf under my Nanaji's guidance and supervision. On the contrary, I was to be pampered, and left to continue my mischievous ways; but more importantly, my inherent business skills would be honed at Jodiya. In short, I was in for a very good time here in contrast to the privations in Mathak.

Jodiya is a port town in Jamnagar, Gujarat, with a population of approximately 14,000. My Nanaji, Jivram Nabheram Pandya, was the Taluka Panchayat Pramukh or the head of the Taluka Council. He was one of the most influential persons in the village, with a towering personality and a government-provided Jeep – necessarily in that order! I moved into Nanaji's prosperous establishment. I now had the company of my cousin, Mahendra Pandya, who was my maternal uncle's son.

The mischief-making continued unabated. Mahendra, my cousin, is an extremely soft spoken, gentle and kind person. Inadvertently, he became the target of most of my jokes and pranks. It was difficult to keep count of the many times he had been at the receiving end because of my mischief. Every evening, it was my Nanaji's practice to relax on the charpay (a rusticstring bed) after work. A diligent Mahendra used to massage his feet, while I sat at a distance, out of Nanaji's sight, looking to play some prank. While Mahendra massaged Nanaji's feet, the latter relaxed with his eyes closed. Taking this opportunity, I would mimic our teachers in school, which made Mahendra burst out with uncontrollable laughter. This would rouse my grandfather from his peaceful slumber, and my cousin would be punished for no fault of his own! The naughty child that I was, I would watch it all secretly. My cousin usually expected a tip of five paisa from Nanaji, who always gave him INR 100 instead (which was a very high amount for those days)! Kind hearted that he was, Mahendra always treated me and his friends with snacks and goodies. More often than not, I used to snatch whatever money he had left with him after the treat, leaving a helpless Mahendra in tears. That is how naughty I was as a child!

In school time too, I was always up to some prank or the other. During the school lunch-break, I used to gather a few students around and showed them my famous thread trick. I used to insert a thread into my mouth, and as the children watched in wonder, I would remove it from my nose, leaving them awestruck! At the end of my show, I would ask each of the spectators to pay me for their entertainment, usually a harmless five to fifty paisa, but anybody who refused would have it from me! Naturally, the complaints started flowing in very soon to my Nanaji.

Mahendra is now settled in the UK and serves as a temple priest. We recently met over a cup of tea and fondly recalled all our old school memories. In his words, 'Batka [as he still lovingly calls me], I was always at the receiving end because of you!' Both of us broke into a laugh. Then he brought up a particularly 'colourful' incident around 'Holi' (major Indian spring festival of colours). It is a custom to light a bonfire (Holika) on the eve of Holi. In those days, neighbourhood children would often go door to door to collect donations to buy firewood and fuel for the deity's fire. On one such occasion, Mahendra and I had reached a shopkeeper's doorstep. I remember that he used to sell firewood and scrap, but he refused to help us. That made me very angry and I was determined to make him pay one way or the other.

On the night of the bonfire, Mahendra and I sneaked into the shopkeeper's scrap yard and broke into the closed shop. We stole all the stored firewood, oblivious of the consequences. The next morning, shocked to discover that his shop had been robbed, the shopkeeper lodged a police complaint. We were promptly caught and locked up in the local police station. I coaxed Mahendra to threaten the officer to let us go, because our grandfather was the head of the village council. Being young and innocent as he was, he shouted at the officer at the top of his voice, only to be beaten black and blue! Later, Nanaji had to visit the station to have us freed. Back at home, however, both of us got the thrashing of our lives and were sent to bed without any dinner, as punishment.

As I have shared earlier, studying was never my cup of tea. I constantly had money-making pranks on my mind. At the Jodiya port, ship and dhow owners regularly bought imported products to sell them in Jodiya. Though I did not have any money of my own, I convinced them to lend me the merchandise on credit. I then sold in the market to earn a little money. A naïve Mahendra was always a silent spectator. This went for a while, till noticing my business skills, a ship owner named Kader offered to take me along in his ship to Dubai. Even at that tender age, I was ready to travel with him, as long as I was able to earn some money! Word naturally reached my Nanaji's ears. He warned Kader to stay away from me and reserved a sound beating for me that night. After this incident, my Nanaji, too, got tired of my pranks and decided to shift me to my maternal uncles' home at Balamba.

Balambha was yet another tiny village in Gujarat, where my two Mamajis (maternal uncles) stayed and worked in a bank. Both Mahendra and I were sent to my Mamas, Ananteai Jivrambhai Pandya and Kantibhai Jivrambhai Pandya. They treated us like their own sons and I continued to be pampered here as well. They never beat me, but taught me discipline and trained me in household chores. I was happy to assist them in any domestic work that was given to me. To add to this, I had the company of rich schoolmates, who always treated me and I never had to shell out a single penny of my own! For the first time in my life, I wore shoes, especially rubber soled slippers. I still remember the brand 'Parag'. I was on cloud nine!

At Balambha also, my pranks and my endless innovative ways of making money continued. The same story continued at my new school as well. I remember that whenever we had a lady teacher with long braids in class, I would wait for her to turn around and write on the board, while I tied up her plait to the back of her chair. The whole class would break out in laughter as I sat back to watch the fun. In the end, I would either get beaten up or sent out of class. Once out of the class, I used to climb up the school terrace and pelt stones at students, teachers and all who passed below. I used to pick up fights with other students and complaints from everyone would often land on my Mamas' desks. Poor Mahendra was a soft target and would often be beaten up by students bullied by me! In hindsight, I regret having put Mahendra through all that trouble, but I was simply an uncontrollable little menace in those days!

I always found creative ways of making money. In Balamba, there was a public garden, frequented by young courting couples. Being a small community, everyone knew everyone else; and the park was one of the few places the 'love birds' could meet in secret, away from prying eyes. In the evenings, I would hide in the park and blackmail the poor couples if they did not pay me! Surprisingly, most of them parted with their money very easily. Of course, I also got licked a couple of times; but to put it in business parlance, that was a calculated risk!

I was crazy about many luxurious things, and riding in a car was one of them. Cars were scarce in rural and small towns in Gujarat of those days. Once in a while, we could watch cars pass by our villages, which would fascinate us. My Nanaji had a government Jeep, as the Village Pramukh, and I always looked for an opportunity to take a ride in it. Let me share a hilarious incident in this connection.

There was a grand religious festival in Balamba, where people from nearby villages had gathered too. The fête was being held along the banks of the village river. When Mahendra told me that Nanaji had also come to attend the event in his Jeep, I couldn't control my urge to sit in it. The car was parked on the other side of the river; and even though I wasn't a very good swimmer, I plunged into the river without thinking of the consequence! When I started drowning, I began to cry for help, till somebody jumped in to save me. It goes without saying that I was taken to task by Nanaji that night!

I also had innate qualities of courage and straightforwardness and never feared anyone or any circumstance. We had a water tank outside our village, with a huge storage capacity. Drinking water was stored here and supplied to the entire village. There were more than 200-odd steps to the top of the tank. Once it so happened that a stray dog managed to climb the tank, fell into it and died in the tank. As usual, we are loafing about the village when we came to know about the incident. I rushed to the tank with the other boys, but nobody dared to climb up there. I couldn't stand it any longer and climbed up to the tank to bring down the carcass myself. Then I confronted the Village Panchayat Officials and made an issue of the poisoned water being supplied to the town without any inspection! I must have been around twelve or thirteen years old then!

Like all good things come to an end, my two years of fun and games in Jodiya and Balamba came to an end sooner than expected. Both my Mamas' bank jobs were transferable and they asked Nanaji to shift Mahendra and I back to Jodiya. Moreover, they too had become tired of my behaviour and regular complaints. So my Nanaji, my father and my mamas decided that it was high time I should be tamed. They decided to send me back to Mathak first, before admitting me into a boarding school in Surendranagar.

• CHAPTER 3 •

GENEROSITY AND PHILANTHROPY: FIRST LESSONS LEARNT

You must be eager to learn what happened next after I moved to Surendranagar. Yes, it was a different ball game altogether and I learnt some fundamental lessons in life. I will continue to share them as we move ahead, but let me share an interesting anecdote before that.

It's said kind heartedness and generosity are inborn qualities. Yet certain incidents leave a lasting impression and change the way we think and act. I am naturally an affectionate person who is always ready to extend a helping hand. What laid a very strong foundation for my generous and philanthropic outlook in life, however, are a couple of incidents that occurred in my life, before I moved to Surendranagar. Today when I participate in the numerous Corporate Social Responsibility (CSR) programmes that our Group is involved in, these incidents flash across my mind, as if it were yesterday.

My father used to sell spare parts for oil engines in Mathak. Back in those days, oil engines were commonly used by our village farmers for their farm machines. We used to source them from nearby cities; and I always accompanied my father on these occasions. We would leave at dawn to reach Rajkot by nine in the morning. My father used to buy these spares and carry the heavy merchandise all by himself – to save INR 5 for the porter's labour charges. Each penny saved was a penny earned!

On one such occasion, when I was nine or ten years old, I went with him to Rajkot to buy liner piston, a spare needed for oil engines. By mid-day, having completed our business, we headed to the bus stand. Since a meal in a decent hotel was beyond our means, we brought some bhajias and ghanthiyaa (popular Gujarati snacks) packed in newspaper from street vendors. Across the bus stand, the road was lined with shops, with narrow passageways between each shop. We hopped across the road to stand in one such narrow passage to get out of the sun's glare and eat in seclusion. It was time for all shops to down their shutters for lunch. The shopkeeper, next to whose shop we were eating, shouted at us to go away and not litter around his shop. 'Get lost both of you and find somewhere else to eat!' I had never felt so insulted in my life, as though my father and I were beggars on the street. The incident left a permanent scar on my soul.

We repacked our food in the newspaper and headed back home. There was no point standing by the road side in that hot noon sun. Sitting in the bus, despite my best efforts to put it out of my mind, the incident kept resurfacing, pointing at our wretched helplessness. This also made me think of millions of people around the world who must bc suffering similar fate every day. That day I decided that once I became self-sufficient, no one would step away from my doorstep without being fed.

Many years later, when we started our own business, I ensured that anybody coming to our premises (whether our home, shop, office or factory) at lunchtime, whether a friend, client, supplier, labourer or even a stranger, would always share the table with the rest of us. This incident was responsible in a way for a very successful CSR programme that our Group successfully manages to this day. As I sit down and look beyond my office window, I remember these words of Winston Churchill, 'We make a living by what we get, but we make a life by what we give.'

Around the same time, another incident occurred. Groundnut trading was also a part of my father's business. We would purchase these groundnuts from our village farmers and sell them at Wankaner, a tiny hill town about 50 km from Rajkot. At the marketplace, the groundnuts had to be heaped up in the yard for prospective buyers to inspect. The process often involved waiting for as long as four hours in the hot sun. On one such occasion, I had accompanied my father to the public auction. After heaping our nuts, we waited patiently for the bidding process to begin. My father decided to take a quick tea break and instructed me to watch our merchandise.

Guarding the nuts from birds was a huge challenge. Every now and then, a flock of birds would descend on our heap. I would shoo them away, but they would come back. In frustration, I picked up a stone and hurdled it at them. The stone hit a bird, which was fatally injured and eventually died. I felt guilty of killing the bird and could not pardon myself. Once more, I made a decision that after I grew up, I would provide food and water to all kinds of birds, especially those who built their nest around us. True to my promise, we made arrangements at home to make food and water available to birds round the clock.

This incident too had a strong impact on me, and today the welfare of birds and animals are part of our Group's philanthropic goals. Feeding birds brings me divine solace and I cannot help but share these beautiful words of Pope Pius XII, who said, 'Feeding the birds is also a form of prayer.'

With such strong impressions even before I turned ten, I moved to Surendranagar, where a new life awaited me.

• CHAPTER 4 •

SURENDRANAGAR: FIRST TASTE OF AN OUTSIDE WORLD

I have always believed that every day we start life afresh. Each day is like a blank page, where we face new challenges and find opportunities to counter them; but more importantly, we learn new lessons and gain new experiences.

My parents, Nanaji and my Mamas, unanimously decided that I needed to be disciplined and pushed out of my comfort zone. All these years, whether in Mathak, Jodiya or Balamba, I was sheltered, protected and pampered by my family. And so a boarding school awaited me in Surendranagar. It was my first taste of the world out of my family cocoon, and life was to test me and teach me new lessons.

Surendranagar is an administrative district of Gujarat. It is the gateway to the Saurashtra region, and stands at a distance of about 80 km from our village. It is a major trade and processing centre for agricultural products, cotton, salt, pharmaceuticals, ceramics and sanitary ware, among many others. Today, it has the second highest number of education institutes and many newspapers are published from there. Moving to Surendranagar from Mathak was like David meeting Goliath!

It is the dream of every parent that their children receive the best of everything, including the best education. As my family lacked the resources to get me admitted into a good school and hostel, my father sought a school and hostel that offered free scholarships with free boarding and lodging. With the help of my Nanaji, I was admitted into a hostel run by an institution called 'Manav Mandir'. It was newly established in 1968 for the education of poor children from remote villages. This institution was managed through donations and charities. The fact that Manav Mandir charged a nominal fee of INR 12 per annum for food and accommodation will elucidate our plight, misery and state of affairs. There was a school in the same complex, but I did not join it because they only taught Sanskrit. Finally, I got admission in the seventh standard of 'Bharati Vidya Mandir', on a freeship basis (or 'Mafi' in Gujarati).

Everybody had said that life in a boarding would be tough, but nobody had told me that it would be so extremely difficult that it would make me cry everyday! To a poor twelve-year-old, it was like being thrown into a dungeon, where everything was controlled by the jailer's stick (or the hostel superintendent's stick). Hostel was full of rules and regulations. One mistake and down would come the stick on you, followed by more punishment. We had to wake up early, learn Sanskrit and attend prayers every morning and evening. Not only did we have to have cold-water baths and wash our clothes, but we also had to assist with some hostel chores. I did everything that I was told to do, but there was one particular errand that still brings tears to my eyes. Our school was almost 6 km away from our hostel and we used to walk to school and back, bare feet.

As part of our hostel rule, we had to get whole wheat milled and ground daily. By rotation, each hostel student had to get this done at least once or twice a week. About 7 kg of wheat would be handed over to students to be ground into flour. The routine was that every day the students would carry the grains with them, dropping them off at the miller on the way to school. On the way back from school at high noon, we had to collect the flour and bring it back with us. The flour used to be very hot and we had to carry the bags on our heads. After every five minutes, we would stop and take a breather, then continue walking down, bare feet, in the sun at high noon till we reached the hostel.

Just imagine doing something like that on an empty belly, at three in the afternoon under a glaring sun! The hunger and hardship would drive me wild; and whenever it was my turn to carry the day's flour, I used to grab handfuls of the plain flour and gobble it down to feed my burning hunger. This was the toughest of all hostel routines!

Today, I am one of the trustees of the ISKCON foundation in Kenya. The 'Food for Life' programme is one of the most important initiatives of this foundation, undertaken in about sixty countries. Through this programme, children are fed free mid-day meals. I often personally serve the children lunch, with tears in my eyes, as I remember my own childhood days of hunger and deprivation. I remember myself as one such child, holding out a small bowl and eagerly waiting for his turn to be served! In those days, 'bajranarotla' (flat bread cooked from the flour of pearl millets) and 'tuvardaal' (Indian daal with split pigeon peas) was our staple diet. The daal served in our hostel was so watery that when poured into our bowls, one could clearly see the bottom of the bowl! To fill my belly, I used to gulp down any food that I was given. I had no complains whatsoever and accepted all that was served with gratitude, for we could not afford to buy anything for ourselves!

Poverty and the struggle to survive make us do unimaginable things. In those days, in Surendranagar, there used to be a funfair ('mela' or 'jatra' in Gujarati) every Sunday at a particular ground. Street vendors would sell food, clothes and jewellery, among others. The entire town used to come down to the fair and enjoy themselves till late in the night. On Monday mornings, I used to clean the littered fairground with a 'savena' (big broom stick) along with the other children. I would often come across small pieces of groundnuts that I would pocket. Later, I would gleefully eat the scavenged nuts to fill my ever-hungry stomach!

Empty pockets teach you a million things in life. As a small boy, the fire of hunger always burnt in my belly, twenty-four hours a day. So much so that I was ready to undertake any work for food. To earn extra food, I used to help out in the households of the hostel manager and hostel superintendent' (gruhapati). Even today, I get goose bumps thinking how I managed to get by in those days.

As I said earlier, each day life teaches us something new. While we are learning our lessons, we are oblivious of how much that experience would help us ahead in life. Believe me when I say that whatever we learn the hard way never goes waste. Here at Manav Mandir, learning Sanskrit was mandatory. Our teacher would give us a sholka to learn every day (sixteen-syllabic Sanskrit couplets that form the basis of most classical Indian literature) that we had to memorise and recite the next day. If we failed, we had to forgo our breakfast the following morning, as a punishment. This teacher seemed to be my biggest enemy, whose very sight filled me with hatred. Years later, however, I realised that it was the tireless efforts of my Sanskrit teacher that helped me become a temple priest.

Right from my childhood, I have always been fascinated by cars. It was rare to catch a glimpse of a car in our tiny village of Mathak. Every once in a couple of months, a Jeep would pass by the village; but we were always privileged to watch the public bus ply through Mathak every evening! We used to wait at the bus stop ten minutes before its usual arrival to catch it in time. The very sight of travellers alighting and boarding it, vendors calling out, the honking of the driver and the bus conductor requesting passengers to hurry up, thrilled me to bits. At times, I used to hang on to the ladder behind the bus to enjoy a joy ride to the end of our village; and at other times, we would hold on to the bus while riding our bicycles!

One Sunday afternoon, while resting in my hostel room, I spied a car parked inside the hostel campus, right outside my ground floor room. I stepped out to take a closer look at it. It was a brand new, white 'Premier Padmini' Fiat model. Unable to control my excitement, I surveyed it from all angles, touching it lovingly. As I was admiring its beauty, an elderly gentleman clad in white, presumably the owner of the car came up behind me. He asked me if I liked it and whether I would be interested in taking a ride. I readily agreed. My happiness knew no bounds, as he drove me for about a quarter of an hour around our campus. Thanking him, I got down and asked him the car's cost out of sheer curiosity – although I couldn't even afford a second-hand bicycle! I was surprised to learn that it had been presented to him as a birthday gift by his elder brother. He asked me whcther I would like to be like him and receive a gift like this, to which I responded with a big 'No'. He was taken aback and asked me why. Looking at his surprised face, I replied with a smile that when I grew up, I would rather be like his elder brother, who could give such an amazing gift to others. Later, I came to know that the car owner was from a Patel family, whose son was a friend of mine at the hostel. Unable to bear the hardships, he quit after two months.

I have always dreamt big, no matter what the situation or circumstance. Even the toughest of times at the hostel did not deter me from dreaming big. But there was one dream that I saw with my open eyes in Surendranagar, which I went on to fulfil many years later. It had to do with riding a helicopter. It so happened that the then Prime Minister of India, Smt. Indira Gandhi, visited Surendranagar for one of her election campaigns and addressed an enormous public gathering at a prominent ground. Being an orator par excellence, thousands flocked to the ground to listen to her. I was one among the many, accompanied by my grandfather.

She was to arrive in a helicopter, and I had never seen one in my life before. Along with the others, I eagerly waited to see what this machine was like! As the crowd cheered, I saw the helicopter landing near the ground amid a deafening roar. While the gathering listened to the Prime Minister's speech, my eyes were glued to the helicopter. I could not imagine how something like this could fly like a bird and swiftly take you to places! It was right then and there that I dreamt I would enjoy a ride in a helicopter one day in my life! This was the dream of a twelve-year-old, with no proper clothes on his back, no shoes on his feet, residing in a charity hostel and studying on a freeship. The same people, who had laughed at my 'absurd' dream, are amazed that I own an aviation company today, with my own commercial pilot's licence, and most importantly, my own helicopter.

Surendranagar was my first experience of staying away from my family. Being the youngest student at the boarding, I missed my parents and my family much more than the others. Normally, the parents of most of the students visited their children on weekends, carrying food and treats for them. I longed for my parents to visit me. Our boarding was in a forested area, and whenever free, I would sit on top of the highest platform facing the city and mistook every person visiting the boarding to be my father. He mostly never turned up, breaking my boyish heart – except for the one time when he came to meet me and took me to a movie in town. That was one of the few good times that I had at Surendranagar.

Life at Manav Mandir continued with its frustrations and hardships. Each year, at the beginning of the academic session, as many as forty or fifty students would enrol in the hostel. Before the end of the year, however, most of them would call it quits and hardly ten or fifteen remained. My parents would visit me once every six months. Each time they came, I shared my plight with them. Every week, I sent a post card to my father with my complaints. Post cards were the cheapest modes of communication and cost around five paisa. I would use every square inch of the paper to pour out my heart. Finally, at the end of the second year, I earnestly requested them to do something about my unbearable situation. My father spoke to my Mamas, and they agreed to shift me out of Surendranagar. My happiness knew no bounds when I came to know of my impending freedom.

As I said earlier, life teaches us something new every moment of every day. The hardships that Surendranagar had inflicted upon me, turned out to be a blessing in disguise, when I faced much bigger challenges later in life. My childhood experiences enabled me to face all challenges and find solutions to them. But the most important lesson I learnt here was the Sanskrit language, which every Brahmin priest is required to learn, since all Hindu rites and rituals are conducted in this classical language.

So in 1974, after studying for two years and completing my eighth standard, I bid adieu to Surendranagar. I stood at the crossroads yet again, not knowing what life had in store for me next. I was to move to Bhuj (another town in Gujarat).

• CHAPTER 5 •

NECESSITY IS THE MOTHER OF INVENTION: MY BUSINESS INSTINCTS

In the words of the Greek philosopher Plato, 'Necessity is the mother of invention.' When one struggles for the very basic necessities of life—food, clothing and shelter—then life teaches one to find ways and means of fulfilling them. Since we had our own small home, we never faced the challenge of shelter; but life had taken a 180-degrees turn after my father separated from my Grandfather's family and business. From a tender age, I had experienced struggle, hunger and helplessness. I have shared how my father used to buy a poor man's beans, karthi, on credit to feed his family. There were also times that we went to bed without dinner or after having dined on a few peanuts only. While in Mathak, we never had the means to buy shoes for ourselves. I still remember the sheer joy on getting my first pair of 'Parag' sandals from my Mama. When I was a child, buying new clothes was beyond our means, and I always wore second-hand clothes (or 'mitumba' in Swahili).

I still remember that 'bell-bottomed' trousers were all the rage in the 1970s. They would cost about INR 120–150, which was unaffordable for us. I remember travelling with my father to Morbi, about 30 km from our village, to buy second-hand clothes. In the city centre, there was a place called Nagar Darwaza, where vendors would sell second-hand clothes in small handcarts. There, we used to get our bell-bottomed trousers only for INR 15–25! Though I never complained about any of this, a fire began to burn within me—to earn money, to support my father to maintain our family, and to pull us out of poverty.

Tough times often stimulate imagination, creativity and ingenuity; and I was no exception. Being the eldest son, I kept mulling over ways to earn money, so that I could assist my family. I have always believed very strongly that no work is insignificant or small. Fortunately, as I was born into a Gujarati family, I was blessed with an innate business sense and the art of making money. To add to this, our circumstances forced me to constantly come up with innovative ideas to support my family in fulfilling our basic necessities.

As a child, I was always curious, inquisitive and creative. While in Mathak, I used to play truant and roam around the village, watching how shopkeepers traded and made money. I also went out to the fields to learn how farmers ploughed their seeds and harvested their crops. I was keen to find out how farmers sold their produce to make money.

While studying outside our village, I would always come home to celebrate Diwali (major Hindu autumn festival of lights) with my family. Diwali is about poojas, new clothes, colourful lights, sweets, crackers and fireworks. Although I longed to burn crackers like other children, the very thought of our finances, held me back. Instead of burning them, I would borrow money from my father to go to Morbi and buy firecrackers to sell them in Mathak. While other children of my age were busy celebrating with family and friends, I spent the festival selling crackers. I would display them neatly on empty jute bags outside my father's shop. I would make a neat INR 300–400 during the festival, handing it all to my father to lessen his burden.

There are numerous festivals and holidays in India. One such festive season is the Shravan Maas (the monsoon month of July–August of the Indian calendar). This is a holy month for Hindus. Important festivals including Janmashtami or Satham–Atham (Lord Krishna's birthday) and Raksha Bandhan are celebrated in this month. One will find funfairs and 'melas' with vendors displaying their wares. One such mela used to be celebrated grandly in a town near our village called Tarnetar. In this town, the globally renowned 'Tarnetar Mela' is celebrated annually. A number of colourful stalls come up with beautiful local handicrafts, ethnic jewellery, statues of deities and traditional attires. There are games, rides, magic shows and many attractions that draw daily visitors. During this festive season, I would set up our own stall in our village, in Tarnetar and surrounding villages. In our stall, we would display accessories for girls and women folk. We sold bangles, scarves, ribbons, costume jewellery and traditional clothes. My objective was to make a decent profit to support my father and my family.

My father managed his shop in Mathak, trading in spares for oil engines. He also traded in cotton, cottonseeds and groundnuts, (moong-fali in Gujarati). So whenever these crops were harvested, I used to visit the surrounding villages to source the crops from farmers in small quantities. In those days, cotton was traded by the 'maan' (1maan is around 20 kg). Being aggressive by nature, I used to pay a slightly higher price than other traders to efficiently source the cotton produce, store them in our shop, hold on to it for a while, before my father sold them to traders in bigger cities for decent profits. There were also instances, when I had to sell at a loss; but in six out of ten deals, I made profits. Over time, I learned to never make a loss. Even today, I always take calculated risks, aiming to make profits.

Not all business transactions or ventures end up in profits, but I have always strived hard to ensure that I negotiate hard and don't end up losing money in the bargain. I still believe that if one loses out after taking a calculated risk, it's understandable; but if one loses money without calculating the risks, then one is not a capable businessman.

I strongly uphold this business principle even to this day and pass down the same to my children. While spending money on oneself or while transacting business, try to negotiate hard, even if it means saving a single penny; but when donating for a good cause or helping others, never think twice, even when donating a million dollars. I want to leave this legacy for all those who want to succeed in their business and in their lives.

Even while studying in Jodiya and Balamba, I would look out for means to make money. During the school recess, as I've shared earlier, I used to gather students around me and show them tricks in exchange for an 'entertainment tax'. Then there was the garden in Balamba, where I would blackmail courting couples for the 'price' of my silence. My objective was always to make some money, so that I could send it back home to my parents.

Circumstances force a man to make innovative choices. Right from my childhood, owing to our financial situation, the only thoughts occupying my mind involved ways of making money. While in Jodiya, I still remember that my Nanaji would give my cousin Mahendra around INR 100 for massaging his feet regularly. Out of this amount, Mahendra used to give us small treats and spend hardly about ten per cent of that princely sum. Needless to say, I always took away the rest of it from him and sent it to my parents.

Back in those days, Indians were enamoured of imported merchandise, especially watches, tape recorders, jewellery, perfumes and clothes. Jodiya, where my Mamas stayed, was a small port where trading ships and dhows used to anchor. Many traders and shopkeepers used to source imported merchandise from the people travelling by these ships and boats. I too saw this as an avenue for making some money. Since I did not have any money of my own, I would source products from these shopkeepers on credit, which I sold for a profit, paying back the shopkeepers their product cost. I still remember selling electronics like National Panasonic tape recorders for INR 1,200 and making a small profit of INR 200 or so. Gradually, I was picking up basic business skills.

I always sought ways of making money by honest means and whenever I got an opportunity or an occasion to do so, I earned profits and took pride in being able to support my family. During my days in Jodiya, I used to walk up to the ships and steamers anchored at port for work. I used to tell people on these vessels to take me to Dubai or Muscat or to give me some work aboard their ships so that I could earn a living and help my family. Observing my business skills, a ship owner named Kader had even offered to give me work on his ship and take me along with him to Dubai. He told me that I had to pass a test, if wanted to go along with him. The test involved jumping into the sea (near the shore) to fetch a fifty paisa coin that he would throw into the sea. I remember willingly jumping into the sea! The objective was to travel with him, learn the tricks of the trade and earn a living. Of course, I was too young for this sort of thing and my Nananji, very rightly, denied this venture from taking off, threatening Kader to stay away from me.

Even during my stay in the Bhuj hostel, I shared my financial difficulties with the temple priests who managed the hostel affairs.

I had told them that I was ready to undertake any responsibilities that would fetch me some money. He had readily made me the gruhapati (the hostel-in-charge) and I was paid INR 150 per month. High school fees in Bhuj were high, and I had to manage some textbooks (the ones not provided by the school) as well as my uniform. I needed money for all of these. I would chant mantras on behalf of devotees, who in return gave me dakshina (religious fees in exchange for performing traditional rites and rituals) that helped me with my expenses.

Though I always dreamt of bigger things, I created a plan to gradually start earning a living to support my family. At that time, I could not see the bigger picture, but I was unknowingly training myself for something bigger in life. Years later, I realised that big things often have a small beginning; and in the hindsight, I thank all those challenging times, which compelled me to think of innovative ideas, shaping me into what I am today. Busy as I was in learning business skills and the art of making money, the Almighty had a much bigger plan for me; and as I headed to Bhuj, the biggest turning point of my life awaited me.

• CHAPTER 6 •

THE FIRST TURNING POINT: BHUJ

Everything that has ever happened in your life is preparing you for a moment, which is yet to come. Sometimes, God closes doors because it is time to move forward, and *He* knows that we won't move on unless circumstances force us to do so. *He* has a reason for making things happen, and though we may never understand *His* infinite wisdom, we have to learn to trust *his* will. My life took me to Bhuj—the last leg of my young student life. It was as if I was touring the entire Saurashtra and Kutch region of Gujarat. At this juncture, realising that God's ways were beyond my ken, I could only hope that *He* knew the purpose of *his* ways! So here *he* was, not only opening the door to Bhuj, but making me climb the first step of my ladder to success. This was the first turning point in my life.

Bhuj is the district headquarters of Kutch, Gujarat, the largest district in India. It is almost 185 km from our village. A mid-sized town with a population of around 300,000, Bhuj is well known for its mouth-watering Gujarati cuisine, especially the 'Kutch-ni-Dabeli' (a typical street food with lots of masala stuffed into a bun). It is a famous destination for handicrafts like bandhini (tie-dye) and traditional leatherwork, as well as for its annual 'Rann festival' (desert festival) held each winter, which begins and ends in Bhuj. Many also remember Bhuj for the devastating earthquake of 26 January 2001. As I continue to narrate my story, I will share an incident about this earthquake. When I landed into this beautiful town, I was unaware that this would mark the beginning of my life as a priest.

In 1974, after completing part of my eighth standard, in Surendranagar, I secured admission in Bhuj and had to repeat grade 8. I attended the Shree Swaminarayan School for my studies and Shree Swaminarayan Gurukul Hostel for my boarding and lodging. Both the school and Gurukul were part of the Shree Swaminarayan Temple, situated next to each other. There were about 600 students in the school and about 200–250 boys residing in the hostel.

My parents continued to struggle and money continued to be a major challenge for us, so we had to look for avenues where we could get concessions in school fees, hostel fees and in securing textbooks. As I came from a Brahmin family, I was given a 50 per cent concession in my hostel fees. Even after this, the boarding fees was around INR 100–200, which in those days was considered a high sum. Knowing our family's plight very well, I was determined to take care of my balance school fees, uniform and textbooks.

The 'Janmangal Stotra' (religious hymn) is perhaps one of the most chanted stotras across the Swaminarayan Temples. At Swaminarayan Bhagwan's request, one of his disciples, Shatanand Swami, is said to have composed the stotra. It is believed that those who read, study or listen to the Janmangal, or even those who make others read, study or listen to it on their behalf, will never experience confusion and chaos in their lives. It is also believed that recitation absolves the reciter from his sins and purifies him from evil spirits and diabolic powers; while his life will be blessed with happiness by Lord Swaminarayan. The stotra has to be chanted by a Brahmin on behalf of any devotee, for a specific occasion or achievement. Usually, one chants it between a 1,000 and 10,000 times, depending on the desire of the devotee. While offering prayers in the temple, I saw that many devotees wanted a Brahmin to chant the stotra on their behalf. Being a Brahmin, I was eligible to chant the mantra. So whenever I could manage, I offered to chant it for devotees. I used to chant this mantra around 500 times a day. As a token of appreciation for my services, the devotees would offer me a dakshina, anywhere from INR 25 –100. I still remember a delighted devotee, offering me INR 500, which was the highest I received. With this, I managed to pay my high school fees, get my uniforms and buy my textbooks. At the request of the temple priest, some devotees helped me with my textbooks. That was how I managed to meet some of my expenses.

Life in the Gurukul (hostel) was bliss after the terrible time I experienced at Manav Mandir in Surendranagar. The hostel was a square, three-storeyed building with a small garden in the centre, offices on the ground floor and a big main gate with a small entrance, always guarded by a Nepali security personnel. Undoubtedly, here in Gurukul, too, discipline and strictness were of the highest order, but the environment was much more conducive for students, and even the quality of our food was much better. I was housed in a small 12’x12’ corner room (No. 37) on the first floor, along with five other students. There were no cots or beds and we slept on the ground after spreading out the cotton mattresses provided to us. Every morning, before stepping out, we had to neatly fold away our mattresses and clean our room. Similarly, we were expected to wash our own clothes (which we normally did over weekends), clean our own utensils and offer daily prayers in the temple. I had no issues about the strict routine, as I strongly believe that discipline is the foundation upon which all success is built, and lack of it leads to failure. Today I am thankful for the discipline of my Gurukul, which has brought me to the zenith of my life and achievements.

Though my stay was comfortable here, I still did not have the luxury of owing a pair of sandals. Walking barefeet, I envied other students who wore shoes or sandals. Though often punished by my teacher for not wearing any shoes, I was too embarrassed to explain the real reason! Unable to bear this humiliation, I decided to steal a pair of sandals. As part of our routine, it was mandatory for all students of the hostel to offer morning and evening prayers.

One day after finishing my prayers, I stole a pair of sandals of some devotee kept outside the temple. Then I stole a second pair after six months. I still did not feel a sense of guilt at stealing someone else's shoes. However, when I stole the third pair, my conscious hurt and I realised that what I was doing was wrong, and decided to return them to the temple. So the next day, I put the sandals neatly into a plastic bag and kept it back at the same place outside the temple from where I had picked them up. On the top of the plastic bag, I placed a small note saying that 'this pair was found here'. For the next few days, I watched for the owner to claim them, but nobody turned up. Finally, after a week or so, on a Sunday morning, I was relieved when a devotee picked them up. He then met the temple's priest to say that he had found his lost property, along with a small note. Though no action was initiated against any student for this incident, unable to carry a guilty conscious, I confessed my sin to the priest, sought his forgiveness and was pardoned. To this day, I vividly remember the incident. I thoroughly enjoyed the two years that I spent in the Swaminarayan School and completed grade 9.

As the Swaminarayan School did not have any facilities for further education, I continued my studies at the Alfred

High School in Bhuj. Founded in 1870, it is one of the oldest educational institutions in Gujarat and the first high school of Kutch. Incidentally, the school was named after Prince Alfred, the Duke of Edinburgh. I continued to enjoy the benevolence of the Swaminarayan temple that paid my school fees until I completed high school.

Though I enjoyed my stay in the hostel and my high school studies, every single moment brought me pictures of my father toiling to manage the shop and struggling to meet the family's needs. Whenever I watched young boys and girls from affluent families, my thoughts would always be with my brother, Bhavesh, and my sister, Sangeeta. I shared my agony and pain with the temple priest, who managed the hostel affairs. He was kind enough to give me a break and made me the hostel gruhapati. I leaped high with joy, when I was told that I would be paid INR 150 per month for my services as a gruhapati. Today, this amount might sound meagre, but back in the 1970s, it was a fortune. I always felt a sense of pride, when at the end of the month, I collected the amount and sent or handed it over to my father. That feeling of happiness can only be felt, not measured. I performed all my duties religiously and sincerely, though this lasted only for a few months.

I often visited my aunt (father's sister) Hiraben and my uncle, Shashikant Bhai, who resided in Bhuj and traded in salt. Though I didn't receive the expected love and affection from them, I always looked forward to help my uncle in his shop. During my visits, I used to help pack the salt in small plastic bags of 1 kg each and load them into their handcart that could carry around 200 such bags. Sweating under the scorching sun, weathering the Kutch heat, bare feet and unmindful of the blisters, I used to drag the handcart through town, selling the salt to wholesalers or big grocers. I was pleased that my hard work used to save my uncle at least INR 20, which he would have normally spent on a labourer.

Though it was neither appreciated nor rewarded, I continued my efforts without realising that I was preparing myself for a bigger role in life.

Till date, I have not forgotten the time I spent with my uncle and his family. My uncle passed away many years ago. His two sons, my cousins, Bhavesh and Hitendra continue their family business of trading in salt. They have financial challenges today; I assist them financially and help my younger cousin, Bhavesh, who has medical issues. Recently, I assisted them in buying a vehicle for their business and one of my cousin's sons is working with us in Kenya. All this I do so that they also grow in life.

Old habits die hard, so on one hand while my struggle with life continued, on the other hand, my mischief-making resurfaced. Today, just thinking about those pranks makes me laugh, but the trouble that I have inflicted on those around me was a matter of serious concern then. Like birds of a feather, I managed to team up with a few likeminded, mischievous hostel-mates. One day, while we all were resting in the hostel, one of the 'likeminded' friend, who now is a successful businessman in Nairobi, approached us and suggested that we slip out of the hostel and watch a Hindi movie. In India, movies and cricket are like religion and the cine-stars and cricketers are demigods. So far, I had watched only a couple of movies and was excited about it. But all of us knew that stepping out of the hostel to watch a movie was like dreaming of flying in the sky without wings! Simply impossible! Notorious as we were, we hit upon a plan. As part of our hostel routine, it was mandatory for all students to offer morning and evening prayers. We were around 200-250 students and were supposed to form a long queue outside the temple and then offer prayers. The queue itself was about a kilometre-long and controlled by the school monitors. However, once the prayers were over, we dispersed on our own, without monitoring. So one day, after finishing our evening prayers around 7.30 pm, the four or five of us, slipped out of the temple and hostel campus without raising any alarm! Since the strength of students was huge, it was difficult for the monitors to watch us escape!

We watched the famous Bollywood blockbuster, *Sholay*, for the nine 'o'clock show. *Sholay* is probably the most popular of all Indian movies till date! Since all my friends were rich, they paid for my snacks and ticket! We sat on wooden benches in the first row, feeling proud, that we could see all the king-sized images and assumed that this was the best sitting place in the hall! It was past midnight when the movie got over and by this time Bhuj had a deserted look and all students in the hostel were fast asleep. Our hostel was a three-storeyed building and since the Nepali security guard was very strict, there was no way we could bribe him and walk through the main entrance. Like thugs, therefore, we went to the back of the hostel, where there was a toilet pipe leading from the ground to the top floor, ending on the terrace of our hostel. One-by-one, all of us climbed the pipe like monkeys and reached the terrace. Our rooms were on the first floor and from the terrace there was a beam at one corner that connected all the three floors, except ground floor.

So all of us, like trapeze and circus artists, slid down the beam, without thinking of the consequences, from third to the first floor and then dispersed to the safety of our rooms! Thrilled by the success of this act, we had the audacity to watch more movies and this became a regular routine for quite some time. In the next few months, believe it or not, we watched this movie about eighteen times. Even today, if I find time, I watch *Sholay* and can recite all its dialogues from start to finish! There were a few other movies that we watched too, but I do not remember their names, except for *Deedar* and *Dhoti Lota Aur Chowapathy*. In those days, the leading cine star, Hema Mailini, was my favourite actress and Govardhan Thakurdas Jethanand Asrani, my favourite actor.

Our movie-watching adventure did not last long and like all good things, curtains fell down too soon. Other students started complaining to the Hostel Superintendent. Initially, he ignored it, but when the water level rose beyond control, action had to be taken against us! It so happened that one night after returning from the movie, past midnight, while we were sliding down the terrace beam to our floor, all lights in the hostel lit up, shocking us!

The hostel-in-charge, the head priest, the hostel trustees and all 200-250 students were watching us climb down! We were shell shocked, knowing not what to do next! When we came down, all of us were beaten up and asked to write an apology letter, mentioning that we regretted our act and this would not be repeated! We did write the apology letter, but this did not stop us... Over the next few days, we were caught again, twice! The hostel rules stated that any student caught violating the regulations, thrice, would be expelled from the hostel without any recourse. We fell on the feet of all the concerned, requesting to be forgiven. For one last time, we were forgiven; this incident had a deep impact on me. It turned over a new leaf.

A few months lapsed; impressed by my changed attitude and responsible behaviour, the trustees appointed me as the hostel superintendent. On assuming officc and on the first available opportunity, I got hold of the file where all our apology letters were filed, and destroyed them permanently. There was also a big '*chopda*' (book) where all the hostel complains were noted. I tore all those pages where our complaints were noted! The object was that if we were expelled from the hostel, this would hamper our education and future too! Today all of us are successful in our lives!

Though mischievous, I have always stood by the truth and never tolerated injustice (mainly inspired by Gandhiji). If I was blamed for any act that I did not commit, I always endeavoured to prove my innocence. While studying in Bhuj, I used to visit Mathak, whenever we had a occasion. On one such occasion, when I was around sixteen years old, I had travelled to Mathak and from there, we had to travel to a neighbouring village, Kankavati, for a religious occasion. It is a very small village, at a distance of 57 km from our village. This is where our Kul Devi's (our community deity) temple stands. Being an auspicious occasion, people from surrounding villages and towns had gathered at the temple. My cousin, Kanu-kaka, had accompanied us. He was as mischievous as I was. This time he played a prank on me by offering me a paan (betel leaf wrap with areca nuts that is chewed as a stimulant or mouth freshener) that contained tobacco, knowing very well that I was allergic to tobacco.

Immediately on chewing the paan, my head started reeling and I had to rest, for a couple of hours, on a cot which was lying at a far end within the temple premises. All present could see my condition and many of them even laughed at me! One girl of my age, pitying my condition, offered me water and was with me for some time... But before I could thank her, she had left. I don't know what trick was up his sleeve that my mischievous cousin spied on her and managed to get all her details! I forgot this incident after we returned to our village, but my cousin played a trick on me! He had a small electrical repair shop and also worked as a postman in our village Post Office (he still works at that Post Office). He wrote a post-card, pretending that it was written by that girl. 'She' wrote that she missed me and liked me a lot and a lot of nonsense like that.

He addressed the letter to me, put the girl's name and address in the sender's details, affixed the necessary stamp and made it look very genuine. He then deliberately delivered the letter to my father. Such romantic letters were unheard of in those days and hence on reading this letter, my father's face turned red. It was around two in the afternoon and I was busy loafing about the village. Fuming with anger, he called me home and without giving me a chance to explain myself, beat me black and blue! To add to this, he searched my wallet and found my favourite actress, Hema Malini's photo in it and assumed that everything in the post card must be true! While my cousin laughed hysterically and the entire family and neighbours watched the drama, I cried at the injustice of being punished for a crime that I did not even commit. I vowed to bring the truth out in open and prove my innocence.

In those days, I used to sell National Panasonic tape recorders, and luckily I had one with me, which was the only tape recorder in the village! Kanu-Kaka and I were very close to each other and we would often spend nights together on our terrace. One night, I invited him to spend the night with us and he willingly obliged. On the open terrace, even before my cousin came over to our place, I had placed the tape recorder in a far corner and the microphone under the pillow. Moreover, the darkness of the night, aided me. When we were lying on our cots, under the open sky, I carefully switched on the recorder button and started conversing with him. I told him that I had forgotten the Kankavati (the girl's name) incident and had forgiven him. Beaming with joy, he started blabbering. He went on to stay that it was he who had written the post card and played the trick on me.

He also told me about his stints with a couple of his girlfriends, oblivious that his entire conversation was being recorded. He went on for almost half an hour, after which we called it a day and went off to sleep. I carefully switched off the recorder and safely stowed away my set. Being the only recorder in the village, we used to play this tape recorder in our shop, with two or three big speakers connected to it. My cousin's electrical repair shop was on the same lane. Since he was a trained electrician, he had pulled a cable from our shop to his and connected it with our tape recorder on one end and two speakers in his shop on the other. So whenever we played songs, the entire lane enjoyed them over the speakers in both our shops!

So the next day morning, armed with the recorded cassette and a big smile on my face, I marched to our shop. I waited for the right moment when my father was working in our shop, Kanu-Kaka's father and his brother were busy in their's, when a few customers were present in both our shops and the street was bustling with activity, I played the recorded cassette! At that time, my cousin was busy delivering letters and could not disconnect the recorder. Everybody listened to the recording as if a play was being acted out! By the time Kanu-Kaka returned to the shop, it was too late! It goes without saying that he was taken to task by his family and my father realised that I was innocent. My objective was not to take any revenge, but to prove that I was innocent. Even to this day, I always stand by the truth, howsoever bitter it may be; and cannot see injustice being done to anyone.

Courage was also an innate trait of mine. Thanks to my courage, even today, I have been able to stand tall and take decisions in the most adverse conditions. I was fond of water and loved swimming a lot! Once, when I was in Mathak for my holidays, I had severe fever and despite my mother's warnings, I went out of the house. My grandfather's farm had a big well in it and I plunged into it and swam till evening! It was late when I returned home and being furious with me, my mother refused to open the door to let me in! Despite my pleadings, she did not budge and told me to go back to my Bhuj hostel! I was stranded outside the house, with wet clothes, hungry and suffering from fever. It was getting darker and my pleading went in vain!

Not knowing what to do, I decided to return to the hostel. Without a single penny in my pocket, I headed to the Mathak bus station. In India, state owned buses have a ladder behind the bus, meant for carrying goods and cargo to the top of the bus. I saw a bus heading to Morbi and went around to the back and held the ladder, all the way to Morbi. From Morbi, I did the same thing to reach Bhuj. By now, I was too tired and extremely hungry. It was late when I reached the hostel and gulped down whatever food was available. It might seem like an act of foolishness, but over the years, my courage has helped me a lot to tide over many tight situations.

The stories of my mischief are abundant that it might warrant writing another book titled *The mischievous adventures of Guru*! It was more than a year now that I had moved to Bhuj, having settled down well in the school and the hostel, despite all my mischief. Even though things were seemingly sailing smoothly, the Almighty had a different plan for me; and my life was about to change completely. The first turning point of my life was about to come.

The Swaminarayan Temple in Pareswar Chowk in Bhuj is the first temple in the Kutch region, built under the guidance of the Lord Swaminarayan. Bhuj is one of the six places where Lord Shree Swaminarayan constructed the temple himself about 200 years ago. This divine thought of the Lord to build a temple here alone, signifies the vast amount of spirituality the land of Kutch offered not only in the past but even today. All the necessary rituals, such as preparing and offering '*bhog*' (food) to the Lord, conducting the morning and evening pooja, etc., are compulsorily conducted by a Brahmin. Non-Brahmin priests and saints are not allowed to perform such temple rituals. Around the time when I was performing my role as the gruhapati of the hostel, a Brahmin Swami Karunanand Bramachari, was performing the temple rituals. One day he slipped on the temple floor and fractured his right leg, which had to be plastered. He was not in a position to walk on his own for a long time.

From the temple's perceptive this meant that there was no way he could conduct the temple rituals for quite some time. An emergency arose and the temple authorities had to find someone urgently to perform all the rituals that had to be conducted by a Brahmin. As this situation was unplanned, the temple management made frantic efforts to find a Brahmin immediately, when my name was suggested by someone to the management. Incidentally, I fulfilled the criteria, which required that (a) the priest should be a Brahmin, (b) a brahmachari (celibate), and (c) should not be married. Understanding the gravity of the situation, I acceded to their request without a second thought, considering it to be God's wish.

I accepted the priest's role without realising that my life was to be totally transformed. My mind was full of chaotic thoughts, of whether I would be able to take up this challenge. Without knowing cooking, would I be able to cook the deity's food? Millions of frenzied thoughts flitted through my mind and I wondered whether I did the right thing in accepting the offer. I went to the temple, bowed my head at the Lord's feet, accepted *His* will and prayed for divine guidance. In the blink of an eye, this chance opportunity was about to set me on a course that I had never planned and a future that I had never dreamt of.

It is said that God does not give us what we can handle, but helps us handle what we are given. True to this saying, I started getting help and guidance in my role as a priest. I was moved from the hostel to the temple premises, where about seventy-five saints resided. Swami Karunanand Bramachari, though unable to perform the temple rituals and cook for the deities, offered to guide me and teach me cooking. He used to sit in a chair and instruct me. Similarly, at the kitchen, he taught me how to cook, when to cook and how much to cook, for the offerings to be made to the Lord. This help was like God sent and I felt that my prayers had been answered!

It is always easier said than done. Studying with the twin role of a priest was never going to be easy. I was given a small 10'x 8'room on second floor of the temple. My routine was both rigid and hectic. Hectic since I had to wake up early in the morning by 3.45 am, when most boys of my age enjoyed their sleep. By 6.30-7.00 am, I used to finish cooking for the deity, said my prayers, completed all other temple duties and washed my clothes. By 7.30 am, I used to get ready and reach the school by 8 am. Food is also offered to The Lord at lunch time around 11.30-11.45 am. As a priest, I had to dine at a designated place and food was served on a banana leaf (no plates)! In one helping, I was supposed to fill my leaf with all the food that I needed and we were not allowed a second serving!

While dining, nobody was allowed to touch a priest, otherwise we had to take a bath again, and that too with river sand, since we were not allowed to use soap! Every time I stepped out of the temple, it was mandatory for me to take a bath with my clothes on my return. All the duties had to be executed perfectly, even if one fell ill! It was God's grace that I did not fall sick and managed to perform well. Thousand of devotees from all walks of life visited the temple every day and it was here that I got an opportunity to understand people, learn their problems, and this helped me in reading their minds. Much later in life, this experience helped me in handling my daily business challenges, understanding our clientele and suppliers as well!

As a fourteen-year-old, performing this duty was becoming a challenge as I used to be in class in the morning. Even while attending classes, my mind was entirely on my priestly tasks that I had to do after class. At that time, I was studying in Alfred High School and our classrooms had big windows, almost six feet tall and about four feet wide. Many a time, fearing that I could get late for my temple work, I used to jump out of the window and head to the temple. On a lighter side, there were quite a few other classmates, who interested in listening to the cricket commentary on the radio, used to jump along with me. Till I completed my studies, this window-jumping never caught anybody's attention! Sandwiched between my role as a priest and a student, and unable to focus on my studies full time, I explained my dilemma to the school management and requested them to allow me to attend classes only in the afternoon, post lunch between 12.30 and 5.00 pm, so that I could manage to conduct all temple formalities. My request was granted and I attended the school only in the afternoons.

I used to complete all the morning temple formalities by mid-day and then head to school. On returning from school, I used to cook the deity's evening offerings, say my prayers and have dinner. I got a lot of love and affection from all the saints in the temple and was treated like their child and they to me were all fatherly figures. In the early mornings, along with washing my clothes, I always washed the clothes of other saints, though this was not my responsibility. Similarly, whenever I had some spare time, I visited the saints to see if they wanted my assistance.

In the evenings after dinner and before calling it a day, when the saints were resting, I used to massage their feet, out of reverence and gratitude towards them. I slowly learnt all the duties of a priest. The Sanskrit I had learnt in Manav-Mandir was of immense help to me now. Life was tough, but at the same time, the temple was paying me a monthly salary for the services that I rendered as a priest. Apart from that, I also used to get Dakshina for other religious rituals. Thus I was able to earn some decent amount. Whatever I earned, I used to send to my father, to support my family, in whatever best manner I could.

As I was settling and learning the ropes of excelling as a priest, my education was suffering because it had now taken the second place. Though I tried to balance both, the writing was clear on the wall. In the High School Board examination for grade 12, I failed to pass in English. I had to re-appear for the English examination and after considerable effort, managed to pass the exam. Though we say that life is in itself a school and teaches us new things every moment, my formal school education drew to its end.

There were frustrating times, especially when I used to watch children of my age enjoy their life, wear colourful clothes, spend time with their families, and enjoy food and drinks in restaurants. My life was way different from theirs. I led a very strenuous and disciplined life in the temple, waking up early, completing the temple routine, working every day, be it a Sunday or a holiday. My clothing was simple, a dhoti and kurta (a dhoti is an unstitched length of cloth traditionally wrapped as a bottom-wear by males in the subcontinent, while a Kurta is a loose, collarless shirt) with no footwear. The temple was my home and my fortress, a terrain that I hardly stepped out of.

I hardly made any friends, except for Amratlal, a professional painter. He stayed in a small room, opposite our temple; and as part of his work and profession, he used to visit the temple regularly and paint the deities. That's how I came in contact with him and we become friendly. Though he was from a different caste (he belonged to the Mochi community), we used to share not only our inner feelings of joy, happiness, frustrations, anger and agony, but I also used to wear his shirts.

As a Brahmin priest, I was not supposed to even touch him and at that time the traditions were so rigid that if I touched him, I had to take a shower before I performed any religious rites. However, so isolated I was that I had limited choices and his company and moral support kept me going all the time. In those days, the Khengarji Park was located close to the temple, which was in the middle of the Hairsar-Tatav Lake. Most families in Bhuj used to enjoy their Sunday evenings here with their children. I used to go Amrtalal's room, change my temple clothes, wear his shirt, trousers and footwear. Both of us also spent many a Sunday evening together in this park, watching children play, wondering how fortunate they were! My friend was a kind-hearted person and once gifted me a new shirt. Believe it or not, it was the first time I was wearing a new shirt! People often mistook us for brothers when we walked in the park wearing those shirts! He filled the void of a brother and friend! Stubborn by nature, he never got married! Though I have not met him for a long time now, he continues his painting work with the temple and resides in his own flat in Bhuj.

The sacred *Bhagawad Gita* states that as human beings, we should work and toil hard, without worrying about the end result or the fruit. It continues to say that our hard work will always bear fruits in proportion to the efforts we make. In my case, I offered my services to the temple, performed my duty towards the deity and the saints. I used to cook for the temple, perform rites, serve the saints, including washing their clothes and at times massaging their feet. I never thought of the result or my benefit when I served them, though my mind was constantly thinking of better opportunities for work, especially avenues where I could travel outside India, work and earn better. There did come one such opportunity, where an Indian contractor based in Muscat, Oman, had undertaken a project in a construction and oil rig. He required a person, who would stay at the construction site and cook food for all his 200-300 employees. I was excited about it and offered to go. Unfortunately, somebody grabbed the opportunity and I felt a bit let down.

I confided my thoughts to the head priest, Mahant Swami Hari Swarupdasji. He simply smiled, patted me on my back and said, 'Son, there is something big coming your way, be patient.' And then this happened. I had completed around three years of my service in the temple. I was performing my evening rituals, when a temple saint came and informed me that the Mahant Swami Hari Swarupdasji had called me to meet him. Later that evening, after completing all my temple routines, I walked up to him. He was resting and lost in deep thoughts. I slowly started massaging his legs. He said, 'Son, we are quite impressed by your dedication and devoted service to the temple.'

I was happy, but felt that there was more to come. He continued, 'You have mastered everything that a priest has to learn, you are ready for something big in life, and it's time for you to move on.' He went on, 'There is a temple in Nairobi, Kenya, called the East Africa Sat Sangh Temple, which is a part of our Swaminarayan temple order. They urgently require a priest, who will be based in Nairobi. Impressed by your dedication, we have recommended your name and they have accepted our proposal. Are you interested in this?' My heart missed a beat. I touched the Swami's feet in gratitude and immediately accepted the offer. At last, my prayers had been answered.

Mahant Swami Hari Swarupdasji, Head of the Bhuj Swaminarayan temple and instrumental in sending me to the Nairobi temple as a priest.

Blessed to meet Pramukh Swami Maharaj—The Head of the Swaminarayan Sanstha

This was indeed the first turning point in my life. I had dreamt of doing something big in life, and always strived to achieve this, but when the Mahant Swami informed me of the salary that I would be getting for my temple services in Nairobi, my happiness knew no bounds. I remember his words, 'Son, the Nairobi temple Management has agreed to pay you INR 2,600 per month. You will be residing in the temple and food will also be taken care of.' My businessman's mind started its calculations and I imagined that once I worked in Nairobi and managed to save at least INR 1 lakh, I would return to India. In those days, banks offered a rate of 24% as interest on deposits.

I figured that if I deposited my savings into a bank, I would easily get a monthly interest of INR 2,000–2,500. Back in those days, with this kind of money, we could easily maintain our family. He gave me permission to travel to Mathak and obtain my parents' consent before proceeding further. Without losing time, I took the next available bus to my village and during the entire journey, I could not even close my eyes for a second! On seeing me, my family was surprised, as I had come without prior intimation and enquired if everything was alright. I tried to remain calm when I broke this news to them. Knowing my mischievous behaviour, none of them were ready to believe me. My father laughed and told that this boy is up to mischief again!

It was only when I repeated my words four times that he decided to call the Bhuj temple and talk to the head priest. When the head priest confirmed what I had said, my entire family was overjoyed. Even today, I can see the smile of happiness and joy on my parents' faces that night. No one in our family slept that night out of sheer happiness.

The process of my travel preparation to Kenya began and an application for my passport was made. I was yet to complete eighteen years, when my passport was applied for. In those days, one had to complete eighteen years to be eligible for a passport. The agent handling our application, manipulated my birth year from 1961 to 1960, and that's how I managed to get my passport. Believe it or not, I had never seen a passport till then and mine was the first one that I was looking at. Today, it is difficult to explain or pen down the emotions that I experienced on the day my passport arrived. My proposed travel to Nairobi had become the talk of our village and in Bhuj too. No one was ready to believe that I was to travel overseas. It was solely due to the blessings of the Mahant Swami of the Bhuj Mandir, who has since passed away, that this was possible.

Finally, it was time to travel. The entire village came to see me off! Tears of joy rolled down each cheek and that scene of leaving my village is still fresh in my heart. This was the first time I travelled to Bombay (now Mumbai) by bus. My father and my elder Mama accompanied me till the Mumbai airport, since this was the first major journey of my life. My Mama accompanied us, since he had travelled to Africa before and he knew all the airport and travel formalities. Once in Mumbai, we took a taxi to the airport and my Mama explained the formalities involved in international travel. Bidding them good-bye, I stepped into the Mumbai International Airport, hardly realising that this was the first step of my new life. Clad in traditional priestly attire of a dhoti–kurta with a suitcase in hand, I headed to the check-in counter. I completed all the formalities, some by myself and some by seeking help from other passengers at the airport. As I headed to the boarding area, I became conscious that everybody around me was staring at me, making me feel insecure.

I wondered why all the passengers at the airport were staring at me and thought that was it because such a young boy like me was clad in a priest's clothing, or perhaps they wondering that I did not have all the necessary documents required for travelling. Sitting at the boarding gate, watching passengers move around, my mind was continuously lost in thought. With my eyes wide open, I had a million thoughts on my mind. Where was I heading to? What will my life in Kenya be like? Would I be able to live, work and survive alone?

I did not have any answers then. I guessed that everything in life happens for a reason. My life was taking a big leap. With a bag of mixed feelings and emotions, I boarded the Kenya Airways flight to Nairobi, which happened to be the most memorable flight of my life.

PART II

PRIESTHOOD
1978-1981

• CHAPTER 7 •

KARIBU KENYA

Every story has an end, but within the circle of life, every end has a new beginning. I made an air journey that was attached with many firsts in my life. It was the first time I travelled beyond my country, the first time I saw an airport and the first time I boarded a flight. I was amazed and awestruck by everything I encountered. Everything around me seemed novel and new.

As I boarded my flight from Mumbai—India's financial and entertainment capital—to Nairobi, I was oblivious to the fact that a new chapter had begun in my life. I was extremely busy watching my co-passengers closely, curious to know how my first airplane journey would turn out. When the announcement to fasten all seat belts was made, I tied my belt very tightly in fear that I would be violently thrown about once the plane took off. The hilarious predicament of a few animation movie characters, who were the only ones I'd ever seen taking a flight, was all that I had to go upon! When nothing of the kind happened for quite some time, and none of us were tossed around in our seats like nine pins, I tentatively asked my neighbour whether our plane had taken off. I was extremely surprised to learn that we were already flying in mid-air!

My list of endless surprises that day did not end there. When the flight attendant served us refreshments, I was surprised yet again to learn that they served food on a flight. Although as a Hindu Brahmin priest, with very strict dietary regulations, I could not eat anything that was offered aboard the flight, the fact astonished me none the less.

During the rest of that fateful journey, my mind was occupied with a string of opposing emotions that quickly followed one another. As I looked out the window high up in the clouds, I was thrilled and apprehensive in equal measure at the prospect of starting my life afresh. The new beginning had the potential to bring about a major change in my family's condition. At the same time, I was filled with sadness at leaving my family and friends, my town and my country—in short, a familiar way of life—behind.

As I settled down, I decided to plan ahead instead of looking back to what I had left behind. I began to dream about all the wonderful things I would achieve as a priest at the temple I was going to serve. I planned to keep the temple sparkling clean, serving the Lord and the community whole-heartedly. I dreamt that on the occasions I stepped out of the temple precincts, I would get to know other youngsters of my age. Making new friends, tasting new foods and new cultures, I would try out the latest fashions that my new friends wore, and learn about new things from the elders visiting the temple. I also planned to start religious classes, conduct sports events for the community, and so much more!

My pipedreams were interrupted when the aircraft finally landed at the Jomo Kenyatta International Airport (JKIA) at Nairobi, Kenya.

Nairobi is more than the Kenyan capital. It is the nation's beating heart, and the most cosmopolitan city of East Africa. Nairobi has a distinctive cultural heritage of its own, while impressions of its British pre-colonial era are also plentiful. With a National Park right at its doorstep, perhaps the only spot in the whole world where wild lions roar against a backdrop of skyscrapers and myriad wildlife attractions, a substantial part of this pulsating city's economy is built around global tourism.

As the gateway to East and Central Africa, Nairobi is a key business hub of this geography. It is home to thousands of Kenyan businesses and over 100 major international firms and non-government organisations, including the United National Environment Programme (UNEP) and the United Nations Organisation (UNO). The Nairobi Stock Exchange is one of the oldest and the largest in the continent.

With a heart full of hopes and dreams, I first landed in this beautiful city as an eighteen-year-old youth. Clad in my traditional garb of a dhoti–kurta, I was ready to encounter my new world. At the airport, I was enthusiastically greeted by a group of familiar devotees from Nairobi's East Africa Swaminarayan Satsang Temple (EASST).

As soon as we stepped into the car and headed towards the Temple, I breathed in the fresh air of an extraordinarily beautiful city. I gazed in admiration at surrounding greenery, the pollution-free, clear blue skies, the lack of traffic on the roads, and the strikingly beautiful wildlife of the Nairobi National Park. I was blissfully unaware that this was the city, which would embrace me with open arms, where I was destined to spend the rest of my life.

Enjoying the drive, we reached the Temple in about half-an-hour. I was impressed by the warm welcome I received there, and immediately began to feel at home in this distant land. I could see that the Temple authorities and devotees were relieved at my arrival, for they had truly been in an urgent need of a priest, and here I was full of enthusiasm to serve at the temple. Deep within me, a voice told me that I was here to stay.

The East Africa Satsang Mandal, founded in Nairobi in 1932, is the oldest Swaminarayan Organisation in Kenya, and probably in the whole of East Africa. It was basically formed to serve the religious and spiritual needs of all Swaminarayan devotees of the region. Under the aegis of the Mandal, the East African Swaminarayan Satsang Temple was built in 1945. It was the first Swaminarayan Temple to be built outside India, as well as the first one to be built in Africa.

This temple was to be my sanctuary for the next three years. As soon as I arrived, I was introduced to everyone around, and shown the premises where I was to stay. That night, when I was finally alone in my monastic cell-like quarters, the enormity of my loneliness hit me like a maelstrom. I felt waves of homesickness wash over me, as I remembered my family and friends back home and realised how far away I was from them in this alien land. I cried my heart out. It seemed as though life had given me a hundred reasons to cry, but determined as I was to get ahead, I wanted to show life that I had a thousand reasons to smile.

The pain that I went through that night made me feel as if the Almighty was crushing me down. Little did I realise then that God was not crushing me, but preparing me for something bigger and better, and that this pain was the first step in that direction. I also consoled myself with the thoughts that I had to tide over these tough days, so that I could earn the best days of my life ahead. Too tired and overwhelmed with warring emotions, my eyes closed of their own volition and and sleep overtook my depressing thoughts.

A new beginning had been made and my journey as a priest in Kenya had begun.

• CHAPTER 8 •

A PRIEST'S LIFE: CHALLENGES AND VICTORIES

It was time for a new chapter in my life, a tougher and more challenging one.

When the Mahant Swami Hari Swarupdasji of the Bhuj temple offered me the opportunity to serve as a priest at the Swaminarayan Satsang Temple in Nairobi, not only was I excited, but also felt that God had answered my prayers and given me a path to walk on. I felt I could now rescue my family from the hard times upon which we had fallen, relieving all our pain and hardships.

Although the Mahant Swami had explained to me that it was going to be a challenging life ahead for me, I never realised the true import of his words until I experienced it for myself. Back in India, I had functioned as part of a team of temple priests, cloistered monks and masters. I always had elders around me to whom I could turn for help, guidance and support; but here in the Nairobi temple, my role was much larger than I had ever anticipated or imagined. As the head priest, I was expected to captain the team here, and have a ready solution for all problems! A lot was expected of me, but as they say, when the going gets tough, the tough get going. Today when I sit back and think about all the steps that I have climbed, I can truly say that:

> *'Life is a building; it rises slowly, day by day throughout the years;*
> *Every new lesson we learn lays a block on the edifice, which rises silently within us;*
> *Every experience, every touch of another's life on ours, every influence that impresses us, every book we read, every conversation we hear, every act of our commonest days,*
> *Adds something to the invisible building...*

At that tender age of eighteen, however, thousands of miles away from my family, with no friends to share my joys and sorrows with, no shoulder to cry on, I could only see darkness ahead of me! It appeared as though there was no light at the end of the tunnel. My work never caused me any fatigue, for I served my duties with the fullest devotion and dedication. It was the feeling of despair and loneliness that exhausted me, more often than not. My life was a varied mix of experiences, with good times and frustrating ones all thrown in together. This was about the time that I began to pray to God–not for an easy life, but for the strength to endure a difficult one.

My task was uphill; but the welcoming smiles and the loving hearts all around me, gave me the motivation and energy to serve the Lord with all my dedication and devotion. My experience in India had aided me immensely in executing my duties at the Nairobi temple. My daily routine was strenuous, and my day typically began at four each morning and did not cease until nine in the evening. I was solely responsible for everything, right from opening the temple at dawn to managing all its daily routines until the doors closed for the day. With the help of the other resident brothers and monks at the temple, I managed to grasp the daily routine within the first two weeks of my sojourn.

My day used to begin as early as 3:45 in the morning, with a cold-water bath, since the temple did not have bath water heating facilities. In those days, Nairobi's temperatures would hover below ten degrees, and only those native to the city would know what it meant to have a cold-water bath so early in the morning! This again was a novel experience for me, but adaptability was perhaps the first lesson that life taught me.

By 4.30 every morning, I had to finish my own prayers before opening the temple and completing all temple prayers and rituals for the first half of the day. By this time, throngs of devotees would visit the temple for their morning prayers. I used to conduct a religious discourse session too, where I would read to the community from holy texts, such as the *Vanchanamrit of Swaminarayan* (the most sacred and foundational of scriptures for the Swaminaryan Sampraydaya or community). It would then be time for the temple's mid-day rituals, such as cooking for and offering food to the deity. This was a tough routine, since I had to mostly manage this task all by myself, except for a couple of devotees who helped me on some days. By the time I could sit down to have my own lunch, it would be time again for the evening service. This included cooking and offering food to the deity once more, which I usually finish by about 5.30 in the evening. This was followed by evening services and rituals (sandhyaaarti), when about 100–200 devotees would visit the temple for their prayers. Then came the evening discourses and readings from the holy scriptures. It was not before all devotees departed around 9:00 in the evening that I could finally call it a day! The deep silence inside the temple helped to keep me calm, but as a youngster barely out of his teens, I felt very lonely with nobody to share my days.

This remained my daily regimen for the next three years. Be it a Sunday or a public holiday, whether in sickness or in health, whether I felt happy or miserable. I imagined my life to be similar to that of soldiers, who away from their homes and families, zealously guard their country's borders day and night, through all seasons, every single day. The only difference, of course, was that they guarded their countries from enemies outside, while I offered my services to the Lord and preached religion and humanity to the temple's devotees.

There is a first time for everything, including addressing public gatherings; even if it is an intimate one. My turn came soon enough. As I have shared with you already, reading out from the *Vanchanamrit* was part of my daily routine. After the reading, one was supposed to expound the verses and passages read out.

A few days after joining the temple, just as I had finished reading the holy scriptures for that session, I was handed the microphone by a temple devotee and asked to address the gathering. I was dumbfounded and shaken with anxiety as I held the mike in my hands nervously. I had never spoken in public on any topic before, and here I was expected to discourse on religious philosophy before a congregation of 200–300 devotees, who were probably much more learned and knowledgeable than an eighteen-year-old! As soon as I stood up to speak, my head began to swim and I had trouble focussing on anybody present there. Flabbergasted, I wondered what to say for a few seconds, before deciding to thank everyone for bringing me all the way from Bhuj and giving me the opportunity to serve at the temple in Nairobi. It hardly took me a couple of seconds to say these simple words and yet I stood there scared and trembling. Even to this day, the incident is fresh in my mind.

****

Soon I found myself contemplating newer ways to attract more devotees to the congregation strength of the temple. Thinking novel ideas has always been my forte; and I have always been in the habit of finding new ways to improve my family's financial condition. In this case, I thought of beginning a series of activities for the children of devotees, calling it 'Bal Sabha' or a council for children. The temple management were immensely pleased with my initiative, when I sought their blessings and permission to begin.

The Bal Sabha was a weekly event that I used to organize every Sunday morning, following the formal temple service. I used the forum to hold story telling sessions for children and adolescents, sharing moral, religious tales and traditional fables. Most importantly, I tried to instil a sense of morality and the core tenets of being a good human being through the stories. Teaching them to stay away from vices like addiction to drugs and alcohol. The initial response to my initiative was lukewarm and only about 20-25 children used to come to attend the Sunday sessions. To attract more children, I decided to serve prasad at the sessions. In Hinduism, prasad is ritually cooked food that is first offered to God before being distributed among the faithful.

I decided to cook the prasad myself and serve it to all the children attending the Sunday sessions after the Sabha ended. Word of the practice spread among the congregation and soon the Bal Sabha began to see more than a hundred fold increase in attendance! Parents were especially happy that their children were being given lessons in becoming good human beings, and much appreciated my efforts. When the number of children attending the sabha increased, the cost of managing the weekly prasad increased as well. I eventually made a formal request to all devotees to contribute to it generously, which they immediately agreed to do. Thereafter, every week a parent or family used to sponsor the Bal

Sabha prasad that I arranged. This particular initiative of mine was a thus a huge success and I managed it throughout the three years that I served the temple as priest.

I have always believed that every moment we learn something new and that the knowledge we gather over the years always comes to our help. In this case, although the Bal Sabha was a weekly affair, I used to prepare for it through the week, and my knowledge of Sanskrit became particularly useful. Moreover, I ended up mastering much of the religious scriptures while selecting the religious tales for the Bal Sabha and preparing my sermons around them.

****

What I appreciate about the Swaminarayan Sampradaya or sect is that they are a simple, hardworking and down-to-earth community that I can relate to. On an average, around 300 devotees or a 100 families attended the temple's daily prayers. I was offered a lot of help by the families in my daily temple duties. I had learnt to cook during my years at the Bhuj temple, but my abilities were limited. In addition, when there were more than 1,000 devotees attending special events at the temple, it became impossible for me to cook for all of them alone. That was when the women of the community would come forward to help me in the temple kitchens. Not only did they assist with the cooking, but also taught me a variety of new dishes and professional methods of managing the kitchens for large gatherings. They treated me like family and helped me in the belief that by assisting me they were helping the Lord in his work on earth. Other celibate men who worked at the temple also helped me in the kitchens. This wonderful experience was much responsible for opening up my mind to a new perspective. As I said before, the community generated a lot of positive energy.

The temple was like a school that taught me something new every day. As part of my daily duties, I had to interact with devotees who were much older to me, which forced me to reach a level of maturity much beyond my years. Despite the challenges, I managed to achieve a modicum of maturity in my dealing with my elderly congregation. In addition, most of them were successful businessmen and highly responsible members of their community, inadvertently teaching me to become responsible as well. Most importantly, I closely studied the lifestyles of the devotees and realized that most of them led a very simple life, down to their simple Gujarati diet of Khichdi-Kadi and Rotli-Saak. This helped me learn simplicity from them.

I remembered, India's father of the nation, Mahatma Gandhi, quoting his philosophy of 'simple living and high thinking'. Unwittingly, the foundation of my life was being laid on this philosophy.

****

Expectation feeds frustration. While I was cruising at an altitude of 35,000 feet from Mumbai to Nairobi, my dreams and aspirations were sailing just as high. I dreamt that I would accomplish a lot in my young life. I would befriend other children my age, wear the latest fashions, catch the latest entertainment, relish food and drinks with my friends—partying and enjoying myself just as any other adolescent or teenager my age would. As my days at the temple followed one another, I watched all my dreams crash around me. With the growing realisation that my reality was very different from the other children I was comparing myself to, I was gripped with despair. In the first place, I hardly ever stepped out of the temple, except to conduct ritual ceremonies at an outside location. Even that was in the company of other devotees, who dropped me back at the temple at the close of the event. I had no chance, hence, of spending any time of my own beyond the temple walls.

The temple stood right in the heart of Nairobi, densely populated by the local community, with hardly any immigrant or expatriate population residing in the area. When I lay alone in my chambers at night, I would hear sounds of people crying in distress, drunken brawls, squabbles and fights, sounds that seemed as though houses and shops were being robbed and broken into. Despite feeling scared, I felt curious about this world outside my walls; but I never stepped out during all of the three years I was there! I used to feel extremely frustrated about not getting to know the people I lived amid. As though I were a prisoner locked into a cell with no freedom of my own.

My attire and diet, too, were traditionally prescribed by my religion and vocation. I always moved barefoot, wore the unstitched priestly ensemble of a dhoti, kurta and shawl, and ate the simple meals that we cooked in the temple for the Lord. My young mind longed for feasts and colourful fashion. I still remember an incident when a devotee had organised ceremonial prayers in the temple for his son's birthday. The entire family was present at the ceremony that I had conducted, following which they left to celebrate the child's birthday at a well-known Nairobi restaurant. I remember closing the temple doors as the family left, and retiring to my cell in loneliness and sadness.

I realise in hindsight that I had been led into a way of life without having prepared for it. As part of my duties, I had to guide and counsel devotees more than thrice my age, which was exceedingly taxing for a seventeen-year-old. I was just a young teenager who was well-versed in the language of the scriptures and had been taught temple rituals. As an eager and hardworking apprentice, I had learnt my lessons well and performed my duties to the best of my abilities. Unlike any other vocation, however, that of a priest entailed a spiritual calling and maturity that went beyond scriptural prayer readings and rituals performed to perfection.

My spirit was still that of any other adolescent, eager to explore all possibilities that life presented. The young may not be told that certain paths are beyond bounds, it stifles their sense of freedom. The youth need to feel that a whole world of opportunities lies waiting ahead for them. The restrictive ways of everyday life, especially that of a formal religious calling, find easy acceptance as one matures mentally and spiritually. As a hardworking and smart young lad whose natural inclination lay in the world of business, it would still take me a couple of years to understand my true calling in life.

In short, when I had accepted to serve as head priest at the EASST, I had virtually agreed to take up responsibilities much bigger than what my young shoulders could bear. Add to this the rigorous routine that I went through at the temple every single day without any break for three straight years, and I now realise how taxing it all must have been. Right from 3:45 am when I woke up to 9:00 at night when I closed the temple doors, I was constantly up on my feet. There was never any break in my day or in my duties, be it a weekend or a public holiday.

Throughout the day, I was happily engrossed in my work, with no time for any thoughts in my mind. It was only at night when I lay alone in my monastic cell that loneliness, doubt and despair crowded my mind. Many nights I would cry myself to sleep. The very thought of waking up before the break of dawn and beginning my day with an ice-cold shower in the chilly Nairobi mornings used to send shivers down my spine.

Testing times at Nairobi temple: Trying to be alone, without feeling lonely

I still remember an incident when I had come down with cold and fever. It was a particularly cold winter that year. As the day progressed, so did my illness, till I had to visit a doctor. That day, somehow, I managed to complete my evening duties and called it a day; but the next day, I woke up with a high fever. Although I was hardly in a position to take up my normal temple services, I had no choice but to take my usual cold-water bath and begin my tasks. By mid-day, I was ready to drop from high fever and extreme exhaustion. The doctor had to be called in once again, after which I felt better.

That day, as on so many other days, I fervently wished I was home, under the loving care of my dear mother and the congenial company of my family and friends. But here I was, suffering all alone in an alien world, so very far away from home. It was on days like these that I used to feel the urge to run away. Yet, knowing that that was impossible, I would cry silently into my pillow for fear of awakening the other temple residents.

I would often take it up with my Lord, however, in the dead of the afternoon when I mostly found myself finishing a task alone. I used to rage against the injustices showered upon my young self, by giving me the responsibility of running the entire temple. I remember a certain incident when I had been foolish enough to reveal the extent of my frustrations in public. We were singing hymns to the Lord, with an eager devotee playing the manjeera (traditional hand-held crash cymbals) next to me. While the congregation enjoyed the festive air, whipped up into a frenzy by the loud clanging of the manjeera, my irritation reached a crescendo and I snatched the instrument from his hands, flinging it to the ground before the shocked gathering!

I walked straight to the deity and cried for a long time, but I could not console myself even after everyone had left. I later regretted my action; but in hindsight, I am thankful to the Lord today for the strength I was given to endure my early struggles. Although frustration and loneliness was setting deep within me, I never gave up my faith in God. I continued my prayers for granting me the strength and courage to face life.

I believe that when we pray with all our heart, God hears much more than we ever say; answers more than we ever ask for and grants us with much more than we ever imagine–all in *His* own way and at the right time.

My prayers seemed to have been answered, for I gradually changed my outlook towards life and began to learn to find peace within myself.

****

Though confined within the temple walls, I began to find ways of reaching out to the larger community beyond my world, which was something that I had always wanted to do. I wanted to learn Kiswahilli so that I could speak the local tongue and be accepted by the community as one of their own. There was a security guard (Askari in Swahili), who worked at the temple and stayed within its premises with his family. In my spare time after completing my daily tasks, I used to learn Swahili from him. He happily taught me the language. In the first few weeks, I was only able to master common terms such as, 'Jambo', 'Habari' and 'Nzuri'; but with time, I was able to freely converse with him in his language. Believe me when I say that even to this day, whenever I meet and greet any security guard in Kenya, it sends me down the memory lane!

Apart from learning Swahili, I also began to add to my temple services. After the tremendous success of Bal Sabha, I thought of expanding the horizon of my temple activities. I needed something that would not only supplement my role as head priest, but also help me earn Dakshina (fees for performing religious rituals) to help my family. And so I began to perform the Tulsi Pooja, which is an annual religious celebration. It is a ceremonial marriage of the Tulsi plant (holy basil) with the Lord Vishnu or his avatar, Lord Krishna, signifying the end of the monsoons and the beginning of the Hindu wedding season. Noting my increased involvement with temple rituals, devotees soon began to invite me home to perform religious ceremonies on auspicious occasions like marriages, house warmings and office or workplace openings, among others. This helped me utilise my spare hours quite productively.

Performing religious rites at the Nairobi temple

Serving the Lord: My daily routine as a priest at the Nairobi temple

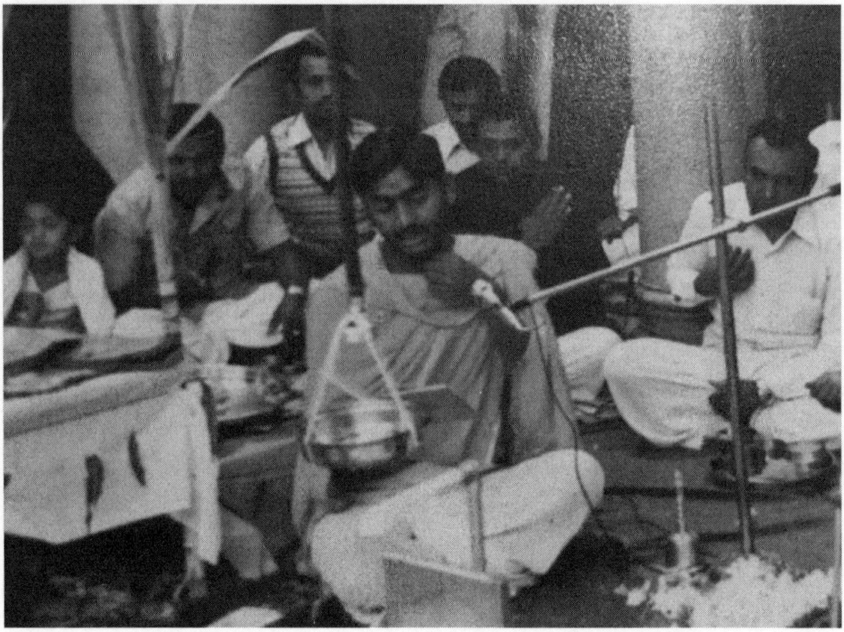

Performing religious rites at the Nairobi temple

In addition, I began to socialise with the temple's many devotees and their families. I took an active interest in their lives, which gradually led to many of them opening up their hearts and sharing their challenges and concerns with me. I sincerely listened to their problems and tried to offer simple and practical solutions that were morally acceptable. In no time at all I discovered that I had managed to create a special place for myself among the immigrant Indian community in Nairobi, earning respect from young and old alike.

An investment in knowledge always pays the best interest. True to this adage, my knowledge of astrology helped me to address the troubles and concerns of many devotees in those days. I had learned astrology from the masters, while serving in the Bhuj temple in India. When I began to practise my knowledge of traditional Indian astrology, many devotees would often stay back after the daily prayers to confide their difficulties to me, seeking a solution for their troubles. Whether it was a personal or family matter, business or professional, they all started consulting me. By this time, I had indeed been accepted as part of their lives and had almost become a part of their families. I was overwhelmed by their love, affection and acceptance. Today, I find it difficult to pen-down these emotions.

I recall a particular incident from the period, which perfectly illustrates the faith and trust that everyone in the community had placed in me. Traditionally, worshippers at all Swaminarayan temples are segregated according to gender, with separate spaces for men and women. As part of my usual temple routine, I used to read from the religious scriptures (katha) twice a day after the daily prayers. All the members of a particular family used to regularly attend this daily discourse. A young couple in the family who had been recently married had begun to attend the temple prayers with the rest of them too. The young bride had newly joined the family from India, and used to sit in the women's wing of the prayer hall with the rest of her female relatives. A very strange thing that was hard to explain began right after I began the katha one day. The young lady in question suddenly stood up and began acting hysterically, screaming and dancing as if possessed by evil spirits, disrupting the congregation and frightening everyone. On that first day we thought it to be a stray incident, calming her down and continuing with the discourse as usual. Her strange behaviour was beyond our understanding. To our amazement and the family's disgrace, her act continued over the next few days, disturbing the proceedings and distressing all devotees present at the discourse.

The worried young husband and his family approached me to intervene in the matter and find a solution for her inexplicable behaviour. Although the young woman acted strangely at a particular moment every day, I was convinced that there was no evil spirit involved in the matter at all and decided to resolve the issue once and for all. So the next day when she began to act hysterically, I stood up with a very thick cane in my hand and marched towards the women's wing. I could see her screaming and swaying wildly as if in a trance and requested some of the women to hold her tightly. I stood before the lady holding up the cane in my hand, as if to strike, and in a very loud and booming voice told her to stop her nonsense, or be prepared to be beaten black and blue till the 'spirits' left her body. There I stood a young priest of barely eighteen or nineteen years, with all eyes in the temple turned towards me, willing me to resolve a delicate and inexplicable matter such as this. I could barely breathe; but believe it or not, my firm behaviour bore results and the lady's strange behaviour stopped as suddenly as it had started.

Later that day when everyone had left the temple after thanking me for resolving the distressing matter, I stood before the Lord, praying. I felt it to be a divine sign telling me to always have faith and belief in the Lord for finding solutions to all problems. I slept peacefully that night. During my tenure, some other similar incidents did take place, but none dared to play tricks or stage acts within the temple again.

Every experience is an opportunity to learn and grow; and the three years that I served at the temple undoubtedly taught me invaluable life lessons. I learnt the power of prayer, the courage to face challenges and to withstand any adversity. The one lesson that life taught me at the temple, however, which I believe to be my biggest learning in life was—*adaptability*. I consider that to be my greatest lesson because as a mere teenager I had learnt the roles and responsibilities of a middle-aged man! I had adapted myself to an austere outlook on life that usually comes naturally to individuals who have completed their life's responsibilities and have no desires left of worldly cares anymore. I had truly achieved to adapt myself to such a mental state. Today when I reflect on those early years of my life, I think that if I could have adapted myself to my circumstances at such a young age, why cannot I do it now, too?

• CHAPTER 9 •

LOVE FOR FAMILY

It is said that we do not choose our own families, but that they are God's gift to us, as we are to them.

As far as I am concerned, my family has never been an 'important' factor of my life—they have been my whole world. They bring meaning to my life and give me reasons to strive to be better. All the values that my parents have ever inculcated in me—the unconditional support that they have always lent, their love and affection as well as that of my siblings—have always kept me afloat through all the trying times and adverse circumstances.

After leaving our grandfather's house, I had seen my father struggle to provide for our family. I had seen him toiling tirelessly to run his tiny business, so that he could provide us with thc basic necessities. As children, I remember times when we had gone to bed hungry, and spent years without any shoes. Getting new clothes was beyond our means and we had to be satisfied with the used clothes brought from roadside vendors at the Nagar Darwaza in Morbi, Gujarat. Even my school and boarding expenses were met through free scholarships, sponsored or borne by the institutions themselves. Despite all these adversities, with love in their hearts and a smile on their lips, my parents had held our entire family together. Indeed, what I am today is the result of the pure love and affection of my parents and siblings. The family love and bonding that we shared always made me think about its welfare. Being the first-born of my parents, I always felt that it was my duty to shoulder my father's responsibility of supporting the family. Even as a school boy, I used to try to find ways of earning money to help my family to the best of my abilities.

When the head priest of the Bhuj Mandir, Mahant Swami Hari Swarupdasji, offered me the opportunity to serve as a priest in the temple, it was this love for my family that made me accept it without a second thought! I had aspired to continue my education, but the very thought of my father struggling to make both ends meet forced me to give up my dream of going to college and head towards Nairobi instead. And once in Nairobi, whenever I found myself alone with my thoughts, they were invariably centred on my beloved family back in India.

I used to feel immensely satisfied each month upon getting my salary and sending it to my parents back home. There were often times when I would be left without a penny after sending home all my money; but as I said, their unconditional love and familial bonding kept me going through all difficulties.

Although I had sacrificed my own education, I always dreamt of my younger brother and sister getting a college education. After completing high school, my brother, Bhavesh, shared his aspiration of becoming an engineer. He confided that he wanted to study at the Vivekananda Institute of Technology in Bangalore, since most of his friends intended to study there. When I heard this, I was overcome with happiness. My heart sank a bit, however, when he informed me that the Institute demanded a capitation fee.

In the Indian education system, capitation fees refer to the payment demanded by institutes over and above the normal tuition fees, during the time of admission. My heart sank further when I learnt that the fee in question was INR 200,000. Putting together that huge amount seemed like a Herculean task for our family. At the same time, I wanted my brother to achieve what I could not, due to our dire financial circumstances. I spoke to my father, and asked him to put together all our savings that I had helped create with my earnings from Nairobi. That did not help either, and my father informed me that we were still short by INR 120,000, even after clubbing all my earnings together. I did not want to let my brother or my family down, and was determined to find a way to arrange for the amount.

Unable to figure out exactly what to do, I approached a few temple devotees, earnestly requesting them to assist me financially. It was Kanji Bhimji Raagvani along with another devotee, who was the son of the owner of Bhimji Devji & Son, who supported me in my hour of need and made arrangements to send the balance ₹ 120,000 to my family. That was how Bhavesh secured admission in the engineering college in Bangalore, and later managed to successfully earn his engineering degree. Over the next twelve months, whatever I earned from my services at the temple were used in repaying my debt to my generous benefactors. In addition, I took up extra duties, such as performing various religious ceremonies for devotees; and whatever Dakshina I earned for these services were also used for repaying the loan.

After struggling for twelve months in this manner, I finally managed to clear my loan. Even this day, I am grateful to those two devotees for supporting me in my hour of need. Not only did they support me financially, but whenever I needed to send money home, they always assisted me by arranging to directly pay my family in India. This is probably the biggest milestone of my life. It has a very special place in my heart because it helped my brother fulfil his dream of completing his education; and because I managed to help him when I was barely nineteen years old myself.

****

As in many other traditional Asian communities, marriage is an important institution in India, especially when there are daughters and sisters of marriageable age in the family. Once my brother's education was taken care of, my thoughts shifted to my sister, Sangeeta's education and marriage. Normally, such a matter is the concern and responsibility of parents and elders in the family; but considering my father's financial challenges in providing for our family, I took it upon myself to help plan for her wedding. My sister's education was taken care of with the money that I used to send home. A wedding, however, was an entirely different kettle of fish that required massive funds. Even in those days, a modest family like ours would need at least INR 100,000–200,000 to organise the simplest of ceremonies. Considering our family's financial condition, even that minimum amount was a pretty sizeable amount for us! Never the less, I asked my parents to start hunting for a prospective groom for Sangeeta and leave the finances to me.

They managed to find a good alliance for her, and once again, some of the temple devotees kindly loaned me the funds for arranging my sister's wedding. And once again, I worked hard and took on extra ceremonial duties to pay off the loan from my earnings and the Dakshina I received during the rest of my tenure at the temple. This was another achievement of sorts that holds a special place in my heart, along with my brother's college education.

I had managed to fulfil two very important family responsibilities, oblivious of the fact that I had completed three years at the temple and that very soon my life was going to face a sea change. All that I earned and saved during my three-year tenure at the Nairobi temple had been utilised for my family, for my brother's education and for my sister's education and wedding, so that they could lead a decent life. I also realised that these milestones had taken a toll on our finances, and once again we were back to square one. Although this was difficult to digest, the love I had for my family made me happy that I had been able to help in their hour of need. Today, in hindsight, I realise that it was all a part of the Lord's larger design for me to play the role of a head priest, work hard and help my family.

What I did not realise at that time, however, was that in those years I was being prepared for playing a much bigger role on a much bigger stage in life!

• CHAPTER 10 •

BOLT FROM THE BLUE

Time flies, but leaves behind memories that last forever.

Nearly three years had passed since my arrival from India as a priest in Nairobi. The intervening years had brought some good times and some tough times, some wonderful memories and challenging experiences. Although time had flown by swiftly, I had begun to feel terribly homesick and lonely by the end of those three years. As if time had come to a standstill! I would often catch myself crying silently at the sight of children and their parents. I clearly needed to take a break and visit my family back home in India.

I finally mustered enough courage to place my request for a month's break before the temple trustees, and sought permission to travel to India. I could not believe it when the temple management flatly refused my request. I completely failed to understand the reason for their refusal. I had efficiently and devotedly served the temple every day for three years, without taking a single holiday even when I was ill. I had initiated popular practices, such as the Bal Sabha, and I had never given the temple committee any room for complaints over my services.

I tried to speak to the resident monks at the temple, the devotees and even individually to the management trustees, but it was all in vain. Each passing day became unbearable with the thought that perhaps I would never be able to leave those temple walls. It was a time before mobile phones were discovered and overseas calls were prohibitively expensive. The only way to reach my family was to write a detailed letter home, which is what I did, telling my parents of my desperate desire to come home. My father made frantic efforts to convince the temple management at Bhuj as well as in Nairobi, to allow me to travel to India for at least a month, but to no avail. While we were busy trying to get a favourable response from the temple committee, my mother fell ill. It was too much for her to bear, learning of my inability to return home for a visit, on top of her existing pain of separation from me.

When my father broke the news to me, I was devastated. He wrote of my mother's serious illness, adding that in case I delayed coming home, it might be too late! I took the letter to the temple management; but they still did not agree to let me go home! Finally, it was only through the intervention of a trustee, who understanding my state of mind, made a strong request to the temple management to grant me leave, for at least a fortnight. After much debate and to my great delight, my request was finally granted. After a lot of persuasion, the management finally arranged for a substitute priest, who would take over in my absence. I was happy for the arrangement, little knowing that the reliever was to take over my role permanently. The only truth I cared about at the time was that I was travelling back home after three long years.

The best journey in life is the one that takes you home.

From the moment I learnt of my impending travel to India, I began dreaming of my hometown, my family and friends. When the day finally arrived, I couldn't wait to get started and was ready to leave much ahead of time! I revelled in the sense of excitement. A cool breeze blew over me as I stepped out of the temple doors and got into a taxi for the airport. That soft breeze felt like 'freedom'. After I completed all formalities at the Jomo Kenyatta International Airport (JKIA), Nairobi, my excitement was almost uncontrollable. When our flight finally took off for Mumbai, I felt like a free bird, just released from its cage, flying high up into the clear skies. Finally, I was coming home, oblivious to the fact with the flight, my life as a temple priest had come to an end…

****

After a seven-hour flight, I reached Mumbai and took an overnight bus home. Throughout that journey, I was just eager to catch the first glimpse of my family and my village. On reaching home, I was given a very emotional welcome. My father had come to the bus station to receive me and I could see how happy he was when he first caught sight of me. My mother waited eagerly by the doorstep, and I could see her tears of happiness when I finally stood before her. I touched my parent's feet before entering our house, and then unable to control myself, I broke down with the sheer joy of homecoming. I felt relieved and at peace. I was home.

The next few days were probably the best of my life. In contrast to my daily temple ritual, I used to wake up at leisure, enjoy the food cooked by my mother, spend time with my family, especially my mother, assist my father in his business, visit friends and generally stroll around the village. In Nairobi, bound by duty, I used to call it a day by nine in the evening. Here in the company of lifelong friends, it was late nights every day. What a changed life! Close family often visited us, as did we. I was in seventh heaven, enjoying my time under the spotlight. I realise that it was a very good change for me at that point in time.

As I said before, time flies, but good times fly even faster. My one-month break was almost nearing its end and it was time for me to return to Nairobi. I was already feeling heavy hearted. I wondered how strange we humans are and how stranger still is our nature. On the one hand, I needed to travel to Nairobi to earn a living and help my family; while on the other hand, I found it hard to leave that very same family that I had to help!

It is rightly said that 'Man proposes and God disposes'. As mere mortals we plan so many things, but it is the celestial design of the Almighty that prevails in the end. One afternoon towards the end of my vacation, as I was busy packing my bags, I received the biggest shock of my life. My cousin Kanu-Kaka, the village postman, handed me a letter from the Nairobi temple. My heart missed a beat. For reasons unknown, I was extremely nervous about accepting the letter. I sat down on the veranda and went through the contents carefully… I read and re-read the letter several times, but I still couldn't believe my eyes!

The temple authorities had written that after my departure from Nairobi, they had received another letter from my father addressed to me, in which he had written that my mother's health was fine and that there was no need for me to travel to India. He had also added that he had exaggerated about my mother's health in the first letter so that I could get leave to travel! In my absence, the trustees had opened my letter and taken a very stern view of its contents. They stated that my father and I had falsified my mother's health condition so that I could get a break, which called for very serious action. Consequently, they had decided to cancel my permit and now there was no need for me to return to Nairobi… It was like a bolt from the blue!

The letter went on to add that they were extremely pleased with the services of the substitute priest, who had been brought in as my temporary replacement. My mind ceased to think and

I was seized with panic. My mother and siblings were all sitting there on the veranda with me and understood that something was clearly amiss; but I could not even look them straight in the eye. With the letter in hand, I ran all the way to my father's shop. He was equally dumbstruck and shocked by the letter. He confirmed that he had indeed written a second letter before my leave was sanctioned, and unfortunately it must have reached Nairobi after I had already left for India. My head reeled from shock and I could only see darkness at the end of the tunnel. My eyes full of tears, I looked heavenwards as if seeking an answer. Strangely enough, as I looked up, it began to rain and I felt that the Lord and his entire creation was crying with me!

It took me a while to come to terms with this new situation. Today I am grateful for that crucial juncture in my life and I realise now that God had very different plans for me; but at that point in time, I felt lost and helpless. I was concerned because all my savings were exhausted and we were back to square one. My father continued to toil hard to make both ends meet, and I could not bear to see all the tough times repeated once more. My father suggested that I should try to find a job here at home instead. Though my heart did not agree, I accepted his wisdom and began to look for jobs in and around our village.

After a desperate search, I managed to get a job at the Ajanta Watch Company in Morbi, which manufactured wristwatches. My role was that of a machine attendant. In those days, wristwatches had pins attached to them and my job was to see that all the watch pins were properly fixed. Once in a while, when the machine stopped, I had to adjust it for the process to continue afresh. My salary was a meagre INR 75 per month.

I worked at the factory for about a month before becoming very frustrated. One evening, while walking back from work, I realised that my life was not meant to go on like this, and that

I was meant for achieving something much bigger in life. The sun was setting in the west and I could feel that the sun of my life in India was gradually setting as well. I also realised that to achieve my dreams, I had to try to find something worthwhile beyond India. After working for a month at the Morbi watch factory, I quit. I spent the next three or four months looking for better opportunities, but nothing materialised, making me feel more desperate than ever. It was as though all happiness had disappeared from my heart in a flash.

My parents continued to console me, asking me to be patient and wait for things to improve, but I was unable to stay calm.

They say that only a mother can truly understand her child's agony. Unable to bear my anguish and misery, my mother sent me to Jodiya, my Nanaji's village, to be with my cousin and childhood friend, Mahendra Pandya. Although I spent a couple of blissful days with him, recalling our childhood memories, the question of my future was always at the back of my mind. Thoughts of returning to Nairobi, to look for a job or to start my own business were constantly hovering in my mind.

Although I was eager to return to Kenya, I was sceptical of what my educational qualifications could fetch me as a job. My parents' continued struggle to make ends meet finally forced me to come to a decision about my future. I knew I would be wasting my time and my life, if I continued to stay back in India. I still had a return ticket to Nairobi, and made up my mind to go back to Kenya. It was a shot in the dark, but under the circumstances, it was the best option for me. I managed to convince my parents and started making travel plans. Believe it or not, I also began to learn the English language at classes that a South Indian family ran near our village. After about a month of taking those classes, I decided to travel back.

My twenty-one-year-old mind was full of dark thoughts of what awaited me after I landed in Kenya. I did not know what the future held for me; but was confident that something positive would turn up if I left my destiny to the Almighty. For *He* sees things that we cannot even hope to see. His plans may not make any sense to us, but once when his whole plan unfolds, we get to see what had been planned for us. And that was how destiny pushed me back to Kenya.

PART III

A NEW BEGINNING
1981-1985

• CHAPTER 11 •

BACK TO KENYA

It is said that every second brings a fresh beginning; every hour holds a new promise, every night our dreams can bring hope and every day is what you choose to make it.

I was starting afresh and making a new beginning. For the second time in my life, destiny was taking me back to Kenya; although this time I was completely on my own! With the exception of the return ticket to Nairobi, my pockets were empty. However, I had plenty of blessings from my parents to carry back with me. I touched my mother's feet to seek her blessings, and with tears in her eyes my mother handed her gold chain to me. She asked me to sell it off should circumstances demanded it. I was moved by her concern and accepted her gift, but believe me when I say that I never sold it off. I have kept it with me to this day, as my mother's blessings.

As this was the second time I was travelling to Nairobi, I had no problems at the Mumbai airport and boarded the flight after smoothly completing all formalities. As our flight took off, my mind was flooded with millions of doubts. I wondered whether I would be allowed to enter Kenya, since my work permit had been cancelled. Would I be arrested at the airport? Would I be deported? With absolutely no money with me, what would I do if

I was sent back to India? During the entire flight, I kept searching for a familiar face, who could help me at the Nairobi airport, but I found none! My stream of disturbing thoughts continued even as the aircraft landed at Nairobi.

I have always maintained that in life nothing is greater than truth, and have always believed that honesty is the best policy. At the immigration desk, I handed my passport to the officer and requested for a visitor's visa. On scanning my passport, the immigration officer told me that I had no reason to apply for a visitor's visa since the work permit stamped on my passport was still valid. I could have easily walked out of the immigration desk, but my conscience did not permit me to do anything illegal. So I showed the officer the letter from the temple, which said that my work-permit was cancelled. Impressed by my honesty, the officer willingly issued me a three-month visitor's visa and all my fears were laid to rest.

A trivial, but funny, incident occurred as I collected my luggage, which consisted of just a suitcase. It was a pretty old and worn-out suitcase, which my mother had received as part of her wedding gifts! During those days, customs officers mandatorily inspected all baggage, and so I was also asked to open my big suitcase.

Believe it or not, my 'big bag' consisted of only two dhotis, four light shawls (khes), my ritual pooja paraphernalia and a couple of books. Puzzled, the customs official asked me, 'Is that all? Where is the rest of your luggage?' He burst out laughing when I said I had nothing else. I was a bit embarrassed. Though trivial, the incident has stayed fresh in my mind.

I collected my bag and stood at the airport, not knowing what to do next and where to turn to. The only place I knew in Nairobi was the EASST, where I had spent the last three years. I had kept searching for familiar faces during my entire flight and found none; but at the airport, I fortunately ran into a couple of devotees I knew. I requested them to drop me to the temple and they willingly obliged. I was silent throughout the drive, contemplating what I should do next.

Once I arrived at the temple, everyone was shocked to see me back, since I had landed unannounced. The temple authorities, however, gave me a warm welcome. They told me politely that they were happy with the services of the present priest and no longer required my services. I could stay at the temple for a few days, I was told, but I would have to make my own arrangements thereafter.

I was tired after the long journey, but sleep eluded me. I stepped out of my room and casually strolled within the temple premises and memories of my last three years there surged back. As I sat there, it all flashed by my inner eye like a movie. The daily temple routine, the rituals, the devotees, the happy and the challenging times—all of it. I became sentimental at the thought that the very place I had served sincerely, no longer required me anymore, suddenly turning me into a stranger within its walls. The night was dark, but I looked heavenwards and prayed to the Lord to show me the way. I did not want to be a burden on the temple. For that matter, I did not want to be a burden to anyone.

By sunrise, I had made my decision. I decided that I would leave the temple at the earliest possible opportunity and travel to Kisumu where my aunt (my mother's eldest sister) and her family lived. The very next day, I met a few devotes I was well acquainted with, and requested them to help me travel to Kisumu. A good samaritan, Rajnibhai Pitadia, volunteered to sponsor my travel to Kisumu and booked me a ticket on the Rift Valley Peugeot service. His timely help was God sent, at a time when I needed it desperately. The Rift Valley Peugeot service was a well-known public transport company that operated passenger carriages in the region. Once the travel arrangements were made, I made my up mind to leave the temple's shelter within a couple of days, although I had permission to stay on a bit longer. I thanked the temple management for their generosity and all temple devotees for their support. Finally, with a heavy heart, I walked out of the temple, never to return to it as a priest again.

• CHAPTER 12 •

KISUMU: FAMILY LOVE AND AFFECTION

Kisumu is a port city located at a distance of about 350 km from Kenyan capital city of Nairobi and on the Kenyan side of Lake Victoria. With a population of more than 400,000, it is the third largest city in Kenya and also the most prominent city in the Western Kenya region. It connects Kenya with Uganda and Tanzania through the lake Victorian Ferries. It has a typical rainforest climate and receives significant rainfall throughout the year, with an average temperature of around 22-23 degrees Celsius. agriculture, livestock farming and aquaculture form a major source of livelihood here. It is home to many Colleges and Universities and places of interest include Dunga Beach and Wetlands, Impala Sanctuary, Hippo point and Kit Mikayi.

I reached this beautiful city at a time when my life was in turmoil. What's more, I didn't even have my Masi's (mother's sister) exact address. By asking around, I somehow managed to reach my Masa's (Masi's husband) shop. Surprised to see me at his doorstep, he welcomed me with a warm hug and a huge smile. The family home was behind the shop. I knew I was home when I was welcomed warmly by the whole family. My Masi and Masa, Ichaben Vyas and Lab Shanker Vyas, had two sons and a daughter. They ran a watch shop named, L.B. Vyas & Co.

I was overwhelmed by the love and affection of the family; and I especially enjoyed the company of my cousins, who were all of my age. I assisted them in the shop as well as in household chores; and before I realised, two months had flown by. Soon I realised that I was becoming a burden to them. So I asked Masa, my uncle, to help find me a job. He made serious efforts, but in vain, till somebody told him of a vacancy for an English teacher at the Bhayani Nursery and Primary School. Masa asked if I was interested in it. The irony of life is that it often makes you do things you are least interested in or things that you are feeble at. I was never very good at English as a subject, and had even failed in it twice in my secondary and high school graduation exams back in Gujarat; and here I was supposed to teach the language! My position, however, did not give me any choices and I readily agreed to give it a try. I attended the interview and was asked to teach the English language to middle school children.

The school was nearly an hour's walk from my Masi's house, but since I could not afford public transport, I decided to walk to and from the school every day. I used to leave as early as half past six in the morning to reach the school in time. It reminded me of my school life at Surendranagar. The only difference being that I was a student then, and now I was a teacher! On the very first day, I realised that teaching English was not my cup of tea, and despite all my efforts, I failed to succeed. To add insult to injury, the students turned out to be smarter and instead of me teaching them, they started to teach me! Today, looking back at those days, I find it hilarious! But believe me, it was quite embarrassing!

After two weeks of struggle, I finally gathered enough courage to walk up to the Principal's office. I told him that I was not capable of teaching English to the children. Incidentally, the school management had also received a similar report of my abilities and had decided to let me go. I was relieved of my painful duties immediately, and that was how my very brief career as a teacher ended!

Now I was back to square one. My visitor's visa was about to expire, and so out of sheer desperation I went up to my Uncle and asked for his help in getting me a work permit. He knew someone, who had helped many Indians with their work permits. The next day, we paid him a visit; and as I waited outside, both of them discussed the matter at length. Shortly afterwards, when they stepped out, the person flatly refused to assist us in getting a permit. I was heartbroken and remember breaking down on the way back home. That afternoon, I hardly felt like coming to the dinner table. I took a great deal of loving effort and consolation from my family before I could be persuaded to come down.

I got my visitor's visa extended. With nothing better to do, I resorted to helping my Masi's family at home and at their shop, very soon becoming an integral part of the family. It was fun and enjoyable, particularly because of my three cousins. However, whenever I sat down with my own thoughts, I told myself that this was neither my dream nor the reason why I had come all the way from India, leaving my parents and the rest of my family behind. I had to find my own way.

We made valiant efforts, but nothing materialised in Kisumu. One evening, all of us visited the Swaminarayan Temple and I prayed for divine intervention. As we were leaving the temple, I heard devotees talking about the upcoming Navaratri festivities, and how religiously it was to be celebrated at Nakuru. On hearing this, I made up my mind to travel to Nakuru. The very next day,

I told the family of my decision to travel to Nakuru. Although reluctant to let me go, they understood my circumstances and agreed to my decision.

I cannot thank them enough for all the love they had showered on me during my brief stay with them at Kisumu. My uncle has passed away since then, and my Masi lives with her children at Leicester, UK.

Coming back to my journey to Nakuru, it was yet another moment in my life when I found myself standing at the crossroads. There lay many paths ahead of me, but right at that moment I did not know which one to take. I knew, however, that the choice I would make that day would probably define the rest of my life.

I chose to travel to Nakuru on my own terms.

• CHAPTER 13 •

GURU: A PRIEST AND AN ASTROLOGER

Before arriving at yet another new town, I began to repeat a pattern (by now familiar) all over again. A family known to my Masi was travelling to Nakuru for the Navratri Festival. When asked if I could join them, they readily took me along and I was off to Nakuru! The town is less than 200 km from Kisumu, taking us about four or five hours to reach. Throughout the drive, I was lost in deep thought once more about what lay ahead of me. I had no idea where I would be staying once I reached Nakuru and I neither did I know anyone to turn to for help.

What if I had to return to India? Thankfully, even before I could pursue that depressing line of thought, we had arrived at our destination. When the helpful family asked me where I would like to be dropped, I did not have the nerve to tell them that I had no idea! I decided to seek divine shelter in the Lord's house. Most Hindu temples usually offered temporary boarding to devotees and pilgrims. So the family left me at Nakuru's Sanatan Dharam Laxmi Narayan temple. I knew that the Navratri Festival was traditionally celebrated here, and thought it would be ideal for me.

Once within the temple, I sought the management and introduced myself as a Brahmin priest seeking shelter for a few days. I was given permission to stay there at once; and thus began yet another leg of my journey.

Nakuru is situated in the beautiful Rift Valley Region and at a distance of about 160 km from the capital city of Nairobi. With a population of more than 300,000 it's the fourth largest city in Kenya. Lying around 1,850 metres above the sea-level, it enjoys a pleasant climate throughout the year. It is famous for its National Park, Lake Nakuru and above all home to millions of pink flamingos. Small-scale agriculture, dairy farming, manufacturing and tourism form the core economic activities here. It is also a centre for various retail businesses that provide goods and services to the manufacturing and agricultural sector. The first and second Presidents of Kenya, Hon. Jomo Kenyatta and Hon. Daniel Arap Moi maintained their semi-official residences in this city.

I arrived here by mid-October 1982, in good time for the Navratri festivities. Navratri is an important nine-day-long Hindu autumn festival that culminates in Vijaya Dashami or Dussehra on the tenth day. It holds special significance for the Gujarati and Bengali communities in India. The celebration signifies the triumph of good over evil and is also a celebration of female energy, Shakti, or the Mother Goddess. The term 'Navratri' stands for 'nine nights', during which nine forms of the Mother Goddess are worshipped. The Gujarati community all over the world celebrates the festival with the traditional Dandiya and Garba Raas dances on all the nine nights. Men, women and children dance all night long in their colourful finery to the rhythmic beat of traditional drums and festive music.

At the Nakuru temple, too, the festivities were celebrated with great religious pomp and fervour. I joined the entire Indian community of the town to offer prayers to the Mother, performing religious rituals, singing bhajans (devotional hymns) and even playing traditional drums (dholki or dholak) in accompaniment to the dandiya and Garba Raas. I joined in the community dances as well. On this auspicious occasion, I prayed sincerely to the Mother Goddess to guide me in my way forward. Long after everyone else would return home, I used to continue my prayers for hours together.

It is said that when we pray sincerely with all our heart and soul, God hears more than what we say, answers more than what we ask for, and gives us more than we can imagine—all at the right time and in the right manner. My prayers were soon heard, and a new door opened in the most unexpected manner. The Lord showed me the way through my scriptural knowledge and my experience as a priest. While serving at the Bhuj temple in India, I had studied astrology, palmistry and the knowledge of preparing and analysing horoscopes. During the festive season, the devotees became aware of my skills and began to consult me. I was more than happy to share my knowledge, preparing and studying their horoscopes, reading their palms and offering them guidance through these methods. Suddenly, I became a very busy person, but with absolutely no earnings! I never charged any fee for my services in these matters for I strongly believed that this knowledge was for the benefit of humanity and not for sale!

People began to invite me to perform religious rites and rituals as well. They started calling me: Guru—the priest and the astrologer. Little did anyone know then that I would be known throughout the world by this the name for the rest of my life.

Word of my knowledge of astrology and palmistry spread across Nakuru and soon 'Guru' became a household name. My simplicity impressed them and I made many friends in that town. It was during those days that I first came across Jayantibhai Patel, his younger brother, Ashok Patel, and their families. I will share with you my relationship with them and their role in my life, a little later. Coming back to my Nakuru days...one day...after a religious ceremony, a respected member of the local Indian community approached me. Dhanjibhai Liladhar Valji Parmar, a committee member of the town's Laxmi Narayan temple, was very impressed by my skills. 'Guru, I have heard a lot about you and would be very pleased if you could come and stay with us and guide our family with your astrological knowledge,' he said, adding, 'You can stay with us as long as your wish.'

For a moment, I could not believe my ears! I looked up heavenwards, bowed my head and willingly accepted the offer. My prayers had been answered and the Lord had shown me the way ahead. That was to be the last time I ever took shelter at a temple. Soon I moved to Liladhar Valji Parmar's family home, where I was treated like an old family member. Very soon, they introduced me to other families of the community in town. I continued to guide people without charging anything for my services. Although I did not earn anything, I was happy with the Parmar family, who took care of all my basic necessities of food, shelter and clothing. More importantly, they respected me.

I stayed with the Parmar family for about three or four months. It was true that I was very happy during my stay with them, not wanting for anything; but my thoughts each day were consumed with that of starting my own business. I could not help it, it was in my blood! I kept telling myself that my dream was different and this was not for what I had come to Kenya. I wanted to return to Nairobi, do something worthwhile and earn a lot of money. The path ahead seemed to be very hazy, until an unusual incident took place.

One Sunday evening as we were relaxing and sipping our evening tea, I was given the horoscopes of the entire family to study. I reviewed them and in very simple terms explained what I had read. I was barely about twenty-one or twenty-two years old at the time and very straight forward with my answers. Based on my readings, I told them that the head of the family, Liladharbhai Valji Parmar's days were numbered and that his death awaited him.

The entire family, including Mr. Parmar himself, was dumfounded and shocked. They did not appreciate my readings; I could sense their stress and anxiety, and guessed that it was time for me to leave their home. A few days later, as I was packing my bags, Liladharbhai, who was reading his newspaper, suddenly stumbled from his chair and fell down.

He had to be rushed to the hospital immediately. I hesitated between picking up my bags and leaving or staying back with the family in this hour of need. Good sense prevailed and I thought it was my duty to support the family that had treated me as their own, and so I stayed back. During his hospitalisation, I was with the elderly gentleman and served him selflessly. I read from the holybooks, chanted shlokas (psalms) and narrated the Satya Narayana Katha (religious story of Lord Vishnu). I became very close to Mzee (elder) and he treated me like his own son. The entire family appreciated my service and was happy that there was somebody to take care of him full time. After two months of struggle, the old man breathed his last. I was grief stricken and felt as though I had lost one of my own family. I could not bear the family's sufferings and for once in my life, I regretted having spoken the truth about his death!

There is a first time for everything. As a Brahmin priest, I had performed many religious rites, but this was the first time that I performed the funeral ritual. I helped the family complete the last rites for their father and stayed with them for almost a month during their period of mourning. Every day I sang bhajans, performed poojas, and recited from the holy scriptures. I was re-living the life of a priest.

Meanwhile, people from the community continued to solicit my help and consulted me for their personal and professional problems. Sometimes, I even visited their homes, read their horoscopes, guided them in resolving issues and conducted various religious rites. They accepted and loved me; and I easily became a part of the community. Although I was happy, my thoughts on setting up my own business continued, as usual. That was when I faced a life changing experience.

A well-know family in Nakuru had lost an elderly member, Tribhovandasbhai Patel, and had organised prayers for about ten days in his memory. I was asked to lead the prayers and recite from the Srimad Bhagawad Gita (a prime Hindu text). The entire community used to attend the prayers. Among them was Mahendrabhai Dayabhai Patel, a businessman from Nairobi, who attended it every day. On the first day after the prayers, I was introduced to him and came to know that it was Mahendrabhai's father-in-law who had passed away. The family told to him that not only was I a good priest, but also a master in preparing and reading horoscopes, and that they were impressed with my abilities. He merely smiled and tested my knowledge with a series of questions. 'Guru, can you read my palm and tell me if my employer will give me a raise? How much will it be? And when will I get it?' The house was packed and all eyes were on me.

Unfazed, I studied his palm and replied that since he was a business person and not an employee, the question of a salary or increment did not arise. Moreover, he was quite a wealthy person. He was not only astonished, but also highly impressed with my readings while the entire gathering was amazed. Mahendrabhai came from a successful business family in Nairobi, and used to specifically travel to Nakuru every day to attend the prayers arranged for the peace of his father-in-law's departed soul.

He shared my palm-reading story with his father in Nairobi, who asked for me to be brought to Nairobi. A couple of days later, as we were relaxing after the prayers, he came to me. What he said thereafter was going to decide my future, although I did not know it then. He insisted that I move back to Nairobi and stay with his family. Yet again, I was given proof of the Lord's miracles and mysterious ways. One simply had to have faith and continue doing one's duty. While with each waking moment I tried in vain to figure out a way to return to Nairobi, here stood a man before me, inviting me to his family home in that very city!

Without a second thought, I accepted the offer; and that was how my brief stay in Nakuru came to an end. Finally, I thought, I could see light at the end of the tunnel…

• CHAPTER 14 •

A DATE WITH DESTINY: MEETING PRESIDENT DANIEL ARAP MOI

There is always a reason and purpose behind our chance meeting with people. Some are there to test us, others to use us, some teach us, while others bring out the best in us.

People walk into our lives for a reason, for a season, or for a lifetime; and when we meet, the groundwork is laid for initiating transformation in our lives. Destiny has strange ways of making us encounter new people and when we first meet them, we hardly realise what role the person may play in our lives. It was in the strangest circumstance that I first met the then President of Kenya, His Excellency the Hon. Daniel Toroitich Arap Moi. I was a twenty-two-year-old youth at the time, without the faintest idea of what the chance meeting was to mean for me in my life. It would go on to lay the foundation of my bond with him in the years to follow. Let me share this incident with you, before moving ahead with the rest of my journey.

It took place in early 1983, during my stay with Liladhar Valji Parmar's family in Nakuru. On that day I had visited Jayantibhai

Patel's shop to study the palms and horoscopes of Jayantibhai and some of his friends. He was a reputed businessman, trading in electronics and hardware equipment. While we sat there, Jayantibhai received a call from the State House in Nakuru. That was when President Moi's semi-official residence was in Nakuru. The caller said that the television at the President's residence needed to be repaired, requesting for a technician to immediately check and mend it. Jayantibhai and his engineer picked up their tool bag and headed to the State House. With nothing better to do, I went along with them. When we reached the State House, we were guided to the drawing room where the TV set was installed. My friends asked me to wait in the drawing room as they got down to inspect the equipment. Unable to find any fault with it, they went out to check for any fault with the wiring and cables. They asked me to keep an eye on the TV as they adjusted the cables outside the room. Except for myself, there was nobody else in the drawing room. It was then that the President, His Excellency the Hon. Daniel Arap Moi, walked into the room!

With a great big smile, he extended his hand to greet me. They say the first impression always leaves a lasting impact. His bright smile touched my heart. He sat next to me and immediately struck up a conversation. He asked me who I was and what work I did. I humbly told him that I was a Hindu priest, and that palmistry and astrology were my subjects of interest. We had a brief discussion about religion, humanity, politics, and astrology. I was impressed by his humility and by the fact that the head of the nation sat conversing so easily with a nondescript and ordinary young man like me. Eager to know more about astrology, he extended an open invitation to visit him at the State House in Nairobi. In that very first meeting, we developed a rapport and bond with each other. I never imagined that I would ever have the opportunity to meet him personally again.

I did not realise then that I had the privilege of meeting the most important personage in the country, whom people seek permission to meet and wait for days before getting an audience! The great honour dawned on me much later. In the next couple of years, I was to meet President Moi quite a few times at The State House in Nairobi. Despite being an ordinary individual, I used to freely walk down to his residence, much to everyone's surprise.

I have always held President Moi in high esteem and looked upon him with reverence and respect. He walked into my life, when I was young and alone in Kenya, missing my parents and family. His parental guidance helped me to emotionally tide over this phase of my life. A few years later, when I was establishing my business, his moral support went a long way in developing my confidence. Without his blessings, I would have returned to India a long time ago, and would not have been what I am today. President Moi has been more than my friend, philosopher and guide. I felt honoured when years later, he laid the foundation stone of our first steel rolling mills at Athi River, near Nairobi.

Despite my closeness with him, however, I have not taken any undue advantage or utilised our relationship for any personal gain. All through my life, I have never transacted business with politicians or government agencies. I have advised him on political matters relating to the realignment of his ministries or on Party mergers, which he appreciated. And thanks to him, I have had the honour of meeting and becoming associated with a many great leaders over the years. Among many important leaders, he introduced me to His Excellency the Hon. Mwai Kibaki, who used to be his deputy and later succeeded him as Kenya's President. Through him I also met His Excellency the Hon. Uhuru Kenyatta, the ruling President of Kenya at present. In addition, my relationship with him gave me the opportunities to meet the presidents of Uganda, Tanzania and the Democratic

Republic of Congo (DRC). I must reiterate that I have never taken any benefit from these relationships or exploited them for my business or personal needs.

I must say, again, that people come into our lives for a purpose. I will be indebted to the Almighty for giving me the privilege and honour of meeting such a great personality, who helped me transform my life.

• CHAPTER 15 •

PRACTISE WHAT YOU PREACH

As Guru at the age of twenty-one, I had earned respect and a special place in the hearts of the Gujarati community in Nakuru. This was not only due to my role as a priest and my knowledge of astrology, but also my simplicity, accessibility and my friendly nature. People consulted me for the tiniest of their problems and guiding them rightly became a part and parcel of my daily routine. This was an enormous responsibility (of course, I did not charge anything for this) and I perceived that unless I practised what I preached, my advice did not mean anything. People watch what you do more than they listen to what you say. I felt that I could inspire, challenge and encourage people to do their best by practising what I preached. I would like to share a small, yet interesting incident, which has left a permanent impact on me.

While staying with Liladhar Valji Parmar's family in Nakuru, every day I used to recite the holy Srimad Bhagawad Gita. Neighbours used to gather to listen to my discourses. One day, after I had finished my recital, a middle-aged man and his eleven-year-old son approached me. With folded hands, he said,

'Maharaj, my son has a habit of eating jaggery [sugar cane or date palm molasses] with his meals, because of which he has developed boils.' He added, 'He continues to eat it every day despite a strict warning from our family doctor. Maharaj, please advise him to stop eating it! Many people in India, especially Gujaratis, eat jaggery as part of their meals. I placed my hand on the boy's head with a smile and requested the father to bring his son back to me after a month. Exactly a month later, he returned to me with his son. Finishing my prayers, I spoke briefly to the young boy and persuaded him to give up his habit. The boy agreed and actually gave up the habit immediately.

Life continued as usual. A week after this incident, as I was reciting the holy scriptures, I saw the young boy waiting for me with his mother. I guessed something was not right, as her face was red with agitation. Immediately after the prayers, even before the gathering had dispersed, the lady rushed towards me. To everyone's surprise, she screamed at the top of her voice. Venting out her anger, she said, 'Maharaj, it took you only two minutes to advise my son, why then did you make us wait for a whole month for such a small thing?'

Everyone tuned to look at me; a perplexed Dhanjibhai Parmar looked at me for an answer. She was his best friend's wife! I waited for the lady to calm down. Looking at Dhanjibhai, who was like a father to me, I requested him to call forward his wife, Shantiben. When she came, I asked her in Gujarati, 'શાંતિબેન, મારે તમને દરેક ભોજન સાથે આપવા માટે શું વિનંતીકરું? [Shantiben, what do I request you to give me along with every meal?]'. She instantly replied, 'Jaggery!'

I explained to Dhanjibhai that when I had the same habit as the young boy, how could I have advised him not to have it? I went on to share that since the day the boy's father, his friend had approached me; I had given up eating jaggery. I practised this for an entire month, before preaching the boy! I could have advised him to stop a month back, but I would have been morally wrong in preaching what I did not practise myself.

My stay in Nakuru will always have a special place in my heart, for it was from here that the foundation of my future was laid. I will always cherish the love and affection I had received from everyone, especially from Liladharbhai Parmar, his two sons, Dhanjibhai and Shantibhai, and their entire family.

• CHAPTER 16 •

SAINT TO STEEL: THE JOURNEY BEGINS

Although I was a priest by profession, I always aspired to be a businessman, earning a sizeable income and achieving exceptional goals in life. I had a very clear vision of doing business and succeeding in it, which is why I was constantly seeking opportunities for a breakthrough. The fact that Nairobi was an important business hub of East Africa made it all the more lucrative for me to start from here. Even though circumstances forced me to travel to Kisumu and Nakuru on my return in 1982, I knew where I had to go. I was always looking out for opportunities to come to Nairobi and so you can imagine the windfall I landed when I received Mahendrabhai's offer of staying with his family in the great city. Back then, little did I understand the significance his offer would have in my life. Today, standing at the zenith of my career, I have often been asked the question, 'Among all businesses and trades, why did you choose steel and hardware?' Let me now begin to answer that question by going back to the point from where it all began…

After completing the prayer sessions in Nakuru, held in the honour of his father-in-law's memory, I travelled to Nairobi with

Mahendrabhai. During our conversations along the journey, he gave an insight into his family and their business. He shared that his father, Dayabhai H. Patel, and his five sons, owned the biggest and the most successful steel rolling establishment of that time in Kenya—the Kikuyu Steel Rolling Mills Limited. The family business also included a trading arm, Steel Wares. He also divulged that was a joint family business though all his brothers resided separately and had their own personal lives. While we were in Nakuru, he had told me that I was to reside with his parents. Our talks continued throughout the journey and before long we reached Nairobi, where I was to reside at his parents' home.

On our arrival, I was astounded at the sight of their bungalow. It was a palatial affair; and probably one of the most modern in the Nairobi of those days. There was a fleet of vehicles parked at the doorstep, with an army of house-helps. I could sense an abundance of wealth and luxury all around. This was way beyond my imagination, for though I had resided in this very city for a good three years, I realised that they had been spent in a very different environment!

I was given a warm welcome by the entire family, who had gathered to receive me. Much more than their wealth, it was their simplicity and humility that touched my soul. I was overwhelmed by the welcome. Out of respect, I touched Dayabhai's feet and emotions overtook me, reminding me of my father when he hugged me affectionately (bending down and touching an elder's feet is a sign of respect in the Indian community, which is reciprocated by the elder's blessings and affection for the young—in age as well as social relationship). That night as I lay in an opulent bed chamber, I had plenty of things to thank the Almighty for. Following my daily prayers, I slept well that night.

I began staying with the elderly couple, Dayabhai Patel and his wife. The Mzee was around seventy years old, and a very loving and caring person. As always, I began practicing religious rituals for the household, offering early morning prayers for their prosperity and continued well being. The family had installed a temple in their bungalow, where the Mzee and I offered morning prayers together. We gelled very well and became close to each other following certain incidents. After our morning prayers one day, I noticed a box in the temple and out of curiosity asked what it contained. I was surprised when the Mzee told me that it contained a 'Shiva Linga' gifted to the family by the Sankaracharya. A Shiva Linga is an iconic representation of the Hindu Lord Shiva, which is worshipped in temples and shrines. I could not imagine why the holy statue was lying unseen and un-worshipped in a box, and requested permission to install it for daily worship.

The Mzee naturally agreed and I began offering prayers to Lord Shiva from that day onwards. I also insisted Dayabhai to perform daily prayers, which he did. The Mzee's diet included a lot of meat, fish and eggs, which many Hindus do not eat; and so I made efforts to change his diet. Initially, he turned a deaf ear and continued as always. As part of our daily routine, I also recited holy sholkas and read stories from Hindu texts. This had a positive impact on him and he gradually became a pure vegetarian. All these events brought us closer together, and we shared a warm bonding during my stay in his home. He treated me like his own son and the entire family accepted me as one of their own. To this day, I cherish the fond memories of the time I spent at Dayabhai's home; and will always stay indebted to him for the love, respect and support his family showered on me.

I had my first glimpse of the steel industry when I began to regularly visit the facilities of the Kikuyu Steel Rollings Mills and Steel Wares owned by the Patel family. I used to spend most of my time with the Mzee, but after completing our morning rituals, I usually had ample time at my disposal. One day after breakfast, as he got ready for office, the Mzee said to me in Gujarati, 'મહારાજ, તમે દરરોજ શામાટે મારી સાથે ઓફિસમાં જોડાય નહી?તે તમને બન્ને સમય પસાર કરવા અને કેટલાક વ્યવસાયના જ્ઞાનને મેળવવા માટે મદદ કરશે [Maharaj, why don't you join me in office every day? It will help you to pass your time, while you gain some business knowledge].'Needless to say, I was delighted by his proposition; but was still oblivious to the fact that his kindness would lay the foundations of my business life!

Having always nurtured a fascination for businesses of all kinds, I was excited at my first sight of the steel rolling plant. Curiosity to understand the business operations and the management of such a big business mounted in me with each day. I had never witnessed anything of this scale before! Initially, I sat in their office, observing how the Mzee and his children conducted the business – how they handled and delegated work, how they spoke on the phone, how they dealt with suppliers, customers, and government authorities. In short, as an cnthusiastic and keen learner, I observed and absorbed as much as I could.

I was more interested in how they sourced their raw materials, sold their final products and how the business made money. Noticing my eagerness to learn the ropes, the Mzee and his sons asked me to step into the factory as a next step. I became an ardent pupil, eager to gain new knowledge every day. With time, I noted and understood how the scrap metal was sourced, transported to the factory and heated in the furnace. I earnestly watched as the cast liquid steel was converted into semi-finished pencil ingots or billets. The process of re-heating and then finally rolling the metal into wire rods, re-bars, angles, channels, sections or flat steel interested me immensely. As I also had the opportunity to spend time at Steel Wares, I became familiar with the sales and distribution of the finals product as well.

My business interests had been kindled.

Staying with the Patel family, I continued playing my religious role by conducting morning prayers with the Mzee and guiding religious discourses for the family. They consulted me many times on business and personal matters, because of my knowledge of astrology and horoscopes; and I was always more than happy to help! They even introduced me to many of their family, friends and associates, whose homes I began visiting for astrological guidance. Once again, I offered my services free of charge, firmly believing that my knowledge was for the benefit of humanity and not for sale!

Gradually, I began to enjoy my life once gain. Despite being penniless, the love and affection of the Patel family, and the mutual respect I found among them, were my priceless possessions. I continued to accompany the Mzee to the factory every day, and each day I learnt something new. During that period, I often felt as though I were sailing on two boats—serving as a Hindu priest on one end and learning to become a businessman on the other. I had finally begun my journey towards my aim in life. It was time to regularise my immigration status in Kenya. I was still residing here on a visitor's visa, but even before I could broach the topic with the family, an opportunity to travel to England came my way, which needs to be discussed before I proceed any further with my story.

• CHAPTER 17 •

MY FIRST UK VISIT: EXPERIENCE OF A LIFE TIME

Every experience in our lives is a 'once in a lifetime' experience. We might experience it again, but no matter how hard we try, it will never exactly feel the same way as it did the first time. Like a Hollywood blockbuster, the experience of my first trip to London was full of action and suspense! It was one of its kinds that actually left me quite stunned.

I was twenty-two years old, staying with the Patel family in Nairobi, when an opportunity to travel to London came my way. Impressed with my knowledge of astrology and horoscopes that I used to share with everyone, the Mzee had suggested that I visit some of his family in the UK. He felt it would be ideal if I planned a trip for his family to consult me on matters to do with palmistry and astrology. He added that I could also perform poojas and havans (consecrated fire rituals), conduct Hindu marriages and organise Satyanarayan poojas. Over the years, I had performed various religious rites for devotees and their families, but never had I travelled all the way to another continent for this purpose!

No doubt, I was interested, but I was also concerned about the travel cost and accommodation. The Patel family had introduced me to quite a few people, who consulted me on religious matters. One such family was that of Dilipbhai Raniga. It was through astrology and common friends that I first met him. Dilipbhai owned a travel, tours and ticketing business named, Kisumu Travel Agency. I was close to him because I had assisted his family with their horoscopes, guiding them accordingly. It was during one such visit to the Raniga family that I informed Dilipbhai of the Mzee's suggestion that I travel to the UK. I also shared that the travel costs were bothering me. On hearing this, Dilipbhai immediately offered to sponsor my travel! He also suggested that many of his relatives who stayed in London would avail my services too.

I was getting excited and shared my feelings with the Mzee, who spread the word of my proposed travel among his extended family. Incidentally, it so happened that a family in the UK was looking for a Hindu priest to perform a marriage in their family; and they were delighted to hear about my travel and requested me to conduct the marriage during my stay there. All in all, many events were lined up at the news of my travel plans. I was still a bit hesitant and discussed the matter with my Nakuru friends, Ashokbhai and his brother, Jayantibhai Patel, who also concurred that it would be a good idea for me to travel to the UK. They added that their elder brother, Ghyanshambhai Patel, would assist me in England. With all arrangements falling into place, I was all set to travel to London – for the first time.

True to his word, Dilipbhai arranged a return ticket for me through Sabena Airlines, which used to be part of Brussels Airlines in those days. It was my first travel to Europe, and even though by now I was well versed with air travel and airport formalities, I remained tensed during that entire journey. There was a stopover and change of planes at Brussels, and finally I was on my way to London. On a bright and sunny morning, I arrived at the Heathrow Airport in London. In those days, visas for passengers travelling from Nairobi to London were issued at the airport on arrival. The drama began after I headed to the immigration counter and joined the visa queue.

When my turn came, I presented myself before the immigration officer, who scanned my passport and documents and asked me a simple question, 'Sir, what brings you to London and what's the purpose of your visit?' He continued, 'How long do you intend to stay here?' I understood his question clearly, but as I was poor in English, I felt nervous and stammered a response. 'Sir, I am a Hindu priest and came to London for a marriage and other religious functions.' He looked in the eye and asked again, 'Marriage, your marriage?' I was a priest who had come to perform someone else's marriage, but by now I was so perplexed and lost that I merely nodded in affirmation. He gave me another glare and asked me to step aside and wait. After clearing the queue before his counter, he ushered me into the airport interrogation cell!

There was a table with four chairs on one side and a chair on the other side. This was now like a movie-scene and I imagined myself being brutally interrogated! As if to confirm my thoughts, three burly, uniformed officers walked into the cell. My heart sank. While one of them asked me the same question, 'Gentleman, what brings you to London?' The other two gave me nasty glares. With folded hands, I gave them the same response,'I am a Hindu priest and came to London for a marriage and other religious functions.' They misunderstood my poor English and construed that I had gone there to get married and intended to stay back in London permanently!

They looked at me and then at each other, before asking me to wait and left the room. The long wait did nothing for my already shattered self confidence. Why was I asked to wait? What was my fault? Would they issue me a visa? Would they imprison me? The thoughts never seemed to cease and after almost three or four hours of waiting, the officers returned with very serious expressions. One of them stepped up before me and said, 'Sir, we suspect that the purpose of your visit is to marry and reside here permanently, hence we cannot issue you a visa.' What he said next, scared me out of my wits. 'A decision has been made to deport you by the next available flight, please handover your passport and wait.' I tried my best to explain the truth, but all my efforts were in vain. They asked me to wait once more, but by now I sat stunned and shell-shocked. Once again, I prayed to the Lord to rescue me from the terrible situation; and yet again, *He* did not disappoint.

Meanwhile, as all this drama was unfolding within the airport terminal, Ghyanshambhai Patel, Ashokbhai's eldest brother, was waiting for me at the international arrivals hall. He became concerned when I did not turn up on time, and after about three hours of waiting for me, he began to panic. He checked with the Sabena Airlines only to be informed that I had indeed travelled with them and had already arrived in London. He immediately notified the airport authorities and was told that I was being held at the interrogation cell, and was about to be deported. He pleaded with the authorities to allow him to see me once, to which they hesitatingly obliged. He came to the cell and asked me what had happened and after I told him everything, he understood that there had been a miscommunication. He managed to explain to the officers the purpose of my visit, but they held on to their stand and were determined on deporting me. All this while, I watched the proceedings like a dumb spectator, and for once in my life wished that had I taken an interest in learning English in school! Ghayshambhai requested the officers to hold me back at the airport, instead of deporting me, while he made serious efforts to find a solution to the problem.

He made a few phone calls from there to all possible contacts, asking for help. That was when one of his friends told him to call the Member of Parliament (MP) of the Surrey County, Mr. Praful Patel, who was a person of Indian origin. Surrey was also where I was supposed to stay during my visit. Ghayshambhai called the MP and explained the situation to him. The MP asked to speak with the immigration authorities. He told them that he was willing to stand guarantee and issue a surety letter of my credentials, requesting them to issue me a visa and allow me to stay in the country, to which the officers agreed. It did not end there, because one of Ghyanshambhai's friends had to go to the MP's office, collect the letter and hand it to the authorities. After completing all formalities, I was finally issued a visa for only a week! My passport was retained at the immigration office and I was asked to collect it when I travelled back. After spending more than eight hours at the airport, I finally breathed fresh air. Again it seemed like a movie to me, as if I were a prisoner walking out of jail!

Owing to the valiant cfforts of Ghanshyambhai and his friends, and much thanks to the Surrey County MP, Prafulbhai Patel, my visa was later approved for two months. Incidentally, it had to be extended by another month towards the end of my visit, and I recall staying in England for almost three months on that first trip. By the time I departed from London, my immigration file had become very thick with all the exchange of correspondence and documents! I believe it must still be resting in their archives to this day.

The drive from Heathrow to Surrey was an enjoyable one, especially after the ordeal I had just gone through. Passing through the beautiful countryside and lush green meadows, I fell in the love with the country at my very first sight. After settling down at my host's residence, I did perform the marriage for which I had come, as well as various religious rites at Dilipbhai's brother's home. I also visited many other families, performing numerous religious rites, preparing and explaining horoscopes, sharing advice on astrological issues and even conducting Satyanarayan poojas. As a matter of principle, I never charged a single penny for preparing and studying horoscopes; but I did accept my dakshina for conducting poojas and leading the Satyanarayan katha. Believe it or not, I managed to earn nearly £ 2,000 by the end of my visit, which was quite a princely sum back in those days. A good samaritan helped me to open a bank account in the UK, where I deposited the amount for future use.

During my stay, I travelled across the country, met people from different cultures and from different walks of life. I enjoyed the hospitality of all the families I stayed with and made new friends. This visit was an exceptional one for me, because not only did I earn money, but also the won the hearts of many, earning their respect, love and affection. The visit had a lasting impact on me, and by the time I returned to Nairobi, I was already a changed person.

Even to this day, after thirty-four years, the devils of that first visit continue to haunt me every time I travel to London, especially when I present my passport at the Immigration desk!

• CHAPTER 18 •

STATUS REGULARISED AND BACK TO SQUARE ONE

I returned to Nairobi after that memorable UK visit—an entirely refined and changed person. Meeting people from varied backgrounds, different cultures and unique lifestyles had left a lasting impression on me. I was also amazed by the country's progress, the modern infrastructure, advanced techniques of businesses and the government's outlook and concern for its citizens. The calm and serene English countryside had gained a special place in my heart. My perception about life had changed and my horizon had broadened.

On my return, I continued to stay with the Patel family and they were more than happy to have me back. I shared my travel experiences with them and settled back into the daily routine of religious rites. I also accompanied the Mzee to their factory as usual, but I was decidedly a changed man after my travels. By this juncture, despite my priestly role in the community and my interests in astrology, my passion for business had mushroomed manifold. I was still on a visitor's visa and realised that it was time for me to regularise my immigration status in Kenya, if I were to run my own business here. It was time to move forward in life.

One afternoon, as the Mzee and I were having our afternoon tea, I divulged my future plans and shared my concern about my current legal status here. He looked straight into my eyes, gave me a big smile and rose from his chair, patting my back and assuring me in Gujarati,'થઇ જશે [it will be done]'. Without saying anything else, he gestured me to get up and walk out of the office with him. Trusting his judgement and wisdom in these matters, I did as I was told and chose not to probe him further. It took me a few days to understand what he had meant when he said, 'It will be done.' One morning, it so happened that instead of going to office, he instructed his driver to take us elsewhere. I was oblivious of the fact that we were headed to the office of Mr. Charles Mugane Njonjo. Mr. Njongo was the Attorney General of Kenya from 1963 to 1979, and when we visited him, he was the Minister of Constitutional Affairs in the Kenyan Government.

On reaching Mr. Njongo's office, the Mzee introduced me to the honourable Minister as a renowned Hindu priest and astrologer. A year before in 1982 Kenya had faced a political turbulence and a failed coup attempt was made to overthrow the government headed by the President, His Excellency Daniel Arap Moi. It was alleged that Mr. Charles Njonjo had abused his office and had tried to take over the Presidency from His Excellency the Hon. President Moi. As the Minister became aware of my astrological knowledge, he insisted that I predict his future. I studied his horoscope and told him that very soon he would be forced to resign from his office, face judicial enquiry, fight legal battles and asked to leave the government. I also told him that eventually things would all fall into place and he would be absolved of all the allegations levelled against him and given a clean chit. On hearing this, his face went red and he was very upset with me. Mr. Patel's face had also fallen. He must have wondered whether he had erred in introducing me to the Minister! We left the office and on our way back, the Mzee did not utter a single word. Within a few days of our visit, all my predictions began to play out.

The Kenyan Government initiated a judicial enquiry against Mr. Njongo, for office abuse. He faced challenging times; he was interrogated, had to run around the law courts and his image was tarnished. It was then that he recalled my predictions and thanked me for my readings. After months of ferocious legal inquiries, he was finally absolved of all charges, just as I had predicted. Soon thereafter, he quit public life; but he continued to seek my guidance from time to time for all his problems, and I continued to guide him. This is another incident that has always remained fresh in my mind even after all these years.

This association with Mr. Njongo had a particularly important role to play in my life ahead. It was during one of my several meetings with him that he instructed the then Principal Immigration Officer (PIO), Mr. J.K. Mutua, to issue an H-Class permit for me. The H-Class permit allowed me to be self-employed and also permitted me to work as a priest. Within the next few weeks, I received my work-permit, which was also endorsed in my passport. When I first held the permit in my hand, my happiness knew no bounds! The entire Patel family too was excited; and when I broke the good news to my parents, their joy was uncontrollable. There were celebrations in my village back in India as well as here in Nairobi, where the entire Patel family got together to congratulate me. My prayers had been answered yet again and my Kenyan immigration status was finally regularised. I could stay here peacefully for the next two years at least; but I was still far away from my ultimate goal. Although the permit meant that I could practise my vocation as a priest and remain self-employed, it also meant that I could not engage in business activities.

I knew that I had miles and miles to go yet, but thanked the Lord for holding my hand and showing me the way!

It is truly said that we cannot plan for the unexpected. Even as things started falling into place, destiny had something else in store for me. The happiness of receiving my work permit had not yet been digested in full, when Mr. Patel's children wanted to split ways. They wanted to disengage themselves from their joint family system and lead their separate lives. A couple of his sons wanted to migrate to the UK, while others wanted to settled down in the US. The next few days were busy with hectic activity; business and family meetings, and of emotions running high; but the writing on the wall was clear. Finally, after a lot of deliberations, the family decided to sell their business and property in Kenya and split their family wealth. It was painful to see the family part ways in this manner. Circumstances had changed within the blink of an eye; and for the second time in my life, I felt the pain of parting from my family. The last few days were extremely painful for me. On the very last day, when all of them parted from each other, there were plenty of emotional scenes. To me, it seemed as though the world had fallen apart, and I broke down completely when I bid farewell to the elderly couple.

Mrs. and Mr. Patel settled down in their native village of Galla in Gujarat, India. He remembered me very often and we stayed in constant touch. He told me that he had continued with our religious routine in India. I was extremely happy to note that he had built a Shiva temple in his village, consecrating it with the Shiva Linga gifted to his family by the Shankaracharya, which we used to worship in his Nairobi home. One day, when he called me from India, as he often did, and we were conversing casually, he suddenly became very emotional and thanked me profusely for transforming him. Unable to hold myself back, I began to cry, for it was I who would forever be indebted to him. He was the one who had held my hand when I was alone, supported me when I really needed help, embraced me like one of his children, taught me the first lessons in the steel business and was instrumental in getting my first permit in Kenya. It was his greatness, generosity and humility that led him to thank me, when in all truth it was I who should be thankful to him for everything! I am happy to share that the last days of this generous elderly couple were spent in peace and tranquillity. Mr. Patel passed away peacefully at the age of eighty-seven and his wife followed him a few years later.

After the Patel family left Nairobi, I was on my own once more. Fortunately, one of Mr. Patel's sons, Mahendrabhai Patel, who had brought me from Nakuru to Nairobi, supported me for some time. He started his own business of trading in steel products under the name, Steel Wares, and asked me to join him. By this time, I had picked up a good knowledge of steel and hardware products. We worked together like a family and progressed well. I gathered my own experience of the steel trading business, especially in marketing them. While working with Mahendrabhai, I noticed cases of pilferage and fraud, which were against my principles. Though I saw and understood these unethical practices, I was helpless to stop it since I did not have much say in the business. I continued to be a silent spectator till, unable to bear it any longer, I decided to leave.

I was back to square one and back on the streets again; but at least I could stay back in Kenya this time, thanks to my work permit. As Mahendrabhai waved in farewell for one last time, I raised my head towards the skies, folded my hands in prayer and asked the Lord to show me the way.

• CHAPTER 19 •

STEEL AND HARDWARE BUSINESS: A SOLID FOUNDATION

My journey so far had been following a distinct pattern. Whenever trouble brewed or I was left stranded with a keen desire to move ahead in pursuit of my goal, help came from unexpected quarters and I always found the support of a 'Messiah'. The pattern I detected was that every time somebody aided me, and before I could forge ahead, circumstances would change swiftly and I would invariably find myself back to square one! The important aspect to note here, however, is that I never gave up on my dreams despite the numerous setbacks, and I always found help around the corner.

Over the years, I have come to realise that if we pursue our dreams with all our devotion, dedication and determination, then doors are bound to open up in places where we least imagined.

One character trait that I firmly believe is fundamental for success in any field is the ability to never give up on your dreams, whatever be the circumstances. I do not mean that in pursuit of our goals, we should never fail or fall; but it is important that every time we fall, we stand up and march ahead again.

I was at a juncture of my life, where I had a clear vision of becoming a successful businessman in Kenya. I had gained some basic knowledge of the steel industry and wanted to advance in life, but when the Patel family wound up their business in Nairobi, I was back on the streets. The only silver lining was that I was now armed with a work permit, and I was determined to knock on all possible doors for the way ahead. It was then that God opened another door for me.

My inherent simplicity allows me to get along with people quite comfortably and I find it very easy to make friends. In Nakuru, owing to my priesthood and knowledge of astrology, I had met many people and had made many acquaintances, including some very good friends. One family that I was particularly close to was that of Jayantibhai and Ashok Patel. Even after moving to Nairobi, I had kept in touch with their family. I always felt closer to Ashok Patel, since he was a year or two younger, and we often met during his visits to Nairobi. On one such occasion, towards the end of 1983, around the time I had to leave the Patel family, we met briefly in Nairobi. I appraised Ashok of my impending situation and asked for help. Understanding my plight, he informed me that their family owned a one-bedroom apartment in the Ngara area, near the Hare Krishna Temple, in Nairobi. It was lying unused and he invited me to stay there for as long as I wished.

With that, my immediate concern was taken care of and I found a roof over my head, thanks to Ashok. He was a partner in a Nakuru-based trading firm, 'Delta Hardware'. The company dealt in hardware products like cement, nails, door hinges, welding rods and plumbing material, among others. Delta Hardware, however, did not have any outlets in Nairobi at that time. During that fateful meeting, I suggested that they set up a branch here in Nairobi, proposing to independently manage and operate it for them. Ashok liked my proposal. On his return to Nakuru, he discussed the plan with his other partners, Mr. Washira and Mr. Baka, who were more than delighted at the idea. They soon gave a go-ahead for me to start their Nairobi business. The first door to my dream of running a business had just opened up!

Delta Hardware's Nairobi's set up was my brain-child. Though, only twenty-two years old, I had taken on an enormous responsibility upon my shoulders. I was excited, full of novel ideas and wanted to seize this golden opportunity. More importantly, I wanted to live up to the expectations, confidence and trust that the partners had placed in me. Right at the outset, I made it clear that my reason for joining them was not for earning a salary, since I considered them to be my family and their business to be my own. This actually turned out to be more challenging than my priest's life; but as long as my basic needs were being met, I was fine. As a matter of principle, we had decided to only carry out wholesale trading through the Nairobi outlet, and not indulge in retail sales. We hired a shed in the industrial area, which doubled up as our warehouse-cum-office and I was good to go!

As my first initiative, I made a list of all the manufacturers of steel and hardware in Kenya. Owing to my experience with D.H. Patel and the Kikuyu Steel Rolling Mills, I already knew quite a few manufacturers and suppliers. I personally visited all of them and informed them of our newly established wholesale trading unit, earnestly requesting them for their support. At that time, our sourcing was purely on an up-front payment basis and we did not enjoy any credit facility with our suppliers. After a few months of serious discussions and stupendous efforts on my part, most of the suppliers agreed to open credit lines for us. This eased our initial cash flow situation and was a victory of sorts for me.

Secondly, I observed that at Delta, hardware products comprised a major part of the supplies. After my discussions with the partners about why steel products did not have a fair share of our supplies, I realised that it was mainly due to their limited knowledge and exposure to the steel sector that they did not actively involve themselves in such products. They say that knowledge is power and once acquired, it stays on and helps you forever. This is exactly what I did. During my 'internship' at the Kikuyu Steel Rolling Mills, I had gathered a reasonable experience (if not expert knowledge) of the steel products they manufactured. So I suggested that items like barbed wires, chain link fences, hollow sections, mild steel angles and plates, reinforcement bars, re-bars, welded mesh, wire nails, etc., could all be added to our supply range. I added that his would not only boost our sales, but would go a long way in increasing our profits. My idea was soon implemented and our supplies swelled!

Thirdly, we primarily sourced our products from local suppliers and manufacturers. I was aware of the fact that if we could resort to imports, we could stand a chance of getting better quality products at competitive prices. I spent a lot of effort towards this and we gradually started importing. Over the years, I have realised that it always helps to think out of the box, especially in business. There is an interesting experience, which I would like to share here, hoping that it will help all of you, especially those who can think out of the box and generate profits in business. It so happened, that in those days, there were a couple of items such as 'hard-board' and 'soft-board', which were manufactured in Tanzania. There was a lot of demand for these products in Kenya, but there were restrictions on their imports. The government had placed a quota system for sourcing them and only those importers who had applied and had been sanctioned the quota were allowed to source them. I sensed an avenue for making money here, and sat recharging my brain cells. I also contacted many importers who had been awarded the 'approved quotas' and stumbled upon the fact that there were quite a few, who did not import them despite having the entitlement to do so. On further enquiry, I found that some of them had cash crunches and others faced technical issues. I planned to capitalise on this knowledge and decided to the buy their quotas. I worked on a premise where we fore-sold these products and based on our commitments, imported them. The idea was not to stock these items and block our working capital. This plan worked and in due course, we were able to buy quotas from most of the importers. In one particular consignment, I still remember that we booked a sizeable order and managed to buy quotas of almost all the importers and committed ourselves. It so happened that by the time the actual products landed in Kenya, prices had shot up and we managed to make a huge profit!

I realised that it always pays to think out of the box!

With time, though our business expanded four-fold, my appetite had also increased multi-fold and I was never content with what we had achieved so far. I was always looking for ways and means of expanding our business and increasing our sales. Profit became a strong motivator for me to keep on going. I still remember having to burn the mid-night oil to ensure that deliveries were made in a timely manner and that there were no complaints from our customers. I requested the partners to expand their business nation-wide and give me the freedom to travel across Kenya, which they willingly did. I started travelling extensively and marketed our products aggressively. I travelled to Mombasa, Nakuru, Thika, Eldodet, Kisumu, Kakamega and some lesser-known places around the country. Eventually, our foresight, hard work and vision paid rich dividends, and at one point during my association with the firm, Delta Hardware became the biggest wholesale hardware supplier in Kenya.

Today, though it is very hard for me to pen down my emotions exactly, I can share that my joy knew no bounds. The achievement was beyond my imagination. Especially for a person like me, who had boarded his first fight from Mumbai to Nairobi just a few years back, with nothing else but his parents' blessings – this achievement was humongous! I could not believe that I was at the helm of a trading business, which had touched its peak in just a couple of years of my stepping into it. A solid foundation for my business career had been laid!

Delta offered me the perfect platform where my inherent business instincts and my skills bloomed, while my confidence and courage swelled. There was much more than business training that I received here, however, for which I will always be indebted, especially to Jayantibhai Patel and his younger brother, Ashokbhai, and their families. Firstly, in this 'Patel family', I found the love and affection that even my parents would not have given me. (I discuss about the relationship I shared with this family elsewhere in my story, and how instrumental they have been in my life's success). Secondly, this business stage gave me an opportunity to travel all over Kenya, meeting people from across cultures and all walks of life, and understanding their aspirations and needs. I made friends wherever I travelled, be it Indians, Africans or even Mzungus (a 'white person' in East Africa). During my sales trips, all my customers welcomed me and we would share our meals. Our meals were simple enough, consisted of only bread and sodas, but they had the ingredient of love in them! Believe it or not, this was also the first time I tasted soda, having been a priest so far with strict dietary restrictions. Thirdly, even after all those years of my association with Delta, I never worked for a 'salary'. I treated it as my own business and till the end; I was extremely well taken care of and treated like more than a family member.

Cars have always fascinated me. Like most youngsters my age, I wanted to experience the thrill of driving a fast car! This dream was also fulfilled during my association with Ashok Patel. He loved car racing and was a Safari Rally Driver. The Safari Rally is a car race held in East Africa. It was first held from 27th May to 1st June 1953 as the East African Coronation Safari in Kenya,

Uganda and Tanganyika (now Tanzania), as a celebration of the coronation of Queen Elizabeth II. In 1960, it was renamed as the East African Safari Rally till 1974, when it simply became the Safari Rally. It is one of the most prestigious and celebrated rallies, as well as one of the toughest. Though it was an expensive sport, Ashok could afford to participate in it since our business was doing well. Whenever he participated in the rally, all of us travelled with him in 'service cars' to cheer him on and to act as his back-up support in case of emergencies. The fun and excitement of driving alongside expert sportsmen was an adrenaline rush that I enjoyed immensely! Thanks to the Safari Rally, I had travelled across some of the most rough roads in the country. In 1983, Ashok and his teammate, Dalbir Kandola, participated in their Datsun 160J, with a total driving time of around 23 hours and 58 minutes, securing the twentieth position in that year's Marlboro Safari Rally. Two years later, in 1985, Ashok and Dalbir finished ninth overall in their Nissan 240RS, driving for 14 hours and 08 minutes. The memories of the celebrations after that 1985 race are still fresh in my mind.

A moment during the Safari Car Rally

The most wonderful thing to have ever happened to me also took place during this period, when I met the love of my life, Neeta. We first met at a hotel party in Nairobi, organized to celebrate Ashok and Dalbir's victory in the 1985 Safari Car Rally. Love blossomed and culminated into our marriage, which also took place during this period. It was an interesting chapter of my life, which I will share eventually, as we move further with my story.

All in all, I experienced some of my life's best personal as well as business milestones during my years with Delta. Not only was the foundation of my business career laid out, but I had also stepped into my married and domestic phase of life. It was when the sailing was smoothest that circumstances changed; trouble brewed and like all good things come to an end, Delta headed to its finishing line. It had scaled great heights and was peaking well, but as is said, growth poses its own challenges, and so it did for this business as well. Witnessing their tremendous growth over the last three or four years, each of the partners now wanted to work independently. It was probably during the first quarter of 1986 that discussions of closing down the firm began. After a few months of discussions and deliberations, the partners finally wound up their business and parted ways. Although I had given my blood and sweat for the business, not being a shareholder, I could only stand around helplessly without any say in the matter. After its closure, a couple of the erstwhile partners of Delta Hardware made me offers to join their businesses. I had worked for all of them at one point, and felt that it would now go against my personal ethics to work for any one of them against all the others. Standing firm on my principles, I turned down their offers.

Life continued to follow the same pattern once again; and just when it looked like it would finally take off, I found myself back to square one, yet again. Till the closure of Delta Hardware, I had treated it like my own business, never working as an employee.

Consequently, I did not have a fixed salary, and eventually, when it wound up, I was left with meagre savings to barely last me through three or four months. Moreover, now that I was married, my responsibilities had doubled. My back was to the wall and a dead-end lay before me.

This time around, my circumstances led me to introspect seriously on my life so far. I noted that every time life seemed to come on track, it got derailed too soon. Every time I seemed to have a firm control over the operations of wherever it was that I worked on, circumstances would change drastically and I would find myself back on the streets. Having to start from scratch all over again.

Neeta and I spent many sleepless nights and many days seriously contemplating our next move. It seemed so dark all around us that we could not see any light at the end of the tunnel. It was during those challenging times that a thought struck me. I thought that if I worked for some company or for somebody else, and if their circumstances changed and their business ceased to operate, I would have to look for another job. On the other hand, if I ventured out on my own and started my own business, I would hold all the reins and everything would be my responsibility. If I had my own set up, I thought, I would be the master of my own destiny.

And so it was under such testing times that I vowed never to work for anybody else again in life, but for myself. I decided to set up my own business. I had by now completely transformed myself from a Hindu priest to a potentially successful businessman.

• CHAPTER 20 •

LOVE AND MARRIAGE

The best kinds of relationships begin unexpectedly, hitting you suddenly like a thunder bolt from the blue. That's why it is said that you don't have to look for love, because it comes to you at the right time and at the right place. And that is exactly what had happened with me! At twenty-three, my entire focus lay on building a successful career and I had never imagined getting married at that stage. Establishing myself was my first priority and I was not ready for marriage. I knew that when I could hardly manage myself, there was no way I could shoulder the responsibility of a life partner. As a matter of fact, I knew a couple of close friends, who were dating at the time, but I was so engrossed in my career that I never gave love and romance any thought. And that was exactly when Neeta walked into my life.

In was in April or May of 1985, when Ashok Patel and Dalbir Kandola had won the ninth spot in that year's Marlboro Safari Car Rally. To celebrate their victory, all of us at Delta Hardware had decided to host a party at the Hotel Golden Candle at Upper Hillin Nairobi. I was very excited as all my close friends, business associates, near and dear ones had been invited. Neeta's uncle, who was one of our suppliers, had also been invited to the party.

As the celebrations began, a very simple and beautiful girl walked into the venue, accompanying him. As one of the party hosts, I welcomed them warmly and ushered them to a table, offering them some refreshments. It was while conversing with him that he introduced me to Neeta, his niece, who lived with her family in Thika (a town about 50-60 km from Nairobi). It was on this beautiful evening of 5 May 1985 that I first met her. We spoke briefly after our introductions and exchanged our telephone numbers (it was the era of 'landlines', much before the age of mobile phones!). After that I became busy with greeting and meeting all our other guests. Although I had been impressed by her beauty and simplicity, thoughts of love or a relationship had not yet crossed my mind.

I never thought that we would meet again after that party. But as they say, when it is time for souls to meet, there is nothing on earth that can prevent them from meeting, no matter how far they are from each other. Neeta and I were destined to meet again, even though she stayed in Thika which was miles away from Nairobi.

As part of my job at Delta, I used to travel to various towns across Kenya, including Thika. On one such sales and collection trip following our first meeting in Nairobi, I happened to pass by Thika and decided to visit her, since their family happened to be related to one of my Aunts. The moment I stepped into their house, I felt at home and was given a warm welcome. It was during this second meeting that I actually conversed with Neeta and began to understand her better. Impressed by her simplicity, straight forwardness and decent family background, I began to like her. I came to know that she was a qualified chemist and worked as a doctor's assistant in Thika. After this first visit, we started to speak to each other regularly over the phone. During those days, their family did not have a 'telephone line' and I had to call up one of their next-door neighbours if I wanted to talk to Neeta.

I also made it a point to visit their home whenever I travelled to or through Thika on my business trips. Similarly, whenever Neeta visited Nairobi, we used to meet at my office, mostly during lunch hours. As I always worked through my lunch, we used to enjoy 'Coca Cola' and 'Chips' and that's how slowly and gradually we developed a relationship. This was the first time that I had ever become so attached to a girl. This was also the first time that I felt a sense of belonging to someone, that there was somebody who cared for me. After leaving India, I had hardly stayed with my parents and missed their love and care, which I found in Neeta's family. Whenever I visited her home, the first thing that her mother or Neeta asked me about was food. They also enquired about my work, my health and my family, but they were never curious to learn about my earnings. Their caring attitude won my heart and unknowingly I began to fall in love with Neeta.

Although I wanted to confess my feelings for her, I lacked the courage. Thoughts of my inadequate financial state held me back from proposing to her. I was also apprehensive of her feelings for me. I felt that we needed to come closer before I could propose to her. It may sound funny and theatrical, but there is a famous line from a well-known Bollywood movie, which goes something like this, 'कहते हैं अगर किसी चीज़ को दिल से चाहो, तो पूरी कायनात उसे तुमसे मिलाने की कोशिश में लग जाती है [they say that if you desire something from the bottom of your heart, the whole universe conspires to get it to you]'. True to this saying, I was madly in love, but afraid to propose; and unknown to me, the entire universe was working to bring us closer. That was when something unexpected happened that was to bring us closer to each other. I was on a sales tour to Kakamega, a prominent town in Western Kenya, around 360 km from Nairobi. I was at one of our customer's outlets, discussing business with him, when a European gentleman approached us. He informed my customer that he was soon relocating to his country for good and was desperate to sell his brand new car, which he had sparingly used and was looking for a good buyer.

On seeing me, he asked whether I too could help him in selling his car. I shared my business contacts with him, stating that I was based in Nairobi and would try to assist him if I could. After finishing my business in Kakamega, I headed back to Nairobi, totally forgetting the whole incident. After a month or so, one fine morning as our business day was about to begin, in walks this European gentleman into our office, parking his car outside. I was taken aback when he proposed that I buy his beautiful car. When I politely refused, telling him that I did not have that kind of money, he said he was ready to sell it to me at whatever price I could offer him. I must confess that I did not have any money with me and whatever cash was in the till, belonged to the company, which in any case was far too less for his car! I could not hold back my temptation, however, when he said that he was willing to part with his beauty for whatever I could offer him. He said that he had the signed log-book with him and was due to travel back to his country that very afternoon. I knew that this car was worth a fortune and that the Mzungu was making a 'distress-sale'. I sought permission from the partners and brought the car from him. Though I could see the relief on his face as he handed over the keys and the log-book to me, he could not see my excitement! I could hardly believe that I had purchased my very first car, bearing the registration number: KWJ 195. It was a left-hand driven car, and I knew that I wanted to share the moment with someone special. It was then that I decided to share it with Neeta and her family.

After office hours, unable to control myself, I drove excitedly all the way from Nairobi to Thika, unruffled by the fact that it was a left-hand drive! On reaching their home at around 8.00 pm or so, I saw the entire family waiting outside their home to catch the first glimpse of my car. I was delighted! I had more surprises that evening, when Neeta's mother prepared my favourite snacks, samosa (a popular Indian savoury pastry filled with spiced vegetables or meat) and batata-vada (a spicy Indian version of potato fritters, a popular street food from Maharashtra). I was overwhelmed by their hospitality, and stayed back overnight. The next day, by 5.30 am, I drove back to Nairobi. Now that I had my own transport, I start visiting Thika at least twice or thrice a week.

Each time I visited them after office hours, only to return to Nairobi late in the night, to ensure that I never missed my office. Notably, each time, Neeta's mother served my favourite savouries. Moreover, because of my frequent visits, Neeta and I became closer. We had time to talk to each other and to understand each other better. During our courtship, we had some romantic moments that we either spent at the Thika Falls or at a restaurant in Thika called the 'Blue Post'. At times, we also met each other at her Uncle's home. Needless to say, Neeta had also fallen in love with me by this time. Even during our courtship, I always talked sensibly with her. I shared my responsibilitics and my dreams of achieving something great in life. I also told her that we were destined to meet and had been made for each other. Our love blossomed and I can say that this car brought us closer!

It is truly said that love is not finding someone to live with. It is finding someone you cannot live without. I had reached a point in my life where I could not imagine myself without Neeta. Even so, although I was eager to tie the knot, I was still hesitant about proposing marriage, because I did not have a regular income. Delta Hardware was like my own family business and I did not draw a regular salary. I was sandwiched between money and my decision to marry! Finally, mustering up enough courage, I spoke to my parents about Neeta. Both were overjoyed to hear this and gave me their blessings. Despite this, I was still in two minds and consulted both Jayantibhai and Ashok Patel, who assured me not to worry too much about it. Finally, I spoke to their mother, whom we loving called Baa ('mother' in Gujarati), seeking her permission. She was eighty at that time. At first, she was very annoyed me, because she said she could not understand what was holding me back from proposing to Neeta. She felt that Neeta was the perfect match for me. Baa had met Neeta quite a few times when we had visited her, and Neeta had always helped Baa with her household and kitchen chores. This had impressed Baa, who was very eager to see us married. She immediately called up Neeta's family, and gave them the marriage proposal on my behalf. About that same time, Neeta's uncle, who was one of our suppliers at Delta, had also suggested that I was an ideal match for Neeta. Her parents agreed and with everybody's blessings, we got engaged on 14 July 1985.

Everyone was happy about our engagement and looked forward to our marriage. Though I too was eager to get married and settle down in life, 'money' was still a million dollar question. I started worrying about my lack of resources and discussed my misgivings with Jayantibhai and the entire family, who comforted me in Gujarati by saying, 'થઇ જશે [it will be done]'. Here I am reminded of John F. Kennedy's famous saying, 'We must find time to stop and thank people who make a difference in our lives.' If there is one family who made a difference in my life and to whom I will always remain indebted, it is this family. Jayantibhai and Sheelaben have treated me like their own son, and even to this day they are like my own parents. Their younger brother, Ashok, supported me in Delta Hardware and his wife, Hina, is more than a sister to me. Their mother, Baa, has a very special place in my heart. My marriage worries were laid to rest when this family shouldered the entire responsibility of arranging our wedding and bearing all expenses. I must admit in all honesty that even my own parents would not have been able to arrange our wedding in the manner in which they made all arrangements!

I have the highest regard for this family, because while I was expecting a simple wedding ceremony, they made it a very colourful and wonderful event, grander than any other wedding even in their own family! Honestly, even to this day, I don't know exactly how much expenses the family had incurred for my wedding! Jayantibhai spoke to Neeta's parents, decided on a marriage date with them and made all the arrangements. While working for Delta, I used to stay at their apartment at Ngara. As the business grew tremendously, Ashok's family and Baa had moved from Nakuru to Nairobi and stayed in the same apartment. A few months before my marriage, I shifted out and rented a small, two-bedroom bungalow on Muthithi Road at Westlands in Nairobi. The landlord was Rameshbhai, a friend of mine. A couple of months before my marriage, my parents joined me here.

All arrangements were finalised and the marriage was to be held at Thika, on 8 December 1985. Since Jayantibhai's family resided in Nakuru, all programmes from the bridegroom's side were organised at their bungalow. The excitement built up on the morning of 7 December, when more than 300 or 400 family members gathered at Nakuru. The celebrations began with the 'Mandva Muhurat' ceremony, when the parents of the couple seek the blessings of Mother Earth and ask her permission to dig the earth for erecting a mandva or mandap (a canopy-covered platform for solemnising the wedding rites). Sheelaben personally cooked for all the wedding guests, while Baa and Hinaben looked after the guests. They were ably supported by all their family members. The atmosphere was electrifying, the arrangements perfect, with laughter and happiness everywhere in the house. My parents were flabbergasted by the grand manner in which the Patel family had organised their eldest son's wedding. The night before our wedding day, I remember that I could not sleep for a moment out of sheer excitement.

Finally, the day arrived. On the morning of Sunday, 8 December 1985, we proceeded from Nakuru to Thika. We had anticipated about 400 or 500 guests to attend the wedding from the groom's side, but the entire Nakuru community, our clients, suppliers, friends and well-wishers, all participated in the event, and eventually more than 1,500 or 1,700 guests turned out from the groom's side! We reached Thika around 11.00 am in the morning. With great song and dance, our 'વરઘોડો' (bridegroom's procession) headed towards the wedding venue, where we were welcomed by the bride's family. Our marriage ceremony was a traditional Gujarati one, beginning with the 'Varmala' (exchange of wedding garlands), followed by 'Kanya-Daan' (ritual of giving away the bride by her parents), and 'Hasta-Melap' (the tying of the wedding knot and the joining of hands to symbolise the union of two souls joined together in holy matrimony). As the priest chants holy wedding mantras to invoke heavenly blessings on the couple, the family and guests all bless them together and shower them with grains of rice and rose petals. We then proceeded with the 'Pheras' and concluded with the 'Saptapadi' (circling a sacred fire together seven times, to the chant of wedding mantras, where each step binds the couple together with wedding vows). Finally, we were married! In her traditional wedding attire, Neeta was looking so beautiful and charming that I could not resist staring at her throughout the rituals!

By one-o-clock in the afternoon, all the rituals were completed and amid a festive atmosphere, we had our wedding lunch. It was soon time to bid good-bye with the farewell 'Vidaai' ceremony (a sad occasion when the bride bids a final tearful farewell to her family, childhood friends and parents' home to become part of a new household). It was an emotional moment for all of us and guests from both sides of the family were in tears. We finally left Thika by 4:00 pm and headed to our new home in Nairobi, where Baa and my mother performed the 'Ghar-ni-Laxmi' pooja, welcoming Neeta into our family. A bride's first step into her new home is considered to be a very auspicious moment. She is welcomed home as Goddess Laxmi (goddess of prosperity and good fortune), where her step symbolises the entry of the goddess of well being into the household. Later when we travelled to Nakuru, this ritual was performed there once again. At last our marriage was solemnised and we were one!

The secret of a happy marriage is finding the right person: Our marriage photographs

Our marriage was like a fairy tale or a mid-summer night's dream for me. All this happened without my planning or any contribution. Everything fell into place so smoothly, as if the Almighty had planned it all through the agency of Jayantibhai, Ashokbhai and their families. I don't have any answers for this miracle. Over the years, the bonding between our families has only strengthened with each passing year. Jayantibhai and Sheelaben, Ashokbhai and Hinaben continue to reside in Nakuru, while their children are well settled elsewhere. This is one family that I will remember for the rest of my life.

Today, after thirty-two years of our married life, I consider myself fortunate to have found a perfect partner in Neeta. She has stood by me like a pillar of strength through all our ups and downs, supporting me in all my business decisions. You will understand the importance of her presence in my life as I continue to share my life's journey. To me she has been a good friend, a loving partner and a caring parent—all rolled into one. Neeta and I are blessed with two sons and a daughter. Our eldest son, Devang, who is now twenty-six years old, has stepped in our business after graduating in Economics from Brunel University in the UK. Our eighteen-year-old daughter, Tulsi, is pursuing her studies in Business Administration at the Brunel University; and our youngest child, Devrath, is eleven years old. He studies at the Braeburn School in Nairobi.

As I have shared earlier, in 1985, we had just stepped in our married life when the partners of Delta Hardware decided to part ways, eventually leading to its closure by the middle of 1986. I had seen this pattern repeating in my life over and over again. It was now time to start life afresh. I resolved never to work for anybody else again and pledged to take up the reins of my life in my own hands. I wanted to be the master of my destiny and decided to set up my own business.

A new chapter was about to unfold in our lives.

PART IV

THE BIRTH AND RISE OF MY BUSINESS EMPIRE 1986–PRESENT

• CHAPTER 21 •

MY FIRST STEP: STEEL CENTRE LIMITED

Call it destiny or blessings in disguise, but each time my life seemed to stabilise, circumstances would change and I would find myself back to square one. However, the last four years that I had spent at the Kikuyu Steel Rolling Mills, Steel Wares, and especially at Delta Hardware, had given me a detailed insight of trading and manufacturing in the steel and hardware businesses. Moreover, my domestic responsibilities had doubled after my marriage. Whatever little savings we had would last us no more than three or four months at the most. I realised that I had to be the master of my own destiny and not always at the mercy of others. It was time to take the first step towards achieving my goals in life. Though the entire picture was not yet clear to me, I made a choice. I decided to set up my own business.

With my experience and background, it was both logical and understandable for me to start my business in the wholesale trading of steel and hardware products. To start with, I decided to put up my own shop, but that was easier said than done. With limited savings, my hands were tied and I had to start from scratch. Added to that, I was left without my own transport after I handed over the company car, following the closure of Delta Hardware. Moreover, being a non-native in Kenya had its own set of challenges; but I had made a choice and was prepared to face its consequences. Thanks to my association with Delta and my knowledge of astrology, I was able to develop a small group of my friends over the years. I got in touch with all of them and asked them for help in finding me a place for my first shop. A couple of my friends helped me, but the person who really supported me in my search was my friend, Vijay Dhanani. He came from a wealthy family, and we had become acquainted when he had come to seek my help with his personal and business challenges.

Gradually, we became close friends and when I told him of starting my own business, he thought it was a fantastic idea. Since he had a car, he took me everywhere in search of a shop for rent. We literally combed every nook and corner of Nairobi, because I was looking for an affordable place. It was during one such hunt that he suggested we look for a place at Gikomba in Nairobi's Central Business District (CBD). Since it was not yet fully developed, there was a possibility of finding a place at a lower rent than other business districts in town. Fortunately, we heard of a warehouse, sparingly used as an automobile workshop, which was available for rent. It was owned by Mr. Nduati Kariuki, a member of the Kenya African National Union (KANU), as well as an Assistant Minister in the Kenyan Government. We decided to visit it with Neeta and some of her family. We found that there were two warehouses standing adjacent to each other. Mr. Kariuki utilised one of them and was offering the other one for rent. At first sight, my heart sank as the place was a mess and Gikomba was not a safe area in those days. I could see that everybody else's faces had fallen too. However, considering the area of 5,000 sq. ft. at a rent of Ksh. 3,500, it was ideal for our purposes.

Although we finalised the lease, the goodwill to be paid to the landlord was Ksh. 65,000, which we didn't have; but again it was Vijay who encouraged me to go for it. He told me in Gujarati, 'ગુરૂ, હું તમને આ પૈસા આપું છું, તમે તેને લોઅને તમારો વ્યવસાય શરૂ કરો [Guru, I am giving you the money, take it and start your own business]'. And that was how we set up our own company, 'Steel Centre Limited'. The company had to be registered under Neeta's ownership, since she was a Kenyan citizen. We finally signed the lease agreement with the landlord and began our business from November 1986. I had finally made a beginning.

In those days, Gikomba was an isolated and dangerous neighbourhood, well known for robbers and riots. When we started out, barring a few shops on our side and the Nairobi River on the other side, there was nothing else in the area. It needed tremendous courage to run a business there and no Asian had ever dared to step into the area. Needless to say, I was the first Asian to set up a business there. Today, it has become a hub for the hardware business and I can proudly claim credit for this!

As Martin Luther King Junior put it, I had taken my first step in faith, even though the entire picture was unclear. I had begun to chase my dreams. Capital was my first and my biggest challenge. It needed lots of planning to begin. With the little money at my disposal, we managed to put up a retail counter at the shop front and a shelf on the side for storage. Rajubhai, another good friend of mine, who owned a paints business, helped us in painting the whole shop. I did not have any further resources to buy the products that I wanted to trade. I approached a couple of steel manufacturers I had dealt with during my years at Delta, to supply me on credit. After a few initial hiccups, they agreed to extend me credit facility and I finally set the ball rolling!

Transport was also crucial in business. When we started, I did not own a vehicle. With Delta's closure, the car that belonged to them was also gone. In those days, we resided on Muthithi Road in Westlands and I had to walk all the way from my home to our shop. I used to leave home by 7:00 am and on my way I would stop by the Hare Krishna Temple in Ngara, seek the Lord's blessings and start my day. At noon, Neeta used to walk down to our shop with the lunchbox. We didn't have chairs to sit on, so both of us squatted on the floor and had our lunch! Whenever I needed to visit any customer or supplier, Neeta managed the shop. At times, we used 'Matatus' (privately owned minibuses used for public transport in Kenya and neighbouring nations) to commute. Although we managed for some time, I perceived that owning a vehicle was imperative for our expansion and growth.

Though keen on buying a vehicle, capital continued to be a major constrain for us. I approached CFC Finance for a vehicle loan. The company was owned by Mr. Charles Mugane Njonjo, the former Attorney General and former Minister of the Kenyan Government, whom I had first met through Mr. D.H. Patel. They approved my request and sanctioned a loan of Ksh. 265,000, repayable in twenty-four equated monthly instalments (EMIs). With that we got our first pick-up vehicle, a Toyota Hilux. I still remember its registration number: KXU 905. There is a first time for everything and this was the first time I owned a vehicle in my name as well as the first time I borrowed from a bank! This gave an immense relief and boost to our business. We used this vehicle for both business as well as personal purposes, and since we could not afford to employ a driver, both Neeta and I started driving.

A famous saying goes like this: 'If you want to go fast, go alone; if you want to go far, go together...' I always dreamt of going far and knew that I could only do so much alone. Initially, our monthly sales were as low as Ksh. 10,000, which would be equivalent of about US$ 100 today! At that time, we employed just one help at the store, who assisted us with everything. After buying our pick-up vehicle, our sales started picking up as well. It was becoming a challenge for Neeta and I to handle everything by ourselves. Multi-tasking became the order of the day and it was hampering our growth. Many times, we had supplier trucks at the door, ready to off-load, while customer deliveries had to be made! Within a few months, both of us realised that we needed a family member as part of our team, without whom, we could not grow. It was time to build our core team. That was when we decided to take Neeta's younger brother, Kaushik Pandit, into our fold.

He was then a sixteen-year-old who had just completed his O levels. He was working as a store assistant with a hardware trader,'Vershi Devshi & Co'. Having observed a couple of friends' parents with their own businesses, he was eager to have his own business and not pursue his studies any further. When I approached him to join us in Nairobi, he was reluctant at first because he was comfortable in Thika. Though he joined us, after every two or three days in the shop, he would run away to Thika. When this happened more than once, I got upset. It took both Neeta and I to sit down and have a serious conversation with him, convincing him that it was a win-win situation for all of us. At last, he realised the true import of his role and willingly joined hands with us. We finally had a team in place. Kaushik stayed with us at our Muthithi Road residence, sleeping in our sitting room and accompanying us to the shop every day.

We complemented each other very well. While I looked after the sales counter, he looked after logistics. He managed the floor, taking care of both incoming and outgoing deliveries, inspecting quality and quantity, liaising with suppliers and customers. He also drove the pick-up and personally delivered products to our clients. Neeta continued to bring our lunch boxes at noon. Since we worked without a break, one of us used to squat on the floor and have lunch, while the other served customers. From that time onwards, Neeta and Kaushik have been the mainstays of our business, standing by like solid pillars. More than a wife, Neeta has been a friend and a confidante. She has always supported my business decisions without a second thought. It has been more than thirty-one years now that Kaushik, too, has stood by my side. We have weathered many a storm together. I will be indebted to both of them throughout my life. Without them, we wouldn't have reached where we stand today!

For the next five years, we fared well and continued wholesaling and re-wholesaling (suppliers to other wholesalers) in steel and hardware products. But before I continue to share my business growth, I think I should share a few other incidents and emotions that occurred during that time.

Though India was my Janma-Bhoomi (place of birth), Kenya became my Karma-Bhoomi (place or land of action). Though I was born in India, it was in Kenya that I made my life and felt at home. In 1986, after my marriage and after setting up our business, I applied for Kenyan citizenship and surrendered my Indian passport. I remember that when I secured the Kenyan passport, it was the Minister, Mr. Angainye, who was in-charge of these affairs. Mr. J.K. Mutua, was the Principal Immigration Officer. I no longer required any business or work permit to stay here. I was here for good.

Moreover, though I became a Kenyan citizen, I continued to support my parents and family back in India. My parents had visited me just before my marriage and stayed with us for some time. My younger brother, Bhavesh, had completed his Engineering studies in 1989 or so. As a part of our expansion plans, I requested him to come over to Kenya and join us in our business. He worked hand-in-hand with Kaushik, who introduced him to our clients and our product profile. After about a year-and-a-half, however, Bhavesh decided to settle down in Kisumu with his own hardware shop. Most importantly, in 1990, Neeta and I were blessed with our first son, Devang. And through all these years, we continued to reside at our Muthithi Road residence.

In addition, I also pursued my hobbies of palmistry and astrology, despite my tight business schedules. We used to return home by about 6.30 pm and more often than not, there was always a queue of people lined up to consult me. Even though I used to feel tired, I always helped everyone who came to me. By the time I finished with them, it would be beyond 9:00 pm or 10:00 pm in the night.

Most importantly, though there were security concerns in Gikomba, I fell in love with the place and the people. It was the birthplace of my business dreams and ambitions. It was the place where my journey began and I took my first step. During that tenure, there was a lot of turbulence and instability in Kenyan politics. There were riots everywhere and the Gikomba area was the hub of all riots. I still remember what used to be known as the 'Machacos Airport', which was basically a bus station, where all riots used to begin. Many a times, innocent people used to be trapped in these riots and sought shelter in our shop. We always protected them from rioters and the police alike. They never harmed us and were always grateful for our protection. These things, however small, have had a very special place in my heart.

Coming back to our business, hidden in the challenges lie our significant opportunities. It was almost five years since we started our business and as we were trying to get a firm footing, we met a challenge on our way up. It so happened that I had travelled to India and Kaushik was managing the business by himself. One day afternoon, Kaushik received a call from the landlord, Mr. Nduati Kariuki, who told him that he wanted us to vacate his premises, since he intended to sell it. He added that we should treat this phone call as a notice. A shocked Kaushik called me straight away. General elections were round the corner. I presumed that since he was contesting, he must be in need of funds and hence the decision. On my return, I met him personally and requested him to allow us to continue as tenants, which he turned down. I must admit that I, too, was disturbed by this sudden occurrence. We had barely settled down in our business and shifting implied so many things. We might even have to begin from ground zero, and I was not prepared for this again.

Our next few nights were spent sleeplessly and our days in convincing the landlord to change his mind. He never budged. I prayed to God to give us a solution, and as always, He showed me the way. My instinct said there lay an opportunity behind this challenge and I made my decision. The next day, when Neeta and Kaushik were in the shop, I went to meet the landlord without telling them what I had in mind. When I met him, I offered to buy the shop. In addition, I also proposed to buy the adjacent warehouse. He quoted a price of Ksh. 5 million, which is roughly around US$ 50,000 today. Though very high, I weighed my options and committed to buy up both shops. Once again, I seemed to inhabit a melodramatic Bollywood movie, where the protagonist proposes to buy a huge property without a single penny in his pocket! I requested for some breathing time to come up with the finances. When I broke the news to Neeta and Kaushik, they were aghast! When we did not have funds to even buy one shop, what in the world made me to commit to two of them?

As I have said before, life is a matter of choices and consequences. There are plenty of options open to us before we make a choice, but once we choose a path, we are responsible for the consequences of our decision. I had chosen my path, and it was to forge ahead with my business. Now, there was no looking back!

Although I had made up my mind to buy two shops, finding the resources was going to be a major challenge. Thanks to my business and 'astrological' connections, I had developed a wide network of acquaintances, friends, patrons, suppliers, and bankers. I felt it was time to knock on these doors. It so happened that I was introduced to Mr. Mohammed H. Habib, the president and CEO of Habib Bank AG Zurich.

I had rendered services to him as an astrologer at one point. So I approached his bank and met the manager. I requested for financial assistance to buy premises for my business. The bank advised me to negotiate with the landlord and request him to accept payments in twelve EMIs. They also suggested that I offer him twelve post-dated cheques (PDCs). They assured me that on presentation, these cheques would be honoured and sanctioned a backup loan, which would be drawn only in the event that I had insufficient balance in my account when the cheques were presented. Moreover, they agreed to give me a five-year window to repay the loan. This was more than I had expected, and I confidentially negotiated with the landlord, who willingly accepted my offer and the deal went through. The bankers kept to their promise and that's how we brought our first property. Over the years, my association with Habib Bank AG Zurich has been cordial and mutually beneficial. I continue to share a good relationship with Mr. Mohammed H. Habib. Their entire team has been supportive, especially their managers, Mr. Bakir Ali, Mr. Salim and Mr. Iqbal Allawallah.

This was the first property that we owned and it was a great experience that taught me many lessons. Firstly, I learnt that there was something called a 'Post-dated cheque' and secondly, I had always been under the impression that we can make a payment from a bank, only if we had sufficient balance in our account. I now learnt that if we have a facility in place with our bank, we can either make a payment or borrow the amount. It also taught me that whenever a bank facility was in place, we could utilize funds only up to the sanctioned limit. I would like to share a humorous incident through which I learnt this lesson. For meeting my normal business commitments, I also had a facility of Ksh 100,000 from Habib Bank in place. The Bank's cheque book was my proud possession and I always carried it with pride. On one occasion, the Bank's Manager, Mr. Iqbal Allawallah telephoned and advised me to visit the Bank. On reaching the bank, I was he informed that my account had been over-drawn by Ksh 27,000 and urgently needed to regularize my account by depositing sufficient cash or cheque in it. Naïve as I was, I promptly handed a cheque from the same account and requested him to deposit in it. Smiling the Manger explained that to regularize the account, I had to bank cash or a cheque from a different account. I promptly deposited cash in my account. This experience broadened my horizon and I started to dream big. It took us about six to eight months to complete the deal and acquire our properties. From a tenant of a 5,000 sq. ft. shop, overnight, we became the owners of two shops totalling 10,000 sq. ft. We broke the dividing wall and created a huge retail outlet for ourselves. With the increase in our store size, our product range widened to include reinforcement bars, re-bars, barbed wires, binding wires, chicken wires, weld mesh, wire nails, and all types of plates, rods, rolls and sections. We also resorted to importing door locks and hexa-blades. Once when a consignment of imported door locks had landed at our old shop, I remember we did not have enough space to store them, and had to take them home to keep them under our bed. Our growth led to our second three-tonne pick-up vehicle, increasing our workforce to eight. We now employed a driver as well. We had graduated from monthly sales of Ksh. 10,000 in 1986, to almost around Ksh. 1,000,000 by 1990.

Steel Centre's delivery truck

By now, Gikomba had become the hardware hub of Kenya and we were the proud pioneers. Our dealings were straightforward and clear. Customer satisfaction was our motto. We also ensured timely payments to all our suppliers. On the strength these principles, we built a strong reputation and goodwill. By the end of the fifth year, we had become Kenya's largest hardware traders.

The first step is always an experience in itself. Mine taught me many important lessons that I would like to share with today's youngsters, especially those who aspire to become entrepreneurs and business leaders. Firstly, while it is imperative for all of us to have a basic education, qualifying as a graduate, postgraduate, securing a masters or technical skills are not necessary for an entrepreneur. I have seen many parents struggle throughout their lives to ensure that their children get the best education. Some sell or mortgage their properties, borrow from employers or banks, some even part with their entire life's savings or retirement funds for this purpose. In short, parents stake their lives for their children's education. But what happens if you graduate and fail to perform or succeed? Failure will have a cascading effect. Your parents' lives will be ruined, your dreams shattered, and you will become a challenge to society. While I agree that a good education on your curriculum vitae (CV) will definitely impress business houses or corporate firms when you look for a job, but it is not compulsory to have a higher education to make both ends meet. Secondly, be courageous and have faith in your abilities. I was neither qualified, nor did I have any resources to support me, but I still dared to take my first step. You have to make efforts to take that step. After you have the necessary basic education and aspire to be an entrepreneur or industrialist, my personal experience is that instead of idling away your time and getting frustrated, dare to start – even if it means starting out with a small kiosk.

My first shop is Gikomba was no more than a big kiosk, with an initial monthly turnover of Ksh. 10,000. For youngsters, looking for jobs, taking that first step; looking for an opening is important. Once you get a job, try to be practical and gain hands-on experience. In the long run, good employers always weigh experience heavily against education. Thirdly, never give up! What I have observed with youngsters of this generation is that they give up too easily. In business, there will be ups and downs, have the courage to face them. You will face numerous challenges, where you will feel like quitting, but never give up. When we had just started our shop, Neeta and I reached home very late one night and discovered that we didn't have enough groceries to cook dinner. I smiled and told her, never mind, we will survive on water. That night we both had two glasses of water and went off to sleep. Never give up, whatever be the circumstances.

Every business has its own challenges. I had taken my first step. It was time to expand.

A privileged moment: With Indian Prime Minister Hon. Narendra Modiji

A proud moment: Welcoming His Excellency Kenyan President Hon. Uhuru Kenyatta at our plant

Welcoming His Excellency Kenyan President Hon. Daniel Toroitich Arap Moi, on the opening ceremony of Maisha Mabati Mills Limited. I have been fortunate to have him as my friend, philosopher and guide

An intriguing discussion with His Excellency Kenyan President Hon. Mwai Kibaki at our plant

A warm welcome by the Devki family to the then Kenyan Vice President Hon. Musyoka Kalonzo, during a visit to our plant

Yoweri K Museveni @KagutaMuseveni 16h

Today, I met with Mr. Narendra Raval, the Chairman of Devki Steel mills Ltd & discussed investment opportunities here

Discussing invesment opportunites with His Excellency Ugandan President Hon. Yoweri K. Museveni

All smiles as I greet His Excellency Ugandan Prime Minister Hon. Ruhakana Rugunda

With His Excellency President of Democratic Republic of Congo Hon. Joseph Kabila Kabange

Welcoming Mrs. Cherie Blair, CBE QC, wife of former British Prime Minister HE Hon. Tony Blair, at our residence in Nairobi.

My son Devang and I were honoured to meet Gujarat Chief Minister Hon. Vijay Rupani in 2017.

Neeta and I outside the British Prime Minister's official residence — 10, Downing Street, London

Kenya Commercial Bank (KCB) featured me on the cover page of its magazine KCB Venture (Photo Courtesy: KCB Kenya)

Addressing the priest community at the Swaminarayan Temple in Bhuj, Gujarat

Addressing the business community in Nairobi

We need to learn the Art of Listening which enables us to respond in the Right Way.
Patience, Positivity and Perseverance are the key factors of this Art.
"GURU"

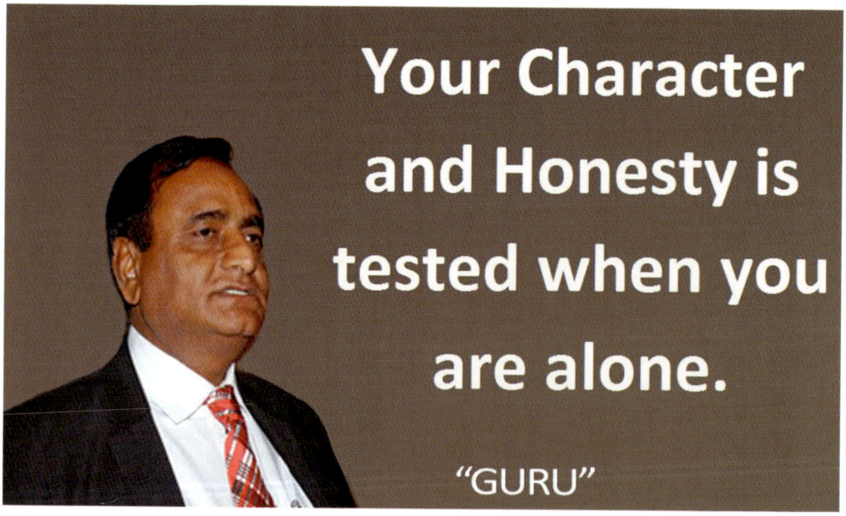
Your Character and Honesty is tested when you are alone.
"GURU"

• CHAPTER 22 •

AN ACCOUNTING NIGHTMARE

The world over, the Gujarati community is well known for two things—their business acumen and their love for Gujarati food. One trait, however, at which every Gujarati is exceptionally good is accounting. Whether a school child, a homemaker, a shopkeeper, a businessman, an industrialist, a doctor or a chartered accountant, they are best at the number game. Accounting is possibly the most boring activity under the sun and it can also be confusing at times. In the long run, however, if your business has to succeed, accounting has to become the lifeline of your business. One small error can have grave consequences on someone's business. Before continuing further with my journey, let me share an 'accounting nightmare' that had once left me shocked.

It was barely two years after we had set up the Steel Centre, when this incident occurred. In the Kenya of 1988, there were only a couple of major steel mills from whom we purchased our products. We enjoyed credit lines with them due to our good payment record. Incidentally, the owners of these steel mills were also Gujaratis and like us—very principled and very good at numbers. We were regular in paying our suppliers and shared a very harmonious and cordial relationship with all of them. Once when I had travelled to India for meeting our overseas suppliers, Neeta was managing the business on her own. One afternoon, the owner of one of the steel rolling mills and our key supplier, stepped into our office. Not finding me there, he confronted Neeta and told her that we owed them Ksh. 3 million for our credit purchases through them. He threatened that if we failed to make the payment, he would ensure that our shop closes down permanently. A very frightened Neeta immediately called me. I was shocked.

It was difficult to digest, because we maintained proper accounting ledgers. It had always been my practise to separate each purchase/invoice to make it easy to track our outstanding invoices. I cut short my India visit and immediately returned to Nairobi. On my return, I asked my best friend, Vijay Dhanani, to come down for a serious discussion. I told him that if the supplier was demanding the amount, then definitely there must have been a possibility of an omission on our part. Neeta and I even totalled our stocks on hand, our receivables and some of our personal effects, which did not even come up to Ksh. 1 million.

I was lost. If the supplier's account was to be accepted, then we would be bankrupt and out of business for good. Vijay suggested that we meet the supplier. Though we shared a very good rapport, I called him up for an appointment with some hesitation. He agreed to meet us the very next day. At this point, Vijay left us, promising to join us the next day morning for the meeting. That night, Neeta and I could not eat a single morsel and sleep eluded us. I kept wondering how we could have owed them such a huge amount. Was there an accounting error on our part? Had I supplied goods to a customer on credit and omitted to account for it? Had there been a theft in our shop? What was it that we were missing? Even before sunrise, I was already waiting for Vijay to join me.

We met our supplier; and with folded hands, I requested him in Gujarati, 'સાહેબ, કૃપા કરીને અમને તમારું એકાઉન્ટ સ્ટેટમેન્ટ આપો અને અમારી સાથે તપાસકરવા અને સમાધાન કરવા માટે એક સપ્તાહનો સમય આપો [Sir, please give us your account statement and allow us a week's time to check and reconcile it with ours]'. I further assured him that after reconciling our account ledgers, whatever amount we owed him would be cleared immediately. Taking into consideration our longstanding relationship, he agreed. Collecting the statement, Vijay and I rushed back. That day I remember that I was not worried about the business, because if we indeed had to pay what the supplier demanded, there would be no business from the next day!

Both of us sat down to check their account statement with our records. We worked for fifteen hours straight, matching invoice to invoice, payment to payment. Neeta continuously supplied us with tea and biscuits. Finally, at 3.00 am in the morning, we had completely reconciled the statement, right from the day we had started purchasing from them. Believe it or not, when we finished, we found that we did not owe them a single penny. Instead, they owed us Ksh. 270,000. There were quite a number of our payments that their accountant had not taken into consideration. I heaved a sigh of relief!

At the first stroke of sunshine the next day, with renewed vigour, both Vijay and I rushed back to the supplier's office. We carried copies of the banking slips of Habib Bank AG Zurich with us, reflecting the amounts that we had deposited with them. I explained to the supplier that his account has not taken various payments into account. On hearing this, he summoned his accountant and instructed him to check it thoroughly. He also requested us to wait in his office. After three long hours of waiting, the accountant finally surfaced and confirmed that they did indeed owe us Ksh. 270,000 after taking into consideration all our payments to them! The supplier's faced turned red with anger and embarrassment. He realised that it had been his accountant's folly and that we were not at fault. He was apologetic about the entire episode, and especially of his behaviour. He agreed to pay the amount owed, which we eventually offset against further purchases.

Much later, I found out the reason why some of our payments had not been credited to our account by the supplier, which is a bit humorous. In those days, technology was not as advanced as it is today. Fax and telex were in vogue. After depositing payments in the supplier's account, it was my practise to fax the banking slips to them. Print-outs received from fax machines used to fade after sometime. Most of the banking slips that we had faxed them had faded away, and all they had with them were blank faxed messages. After resolving the matter, Vijay and I walked out of their office with a spring in our step. This incident did not hamper our relationship with the supplier. Even to this day, though we are competitors, our relationship continues. Incidentally, years ago, before I had set up my hardware shop, I had performed a pooja for their plant as a priest!

I was totally at peace that day. This accounting nightmare would have brought me on streets again. Returning home, I slept like a baby for the next twenty-four hours. The incident taught me another important lesson that I would like to share with you, especially those who aspire to be entrepreneurs or businessmen. I learnt that accounting is the heart and soul of your business; in your quench for increasing your business or revenues, don't ignore accounting and book keeping. A small error, if not nipped in the bud, can bring down a well-established business. Always keep this in mind, whether you run a small kiosk or a huge business empire.

Learning from mistakes is not the first step to success, but correcting them definitely is.

• CHAPTER 23 •

THIS TELEPHONE RINGS

On 10 March 1876, when Dr. Alexander Graham Bell, the inventor of the first practical telephone, called his assistant, 'Watson, come here! I want to see you,' he might not have imagined that one day his invention would bring people on earth closer to each other. Today, when we pick up a phone and call people across the globe, it gives us the happiness of being together despite being thousands of miles away from each other. Many years ago, Dr. Bell's invention not only helped me to stay in touch with Neeta while she was away, but also saved my pocket quite a bit, especially when our hands were tight! I thought of sharing this funny, yet thought provoking incident, which once again proved necessity to be the mother of invention.

Steel Centre and our family life advanced hand in hand; challenging yet progressing well. A couple of years after our marriage, we were eager to have our first child, but Neeta had challenges in conceiving. Neeta did a lot of research and consulted many medical specialists. During this period, she read about Cromwell Hospital in London, which specialised in fertility treatment through in vitro fertilisation (IVF). She communicated with the hospital through fax, and obtained all the details about the procedure, time and cost involved. The entire treatment would costs us around £ 10,000, which was all that we had saved from the two or three years of hard work at the Steel Centre. Family was important to us, however, and we decided to use our entire savings for her treatment. Neeta booked her appointment with Dr. Mike Simmons at the Cromwell Hospital and travelled to London.

In the winter of 1989, Neeta landed at Heathrow Airport. Treading on a thin line of savings, we had agreed to keep a tight vigil on her expenses there, so that we could save as much as we could for her treatment. In an effort to save costs, she stayed at her Kokila Masi's (maternal aunt) home and commuted to and from the hospital by the 'London Tube'. She continued her treatment in London, while I managed our business at Gikomba. Though I was anxious to get daily updates of her health, it was beyond our means for her to call me every day. We agreed that she would call me from a public pay phone twice a week. The treatment progressed well and through her calls, I got regular updates.

One day as usual, after her treatment, Neeta picked up the phone to call me. In those days, she used to insert a 50 pence coin (equivalent to US$ 0.64) to call. She had plenty of these coins in her purse, which she had kept together with Kenyan coins. That day, in her hurry, she inadvertently picked up a Kenyan five shilling from her purse instead to call me in Nairobi. The telephone rang and we spoke, oblivious of what had just happened. Seated on the London Tube on her way home, she realised what she had done. She immediately opened her purse and compared the coins. To her surprise, the Kenyan five shilling exactly matched the 50 pence in size and shape. As I shared earlier, Gujaratis are good at number crunching; and she immediately calculated that her unintentional mistake had saved her 45 pence. On alighting from the Tube, unable to control her excitement, she called me again with a Kenya five shilling coin and 'the telephone rang'.

At her second call, I became concerned, but both of us had a hearty laugh when she narrated the incident. From that day onwards, using the Kenya five shilling coin, she began calling me frequently. A few days later, I also travelled to London to be with Neeta for some time. I carried a lot of Kenyan five shilling coins with me and handed them over to her. At the Nairobi airport, while scanning my handbag, a curious security officer asked me why I was carrying so many coins with me. I politely replied that I loved to carry coins instead of currency notes. From that day till she completed her treatment in London, Neeta called me with the Kenyan coins; saving us a lot on costly telephone calls. Whatever we saved helped us in her medical treatment. This came like a blessing in disguise. As I said, necessity is the mother of invention.

After a successful IVF treatment, Neeta returned to Nairobi. In 1990, we were blessed with Devang, our first born. Even today, we have a hearty laugh recalling this incident, but in those days every cent saved meant a lot to us. It was purely the need of the moment that forced us to do this, but I do not suggest that any of you should try the technique!

• CHAPTER 24 •

MY ASTRAL TRAVEL: A SPIRITUAL EXPERIENCE

The foundation of my life had been laid on many strong axioms. Early to bed and early to rise was one of them, which I had been following from the age of nine. Barring a few instances of illness, I hardly remember a single day of having woken up after sunrise. Truth has been another important trait that I have followed throughout my life and have formed a habit of assessing myself at the end of each day. I introspect and evaluate whether I have done something wrong that day, whether I have knowingly or unknowingly offended or lied to someone. I have always made it a point to correct myself before retiring for the day. Due to this habit, I am blessed with 'peaceful sleep'. Every time I lie down, I fall fast asleep and wake up straight in the morning. Serving as a priest from an early age, I have always felt spiritually connected with the Almighty, but my unbelievable experience of 'astral' travel left me astounded. Before continuing with my business journey, I would like to share this 'spiritual' experience.

In 1986, sometime after our marriage, when we had just begun our hardware business, I had this strange but other worldly experience. Some nights I would dream of travelling throughout the universe. Surprisingly, I always saw myself either in the form of a white leaf or light feather, but never in my usual human form. At times, I saw very tall buildings and sometimes I found myself very high in the sky. In milliseconds, I could reach any corner of the globe, travelling to my home town of Mathak as well. From the top, I could see many people below, whom I had never met before. I would experience the same dream for three or four nights at a stretch. This scared me, but I never woke up and always rose fresh in the morning after each dream.

Strange but true, in these dreams, at least two or three days in advance, I could foresee natural calamities like earthquakes, floods or tsunamis that would occur anywhere on earth. On waking up, I used to share my dream with Neeta. In 2004, a few days before the great tsunami hit the earth, I dreamt that a calamity affecting water was about to occur. I saw animals running to safety, up to the hills and mountains. Though I could not understand what it was exactly, I told Neeta that something was wrong with the oceans and that I could foresee a major disaster. A couple of days later, the great tsunami hit our planet and the rest is history.

Believe it or not, during these dreams, I would effortlessly find solutions to many business challenges. Waking up in the morning, I used to implement my 'dream' solutions without a second thought, and the challenges would be resolved! Amazingly, I also found solutions to personal problems (mine as well as others') and many times solutions to problems affecting the globe in general.

Between 1986 and 1990, these dreams occurred many times. Initially, I was both scared and worried, but eventually I accepted them as part of my life. For many years, I did not know what this meant till a couple of experts recently told me of 'astral travel' or 'astral projection'. The terms are mainly used to describe a wilful, out-of-body experience (OBE), a supposed form of telepathy that assumes the existence of a soul or consciousness called an 'astral body' that is separate from the physical body and capable of travelling throughout the universe without its physical cage. I was also told that it was a rare occurrence and a good omen; probably one human being out of millions experienced it. Though these dreams stopped after four or five years, I continue to find solutions to my business problems in my dreams! Very recently in June 2017, I experienced these dreams again for nearly a week. I will never forget these dreams and feel blessed as they provide me with workable solutions to my challenges!

• CHAPTER 25 •

BIRTH OF DEVKI STEEL MILLS LIMITED

Change is an inevitable part of our life. Life is actually fuelled by change, though most of us want it to be stable. Without change, there would be no life at all. If we have to progress, there has to be change, because change precedes growth. Embarking on Steel Centre was the first step in my business journey. I had a strong desire to grow and realised that all my achievements and progress largely depended on my vision. It was time to grow and change; for change was the only way to turn my vision into reality. The time had come for this trader to widen his horizon from trading to manufacturing.

By 1992-93, seven years after starting out, we had established ourselves as the largest hardware trader in Kenya. Our business grew exponentially and sales volumes increased substantially. This was mainly because we no longer restricted ourselves to wholesaling/re-wholesaling, but had stepped into retailing and supplying to end-users. At that time, there were only two major steel manufacturers in Kenya; and we were their biggest customers. There came a stage, when demand outweighed our supply and the manufacturers were unable to cope. More often than not they lagged in supplies and this hampered our progress. Our supplier's manufacturing locations were in the industrial areas of Nairobi and visiting them became part of my routine. I used to perch myself in their offices, pressurising them to expedite the supplies.

Many times, I used to spend entire days in their offices, while Kaushik and Neeta managed the shop. We even resorted to bills of exchange or promissory notes to make upfront payments.

Despite my valiant efforts, our suppliers could not meet our requirements with timely deliveries. With only a couple of steel rolling mills in Kenya, they ran a monopoly and we had no choice, but to accede to their whims and fancies. This became a nightmare and we weighed the option of importing the products. However, considering the impact of foreign exchange fluctuations and undue supply delays, we ruled it out. It was then that I thought of setting up a small manufacturing facility to cater to our growing demand.

Having spent five years in steel and hardware trading, I was aware of the fact that though manufacturing meant higher risks, the margins were even higher! I was ready to take a calculated risk to earn more. At the same time, every morning when we opened for the day by 7:00 or 7:30 am, I saw many destitute sleeping outside our shop. Housing was a major challenge, and because of their monopoly, the prices of steel and other infrastructure products were high, rendering it difficult for the 'wananchi' (ordinary people or the public in East Africa) to have their own 'nyumba' (meaning house in Swahili). I felt it was my responsibility to do something for the wananchi and thought that if I set up a small steel manufacturing plant, I could supply them with construction material at affordable prices.

I had toyed with the idea of manufacturing for some time. Over the next few weeks, while Neeta and Kaushik managed our daily operations, I did a lot of my own research and feasibility studies. Plenty of questions lingered in my mind.– Where would we set up the plant? How much land did we need to begin with? What would be our capital requirement? What type of products should we start manufacturing? What type of buildings should we construct? Where would we source the machinery from? What about the labour force? How much capital would we require? Would we be able to sustain competition from existing suppliers? These thoughts never seemed to cease; and as Eric Thomas beautifully portrayed, 'Don't think about what can happen in a month. Don't think about what can happen in a year. Just focus on the twenty-four hours in front of you and do what you can to get closer to where you want to be!'

I perceived that unless I crossed the bridge of my insecurities, I could not begin to explore all my possibilities. As a first priority, I decided to look for a site to set up our plant. We explored far and wide for this. While ferreting around, one of my acquaintances told me of a large 20 acre plot belonging to a Masai group that was available for sale. This land was at Athi River, off the Nairobi–Mombasa Highway, around 50-60 km from Nairobi. Upon visiting the site, we liked it and expressed our interest to buy it. After much negotiation, the owners offered to sell the land at a rate of Ksh. 35,000 per acre, which came to around Ksh. 700,000 (equivalent to US$ 7,000 today). We decided to buy it. I was delighted and excited with our first experience of land acquisition.

For ease of operations and accountability, we resolved to incorporate a separate entity for our proposed manufacturing activity. After much deliberation, we chose to name it, 'Devki Steel Mills Limited'. Coming from a Hindu Brahmin family and having been priest myself, I wanted an auspicious name with religious significance. Devki was Lord Krishna's mother, who had borne much hardship and sufferings in life. I thought her sufferings reflected my own trials through life. Moreover, it was also a combination of my eldest son (Devang) and my younger brother, Bhavesh's son's name (Kishan). In 1993, we successfully registered our company. We then proceeded to conclude the land deal and in the next few months, we registered the land title in our company's name. By God's grace, our hardware trading business was doing well and we managed to buy these sprawling acres at Athi River from our profits, without seeking any external loan. This, to me, was an achievement of sorts, considering where and how I had begun my journey.

The renowned American author, educator and businessman, Stephen Covey, once said, 'The key to creativity is to begin with an end in mind, with a vision and a blue print of the desired result.' Once the land was acquired, I began visualising what our factory would ultimately look like. Believe it or not, many a times, I drove in my pick-up van to the site, stood in front of it for hours together and literally imagined the factory functioning. I had to work my mind backwards through the process to make my next move. Once the title was transferred, we fenced the land with a perimeter wall. Over the weekends, we used to transport materials to the site and supervise the progress of the perimeter wall. Once this was complete, we built a tiny room so that we could visit it frequently. Neeta and I often used to stay over for the weekends. We began contemplating what to start manufacturing. From our trading experience, we knew that steel bars formed our core business, but for this we had to put up a hot rolling mill, which would involve huge capital investment. So we decided to begin with a tube mill (sheet cutting mill). We would require lesser capital for this, which would mean investing in a small sheet-cutting machine, imported coil, and the cutting and the marketing of the sheets. We had to plan the construction of our plant and other infrastructure for the tube mill. But by now, we had utilised all our profits and emptied out our pockets.

It was imperative for me to seek assistance from banks and financial institutions. Again, it was my friend, Vijay Dhanani, who helped me out. Early in 1994, we approached the Kenya Commercial Bank (KCB) for financing to set up our steel rolling mill. The bank asked me to prepare a business plan for them. Though I was aware of the process and the costs involved in setting up one, preparing a business plan was new to me. I decided to give it a shot. With Vijay's help, we presented a project report to KCB for funding US$ 100,000, which was around Ksh. 3.6 million. This was a little shy of the bank's expectations, since the contract for constructing the factory itself was around US$ 138,889 (Ksh. 5 million). The bank then advised us to re-work the business plan to include the total cost involved in setting up the plant.

This time, we hired an experienced professional to assist us with a proper business plan. A KCB manager, Mr. Ndambuki, who I fondly remember, kept encouraging me during the entire loan application process. Finally, we put up a proposal for a loan of US$ 500,000. KCB considered our application favourably and sanctioned a term loan as well as a working capital facility. The term loan was for the construction of the plant, other infrastructure and machinery, repayable in five years' time. This gave us the impetus and the resources to move ahead. I owe a lot to KCB for what I am today.

In the second quarter of 1994, with the bank facility in place, our plans for constructing the factory and acquiring the required machinery began in earnest. We simultaneously began to build the factory and make enquiries with suppliers for the tube mill. Our business at Gikomba progressed well. We devoted our time between trading and overlooking the building construction at Athi River. It was a challenging time for all of us; Devang was hardly four years old and Neeta had to take care of our household as well as our business. Kaushik had settled in by now; we complemented with each other very well. While he managed the shop, I supervised the factory construction; and while he was out for deliveries and supervision, I manned the shop. At times, both Neeta and I used to sleepover at the plant site to ensure that things stayed under control. Both our business activities progressed steadily.

One incident that I will always remember is that of a trip I made to India in search of the tube mill. Delhi and Punjab in Northern India had many reputed suppliers. I was slated to travel by train from Delhi to Ludhiana (Punjab) to meet a supplier. During my travel, Punjab had experienced unexpectedly heavy floods and everything had gone haywire, including the transport system. On reaching Delhi, I headed to the railway station, only to find that most of the trains plying to and from Punjab had been indefinitely delayed. The sight at the railway station was unimaginable. There was chaos everywhere; the place was overcrowded with scores of stranded passengers and confused officials, with hardly any space to stand. We were initially informed that our train had been delayed by three hours, which eventually turned out to be twenty-four hours! This was my first travel to Delhi and North India, and I was clueless at the railway station. As night fell, I managed to find a small place outside the waiting room and decided to rest there on the floor. I placed a small bag with my important documents under my head as a pillow, placed my big suitcase next to me, and dozed off in minutes, so tired and exhausted I was. Delhi is well known for thugs, and unfortunately that night, I was robbed of my shoes and my suitcase as I slept peacefully. When I woke up the next morning, I realised what had happened. Fortunately, I still had the bag under my head, which contained all the important things I really needed. Unfazed by the incident, I decided to continue with my trip.

The train that I travelling by was called 'Shane-E-Punjab' (Pride of Punjab) and ironically, I could take no pride in travelling in the state I was in. When the train finally arrived in Delhi a day late, there was hardly any space to even board the compartment. Bare footed, I squeezed in somehow and managed to find a space to stand. Standing there in the train, I realised that most of the travellers appeared to be uneducated labourers or from the lower-middle segment. Standing amid them I saw a young girl travelling alone, who appeared to be decent and educated. I learnt that she had recently got married and was residing in Malaysia. This was the first time she was returning to Chandigarh after her marriage to meet her father. I noticed that men around her were harassing her. Unable to stand their behaviour, I told them that we were travelling together, thus managing to keep them from troubling her. Introducing herself, she thanked me and started a conversation. She saw my bare feet and asked me what had become of my shoes. Smiling, I told her that I had been robbed at the Delhi railway station. Pitying my condition, she requested me to wear a pair of new sandals that she had bought for her father. We continued to stand in that crowd; but I soon realised that it would be next to impossible to travel in that manner. Sometime later, when the train halted at a major station, I requested her to alight and looked for the First Class compartment. Although we didn't have first class tickets, I convinced her to board it. As we did not appear to be local residents, none of the First Class passengers questioned us. Luckily, it was an air-conditioned compartment and we managed to find some space to sit. I was prepared to pay any additional charge or fine in case a ticket collector questioned us. Fortunately, no railway officials turned up and I reached Ludhiana with some modicum of peace and dignity. I thanked her for sharing the sandals and returned them while alighting from the train.

The supplier's representative came to receive me at the Ludhiana station. We headed straight to their plant on his 'Piki-Piki' (motorcycle in Swahilli), I inspected the machinery and returned to Delhi that same night. Even to this day, whenever I happen to travel by train in India, I recall flashes of this incident! In Delhi, I met a couple of more suppliers and eventually settled for a tube mill manufactured by G.R. Mechanical, at a total price of US$ 62,000. My banker, KCB, made the payments to the supplier in instalments, based on the machinery despatch.

Our trading activity in Gikomba and the construction of our steel rolling mills at Athi River moved simultaneously. Our family life kept pace too. Kaushik got married to Bhavni in 1993. Incidentally, her family was a neighbour of ours from Muthithi Road and that's how they both had met. Devang too was growing up and our domestic responsibilities had increased. As our family expanded, it became necessary to look for a bigger place. During this period, we shifted our residence from Muthithi Road to 5 Parklands Avenue, Nairobi.

By end of October 1995, our factory building was ready, the tube mill imported from India had been commissioned, and all electrical installations, fixtures and fittings were also in place. We built a small administrative office within the premises, and a residential space above the office for our engineers. As we began our trial production, I was exhilarated. My vision of diversifying into manufacturing was finally becoming a reality. We were all set to begin commercial production; we were all set to take off!

And that was how Devki Steel Mills Limited was born…

• CHAPTER 26 •

A LANDMARK: TRADER TO MANUFACTURER

My life's battles so far had all been fought uphill. Right from the time I had boarded my first flight to Nairobi in 1978, to my return to Kenya in 1982, the birth of 'Guru', the priest and astrologer in 1983, to learning the tricks of the trade from 1983 to 1985, and embarking on my trading business in 1986 – all along—it had been a hard fought battle. Against all odds, I overcame the challenges that I met as a trader and reached the top of where I stand today. A bigger battle awaited me when my manufacturing button was to be switched on. Little did I know that when I began this segment of my business journey, it would test me to my wits end! This experience would be another turning point in my life and change my perception for good.

Soon after commencing our production, we faced a major setback. By October 1995, we were all set to take off. We planned our staffing requirement and began with a strong workforce of seventy-two. The KCB had already sanctioned us a term loan and working capital funds. Letter of credit facilities were part of the working capital funding that helped us to import our first consignment of raw materials from South Africa. Our initial import of steel was at US$ 370 per tonne and was sufficient to cater to one month's production. In November 1995, commercial production finally commenced and we began with a bang. Our tube mill functioned at its optimum capacity; we managed to market our entire production; our supplier's, employees and bank commitments were fulfilled in a timely manner. Our trading business too did well. I started dividing my time between Gikomba and our Athi River plant. In the mornings, I devoted my time to our trading business and by noon I supervised our manufacturing operations. Suddenly my work-life had turned hectic; but I never felt exhausted because here I was finally chasing my dream! This was more than expected and a perfect beginning.

Encouraged by our first month's performance, I decided to import a few months' requirements all at one go and expressed my intentions to our bankers, KCB, who advised that I utilise the Letter of Credit (L/C) facility for this. Motivated by the bank's support, I signed the contract and opened the letter of credit to buy steel at the rate of US$ 370 per tonne from the same South African suppliers, who were more than happy and promptly shipped the raw materials. I was thrilled at the prospect and started building castles of profit in the air! That's when thunder struck. It is the things that you least expect that hit you the hardest. The global prices of steel crashed spectacularly to US$ 200 from US$ 370 per tonne; and my world came crashing down. With so much stock on hand, I was constrained to continue production, hoping that even though at a loss, we would be able to sell our production and fulfil our commitments. But that was not to be.

As the saying goes, 'Everybody loves you until you become competition.' As traders, we were the darling of the local manufacturers and their biggest customers. The moment we began manufacturing, we became a threat. They were bent upon running Devki out of business and ganged up against us by undercutting us on the prices. The market was flooded with cheap products. As a consequence, we could not sell our production; huge inventory piled up and we failed to honour KCB's letter of credit commitment. We could not meet the obligations of other local suppliers; and most importantly, we had no money to pay to our staff. My heart sank. There seemed to be no light at the end of the tunnel, and I felt as if I had reached a dead-end. But there was no way, I could cave in. I met KCB's officials and appraised them about my situation. The bankers then asked my opinion and expectations on the steel prices trend. I told them that this was a temporary phase; and markets would bounce back and we would be able to sell our production. All that I requested was their understanding at this stage to grant me a moratorium of a few months to honour their commitments.

KCB did not push me for repayments, but instead restructured the facility until the markets recovered. I had not paid salaries to my workers for three months now. This hurt me badly because I used to work with them on the production floor. So one day, I sat down with all seventy-two of them on the shop floor and explained that it was my intention that both the company and the employees progress together; I would clear all their dues, but currently had no funds to pay them. My workers were understanding and responded to me in Swahili, saying '*Guru, muda mrefu kama wewe kutupa kitu kama shilingi 1,000, sisi kusimamia familia zetu. Mara baada ya kusimamia na kuuza bidhaa zote, unaweza kulipa sisi usawa. Sisi ni na wewe*' [Guru, as long as you give us something like Ksh. 1,000, we will manage our families. Once you manage to sell all the goods, you can pay us the balance. We are with you]'. I was touched by their generosity and support. I went back to my office and cried a lot. With folded hands, I looked heavenwards to the Almighty Father to show me the way forward. My prayers were soon answered. The markets recovered and steel prices shot to US$ 500 per MT in three months' time. We were the only supplier in the market, who had ample steel to sell! In an effort to wipe us out of the market, all our competitors had cleaned their stocks by selling cheap. So after five months of frustration, patience and uncertainty, we sold the entire production and made a clear US$ 1 million in profit.

I had graduated from a trader to a manufacturer. This was the first experience of mine in manufacturing and I tasted the sweetness of making profits. This was a landmark achievement in my life; and a major turning point too. This experience was orchestrated by the Almighty to teach me that I needed to move forward. I will always remain grateful to all my seventy-two employees, who stood by my side in that hour of need. Even after twenty-two years, some employees continue to hold my hand to this day. In many cases, the children of those employees work with us now. My team has played a vital role in my growth and success. This taught me a very important lesson early on in my business journey – that all things being equal, human resource is the most critical resource. In addition, it was very nice of KCB to act so kindly towards me.

That's why till today, I keep telling my board of directors that, 'We will never leave KCB, because they understand the Kenyan market; they understand the people, and the business way of Kenya. I have stopped doing business with many other banks, but I will never leave KCB and will always remain indebted to them.' The support of KCB and my employees taught me that alone one can reach one's target fast, but together one can reach very far. Moreover, the battle the competitors fought, made me realise that 'everything is fair in love, war and business'. I am thankful to them. For had they not challenged me, there would have been no struggle; and without struggle, there would have been no success. For without anything to struggle for, there would be nothing to achieve. Lastly and more importantly, the sudden movement of steel prices taught me that business is dynamic and cyclic in nature; one has to be vigilant all the while and there is no room for complacency.

Towards end of 1996, our Athi River plant's manufacturing processes had stabilised. Initially, we marketed most of our production through our trading arm, Steel Centre Limited. Both Kaushik and I were now focussed on our plant and we had a management team to handle the trading activities. After some time, we realised that there was a clash of interest between the two businesses because of some customers. To foster growth, it became imperative for us to give up our trading activity. By the year-end, we ceased trading through Steel Centre and let out our shop on rent. Even to this day, the existing tenants manage a hardware business from the outlet.

I had conquered the first battle; it was time to grow further.

• CHAPTER 27 •

THERE IS NO RELIGION GREATER THAN TRUTH

Even if you are the minority of one,
The truth is still the truth.

—Mahatma Gandhi

Mahatma Gandhi has always been one of my inspirations; Saint Theresa being the other one. Gandhiji had very truly said that, 'There is no God higher than truth.' Honesty and truth have been the fundamental principles upon which my professional and personal lives were founded. Let me share one more anecdote before I move ahead.

Outside my Westlands apartment, I had placed a wooden plaque reading, 'सत्य समम धर्म न देसरा', which means there is no religion equal or greater than truth. These lines form a part of a famous chaupai (a four-line poem) from the great Indian epic—Ramayana. As a teenage priest, serving at the Swaminarayan temple in Nairobi, every night I used to read holy scriptures and texts, including the Ramayana. These particular lines had such a profound impression on me that speaking the truth became imbedded in me from an early age. Due to this fundamental principle, many times, I have found myself in precarious and embarrassing situations, but as Gandhiji said, 'Even if you are in the minority of one; the truth is still the truth.' I have always stood firm on speaking the truth and have never diverted from my stand. As a priest, once I had expressed my honest opinion about a management committee member, who aspired to join the temple committee. Being aware of the mala fide intentions of this person, I voiced my true opinion to the committee; which they didn't appreciate at the time. Later when the member displayed his true colours did they realise the importance of truth.

A very intriguing incident took place in the early 1990s that strongly reinforced my belief in the principle that truth always prevails. This happened when our trading entity, Steel Centre, had reached its zenith. Officials of the Kenya Revenue Authority (KRA) were conducting their normal annual revenue audit of our books of accounts in our premises. I was not directly involved in the process as our team of tax and accounts consultants and our financial controller took care of all the queries raised by the officials. At the end of the audit, the officials disallowed an amount of Ksh. 7 million, which was shown as 'bad-debts' and written off against the profits of a particular year, thus bringing down our taxable profits. While our team argued that the customers who owed us this amount had failed to pay us, hence the claim; the revenue officials maintained that this was not a genuine claim and hence their decision to disallow it.

Unable to resolve the issue, the KRA officer in charge of the audit asked me to clarify their doubts. We all sat together; the official on one side of the table, our team and I on the other end. I was unaware of the discussion at hand. The officer began by asking me about my business, its ownership, turnover, profits, etc., which I promptly answered, and then he brought up the disputed amount.

He explained that though all the papers and documentary evidence for this claim were in order, he was not satisfied and wanted my explanation to clear his doubts. I told him that yes, the amount was outstanding from our clients, but I had personally collected from them and had utilised the funds for my proposed residential apartment. I added that he was right in doubting the claim.

Shocked and dumbfounded, my financial controller angrily spoke to me in Gujarati,'જ્યારે અમે તમને બચાવવા અને ટેક્સ જવાબદારી ઘટાડવા નો પર્યાસ કરી રહ્યાં છીએ, તમે શા માટે સત્ય બોલો છો? હું હમણાં જ રાજીનામું આપું છું! [While we are trying to protect you and reduce the tax liability, why are you saying the truth? I am resigning right away!]'; and he threatened to resign on the spot. I put my hand on his shoulders and told him, 'Young man, as long as you were handling the matter, it was fine. But the moment, the officer asked me to clarify his doubt; I had to tell him the truth as a matter of principle. Whether to continue to work with us or not, is entirely up to you, but I will never deviate from my principles.' The revenue official was equally amazed. He confessed that this was the first time he had come across a businessman who dared to present the true picture! Impressed by my honesty and considering the documented evidence, he decided to allow our claim! I told him that it was his prerogative to allow or disallow our claim, but I had fulfilled my obligation of sticking to the truth. From that moment, we became friends. The official eventually reached a very senior position and retired a few years back. Our bond continues even to this day. Incidentally, my financial controller never resigned and continues to work with me till date.

What I am trying to impress upon you is that be it in your business, professional or personal life, never hesitate from speaking the truth. You may find it bitter and it may even land you in awkward situations. But remember: in the short run, you may get away with lies; but eventually the truth will always prevail.

There is no religion greater than truth.

• CHAPTER 28 •

EXPANSION AND GROWTH OF DEVKI STEEL MILLS LTD

My vision and dreams have always been larger than life. Way back in 1978, as a ten-year-old, when we could not even afford a second-hand bicycle, I dreamt of riding a helicopter. I had been fascinated by the chopper used by the then Prime Minister of India, the late Smt. Indira Gandhi, for her election campaign in Surendranagar, Gujarat. I began my journey into the steel industry through Kikuyu Steel Rolling Mill Limited, which was the largest steel rolling mill in Kenya at the time. Later through my vision and foresight, Delta Hardware became the country's largest hardware trader. Similarly, my own venture, Steel Centre Limited, was acclaimed as Kenya's single largest hardware merchant within about five years of its commercial operations. This had given me the confidence to dream big and achieve them in my life. Having scaled great heights in hardware trading, I wanted to be a one-stop manufacturer for all infrastructure products. Having begun as a hardware trader, I was keen to manufacture all that a hardware trader dealt with. I aspired to establish Devki Steel Mills as the one of the key players in the East and Central African steel industry landscape. I set my mind on expansion.

The erratic fluctuations of international steel prices in the beginning of 1996 had drained my energy and tested my endurance limits, before eventually leaving me richer by more than a million dollars. This boosted our cash flow position and helped us gain a firm footing in the Kenyan steel industry. By the year-end, we gave up our trading activities and concentrated entirely on our manufacturing arm. The year 1997 witnessed a stable and gradual growth in our production and sales; our production of square and round tubes, and hollow sections clocked around 300 MT per month and supplies at around 250 MT. It was during this phase that the seeds of investing in a hot rolling mill germinated in my mind. This would facilitate the manufacturing of reinforcement bars from billets. By this time, bank lending rates in Kenya had hit the roof and were hovering at around 35-40 per cent.

Many industries either raised their hands in bankruptcy or sustained heavy losses. Fortunately, we had no external borrowing; it was an ideal platform to expand. My search for this mill took me again to India. I visited quite a few manufacturers, and though keen on automated and bigger mills, I finalised a good, manual hot rolling mill, manufactured by AMT International at Mandi Gobindgarh in Punjab. It was a bargain deal. Our total monthly supply was around 250 MT, and taking into consideration an increased demand, I aimed at manufacturing around 500 MT per month. Incidentally, by the time the mill was commissioned and started operations in 1998, our demand had shot up beyond my expectations and we were unable to cope up with it!

The installation of the new hot rolling mill boosted our production of thermo-mechanically treated (TMT) bars. Very soon we realised the need for a galvanising plant (process of applying protective zinc coating to steel or iron, to prevent their rusting) as well. We had started as hardware traders and now wanted to manufacture those products that a hardware trader deals in. We were happy with the tubes and pipes that we produced through our tube mill and hot rolling mill. This was just the beginning and I never looked back. We embarked on an expansion drive and invested in reinforcement bar as well as suction mills. They went into commercial production by 1999.

In a steel rolling mill, a billet is a key raw material. Billets are created directly by continuous casting or extrusion or indirectly by hot rolling an ingot. Bloom billets are further processed through profile rolling and drawing. Imports posed two challenges. Owing to unstable economic conditions, the Kenyan Shilling erratically fluctuated against all major currencies, resulting in foreign exchange gains or losses; consequently, varying our import costs. Moreover, because of delays in shipping, logistics and transportation, we were always running short of raw materials. This affected our production and hit our supplies as well.

As a first step to break the shackles of our complete dependency on imports, we decided to backward integrate our operations and came up with a plan of setting up our first induction furnace or melting furnace. The rationale was to source metal scrap locally, metal it using this furnace and manufacture ingots that we could use for converting to billets, eventually using a raw material for our final steel products.(In steelmaking, ingots are semi-finished casting products of relatively pure metal). In 2000, we commissioned our first melting furnace. It was probably the first of its kind to be installed in Kenya and was inaugurated by the then President of Kenya, His Excellency, the Hon. Daniel Toroitich Arap Moi. I felt blessed and fortunate and his presence reminded me of the first time I had met him in Nakuru in 1983.

Inauguration of the induction furnace in Year 2000, by then President of Kenya, His Excellency the Hon. Daniel Toritich Arap Moi

Napoleon Hill put it beautifully when he said, 'Strength and growth come only through continuous effort and struggle.' I have always believed that it was imperative for me to put in my best efforts, while growth and success would follow. Setting up the first furnace helped us to manufacture ingots in-house and reduce our dependency on imports to a certain extent. But this was short lived, as demand outweighed our production capacity and we had to continue importing billets hand-in-hand with our manufacturing. When we could still not cope with the demand, we decided to set up our second induction furnace. After successfully commissioning the plant by 2001, our production increased to 1,500 MT per month from a mere 300 MT back in 1996. Between 2001 and 2006, we atomised our plants. For this, we merged the two furnaces into one, thus increasing the output. Then we installed additional tube and pipe mills, before increasing the capacity of the suction mill as well. My hardware trader instincts insisted that we expand our product profile and target to become the one-stop shop for any hardware trader. That was when I began toying with the idea of acquiring Nailin Nail Works Limited (NNWL).

Established by an Indian family thirty years ago, NNWL was undoubtedly the oldest and the largest mill for wire products in Kenya at that point in time (1997-98). With a workforce in excess of 2,000, it had two manufacturing plants on Addis Abba Road in the industrial area of Nairobi and at Ruiru on the outskirts of Nairobi. Their product range included nails, weld-mesh, fasteners, nuts and bolts, galvanised products and chicken wires, among others. We had very close business ties with them, since it was one of the top steel plants in Kenya and a major supplier of our trading outlet, Steel Centre.

In the 1990s, the Kenyan economy witnessed an increasing inflationary pressure and deteriorating economic conditions. Owing to this, banks shot up their lending rates to more than 38%. Consequently, unable to sustain the high interest costs, most of the business houses and industries collapsed. Nailin Nail met a similar fate and succumbed to financial pressures and cash flow challenges. Somewhere around 1998–1999, it went into receivership and the owners migrated to the UK. The Kenya Commercial Bank, their bankers (who were incidentally our bankers as well) handled the auction and sale of the company. They had fixed an asking price of Ksh. 500 million (equivalent to US$ 4.8 million today, but back then it would have been around US$ 6.5–7 million). This was beyond the pockets of many a prospective investor due to the high interest rates, lack of visionary entrepreneurship, lack of knowledge of managing the industry and also possibly the lack of courage to risk funds under such volatile market conditions.

I was aware of the fact that acquiring NNWL would be advantageous for us. Not only would it expand our horizon and multiply our revenues, it would also increase our bottom-line. I stayed calm, bid for my time to come and waited for things to settle down. For five long years when there were no buyers and interest rates had substantially reduced, I made a major decision to acquire NNWL in 2004. We approached KCB, also our bankers, and expressed our interest in buying it for Ksh. 500 million, the price fixed by the bank. Since we had an existing relationship with KCB, I requested them to sanction us a term loan to facilitate the deal. The only condition I stipulated was that in the event of the deal going through, the bank would immediately transfer the ownership of the company to us. Since NNWL had a facility in place with KCB, the bankers advised that it was not possible for them to sanction a second facility under the existing company.

They advised us to apply for a fresh term loan facility under Devki Steel Mills Limited. At that time, our record with KCB was clean and we had no existing loan or facility with them. Since this matter had been prolonged, the bank carried out a revaluation of NNWL's assets, which incidentally were worth more than the asking price. KCB then gave us a green signal, and sanctioned us a long-term loan. Considerable time had lapsed between the offer made in 1999–2000 and our bid in 2004; and since the company was in liquidation, substantial documentation and paper work were involved. After nearly six months of complying with all legal documentation, the deal went through and we were the proud owners of NNWL, which was finally merged with Devki. At that point (2004–2005), this was the biggest risk I had ever taken in my business life!

There was a lot to be done even after the acquisition. The company had ceased operations for more than seven years now. Since the machines had been lying idle, it was a daunting task to assess their working life. It took us nearly a year-and-a-half to refurbish most of the machinery and bring them to their normal functioning mode. A few obsolete machines had to be scrapped. Similarly, we had to import plant and machinery from Germany and India. After much hard work, we succeeded in beginning production from both plants. From owning one manufacturing facility in Athi River, we now had three plants in our kitty. With this acquisition, our production capacity had more than doubled.

In hindsight, I perceive that my decision of acquiring NNWL had paid us rich dividends over the past decade or so. My vision of thinking and dreaming big resulted in this decision, and consequently we rose from strength to strength.

With NNWL in our fold, we became the largest steel mill in Kenya. My aim was to go further, because our demand continued to outweigh our production, despite importing billets and churning out ingots as well as billets from our furnaces at Athi River. Our billet imports increased, but still we were unable to match the demand. Metal scrap sourced from the vicinity of Nairobi was inadequate to feed our furnace. It became inevitable for us to expand once again. We found out that there were large deposits of metal scrap on the Kenyan costal belt. In 2008, we set up a melting furnace plant in Mombasa. To maximise the benefits of backward integration, we also set up a billet casting mill within our Mombasa plant. These billets were utilised as a raw material for our Athi River plant. We had now become a player to reckon with in the East African steel industry.

Challenges bring change and change brings challenges with it. The acquisition of NNWL and the establishment of the Mombasa plant had facilitated expansion and growth, but overlooking three units in Nairobi posed a challenge in itself. It was then that we took a couple of major decisions. After operating the Addis Abba Road plant for two years or so, we ceased our operations here in 2009 and shifted the nail machines to the Ruiru plant. This enabled us to have a better control of our production facilities. We then leased out the Addis Abba plant, which continues to this day. Most importantly, in 2011, we took another strategic step. To centralize our administration, we relocated our Group administrative headquarters from Athi River to Ruiru, where it stands at present.

My business journey, which had begun from a hardware shop in Gikomba, manned by only Neeta and I, had culminated into a vast caravan of the Devki family. What had commenced its journey with less than ten people grew from strength to strength as we crossed one milestone after another. Today, the Devki Steel Mills family has a strong, dedicated, loyal and hardworking workforce in excess of 2,500 within its fold.

Steel and hardware products manufactured at Devki Steel Mills

With my team at Devki Steel Mill's plant at Athi River

With my team at Devki Steel Mill's plant at Mombasa

Our Group's Headquarters at Ruiru, near Nairobi, Kenya

Devki Steel Mill Plant at Ruiru, Kenya

The times have continued to remain challenging and tough, but the Almighty has been kind enough to shower us with blessings and guidance to bravely face all challenges successfully through the years. Like any successful corporate house or businessman, my success is founded on certain core principles and I have learnt numerous lessons on this path. I have always believed that there is no religion greater than truth. I highlighted the importance of truth in my previous chapter and narrated a real life incident. Whether it is dealing with our suppliers, clients, employees, taxman or anybody else, I believe in sticking to the truth, irrespective of the consequences. Even our management team has been so trained that whenever we give a presentation, I advise them to present the negative facts before the positive ones. Even in the toughest of times, when securing facilities, loans or borrowings was a challenge, we managed to get them from our bankers, solely by presenting a true and honest picture.

While submitting projections to our bankers, we always present conservative figures, so that we always achieve either what we present or much higher than that, but never lesser than our projections. This is how we managed to gain our banker's and supplier's confidence. This principle of telling the truth has helped me sleep well every night. In addition, my courage and attitude of never giving up has seen me through the most difficult times. There have been numerous occasions when my courage has been tested; it takes courage to grow up and become who you really are. Moreover, I have had unfailing faith in the Almighty; and *He* has always been my guiding light, showing me the way ahead.

Additionally, my virtue of thoroughly thinking through everything has always stood me in good stead. I am an early riser; I wake up around 5:00 am every day and think about how to expand and grow our business. Furthermore, I've always had a long-term vision of our business and its expansion. My principles of offering the best quality products at competitive rates, with timely delivery and prompt customer service has helped us withstand all competition and allowed us to build a firm foundation for our business. More importantly, having seen poverty and destituteness from childhood, I have always been humble in dealing with people and have maintained simplicity in life. It is my sincere advise to readers across the globe and across generations, to always remain grounded, no matter who you are or what you do. In simple terms, leave the ego, otherwise everyone would leave you. Lastly and most importantly, the welfare of my employees and their families is my top priority. The furnace blast incident of 2007 (which I have shared in the next chapter) has increased my commitment to them.

Until we spread our wings, we will never have any idea how far we can fly! I have always pushed myself to do more and more; all of us hold tremendous potential within ourselves to achieve our dreams. We have to tap into our own dormant potential to achieve them all.

• CHAPTER 29 •

TESTING TIMES: THE FURNACE BLAST EPISODE

They say it is easy to stand with the crowd, but it takes courage to stand alone. Before I continue any further, I would like to narrate an untoward incident that occurred at our Athi River plant, on Monday, 24 September 2007. It has left a permanent scar on my heart. This day will go as a black letter day in my life. Being a priest, I have unfailing faith in the will of the Almighty. I trust *Him* completely, because I know that if God pushes me to the edge, there can only be two eventualities—*He* will either catch me if I fall, or *He* will teach me how to fly. This incident not only tested my courage, but also deepened my unfailing faith.

As part of our operations, we buy all forms of metal scrap from various sources across the country. This is then transported to our Athi River and Mombasa plants for storage. Employee safety has always been my highest priority and concern. Hence, before melting the scrap, we always carry out a thorough screening to ensure that any hazardous chemical, dangerous liquid or explosive metal is separated, eliminated and destroyed. Once assured of the lack of any risk, the scrap is broken down and melted in the furnace for further processing.

Life on this fateful Monday began normally. All of us carried out our routine tasks; by the evening, all the administrative and office staff, including myself, called it a day. Our plant operated round the clock and production employees worked in shifts. At any given point, around 200-300 workers would be engaged in the plant. In the evening, shifts changed; the morning operators left and the evening ones took over. Production continued as usual, with over 250 workers carrying out their normal duties. Like any typical workday, the usual banter and laughter, went on as everyone went on with their business. Life was perfect until the catastrophe struck. At around 9:00 pm in the night, the furnace exploded. The blast was so tremendous that the entire vicinity of the Athi River area heard it! Red hot metal splinters flew around like meteors falling from the sky; or as if a volcano had erupted. All the twenty workers at the furnace were gravely injured; four of them died on the spot; and the rest were immediately rushed to nearby hospitals. Another five fought a losing battle before passing away in the hospital; while eleven of them survived.

I had just finished my evening prayers, thanking the Lord for everything, when our Group's human resources manager, Mr. James Karuiki, called me. His nervousness and the loud noise in the background made me feel uneasy. I sensed immediately that all was not well. I was thunderstruck when Karuiki finally managed to convey the terrible news. The earth beneath my feet seemed to have opened up. In no time, I was flooded with calls from everyone, cautioning me to stay indoors. Many advised me that if I dared to visit the plant, I would be killed! My family was trembling with fever; panic had overtaken us. How could I dream of staying back at home when my entire work force was battling for their lives? In tears and with folded hands, Neeta and I rushed to the prayer room to seek the Lord's help. As always, I prayed for a way forward in these testing times; and within the next second, I was out of the house, headed to Athi River.

All through the drive, I continued to pray to God. On reaching the site, I saw that all hell had broken loose at our plant, thousands had gathered outside shouting, screaming, crying, running up and down to help, but the situation was uncontrollable. Fire had broken out in the furnace and the firemen were frantically trying to put it down, while Policemen had cordoned off the area to control the mob. The Area Deputy Commissioner (DC) himself had driven down to the site, all the way from Machakacos. People from all around the region sprang into action to help us in all possible ways. Mustering enough courage, I made my way to the furnace, which looked like a war zone with bodies of dead and injured soldiers all over the battlefield.

One employee who stayed close to the site told me,'Guru, I heard a loud explosion and saw huge flames shooting up into the sky. I could even feel the heat.' On hearing this account, I felt like a hapless army commander, shaken from within. My workers were like my family, they depended on me; and as the family head, it was my duty to stand by them in this hour of need. Though panic stricken, there was no way I could cave in. While the relief work was in process, I gathered all the employees, their families and the rest of the people there. I addressed them all, assuring them that come what may, I was with them and their families. The DC also managed to calm down the people standing around. It took a lot of courage for me to stand there; I could have been killed. From there, I rushed to the hospital where the injured had been admitted. It was chaos all around and the entire hospital was filled with weeping and mourning families of the injured or departed employees. I met each injured employee and tried to console them and their families. I left the hospital in the wee hours of the morning, but the weeping continued.

The real ordeal began after the incident. The entire workforce was deeply distressed and the blast survivors were traumatised. To facilitate investigation and to repair the damage, we had to close down the plant for the next thirty days or so. During this period, we held prayers and prayer meetings every day in Athi River for the souls of those who had passed away. Being a priest myself, I conducted these prayers myself. I regularly visited the hospital to ensure that the injured employees were properly attended to; I also visited the homes of my deceased employees and assured employment to their next of kin. The children of some of them are still working with us. Consoling the traumatised employees was a major challenge.

I still remember a couple of them could not swallow a single morsel nor utter a single word for days together; they would simply sit outside the furnace and cry. It was hard to bear their pain. To top it all, a few wily politicians tried to influence our workers to revolt, in order to gain political mileage from the tragedy, because elections were due in December 2007. Some even went to the extent of blaming the entire Asian community for being negligent of their employees. But my employees stood united and showed their solidarity towards me. They managed to drive the politicians out of the scene. I was touched by their gesture and will remain indebted to them throughout my life. Some of the workers involved in the terrible accident continue to work with us, even to this day. The community around our Athi River plant supported me as well. On the night of the incident so many of them had turned up at the disaster site asking, 'Can we help you in any way?' I felt that God was with me.

Handling the government agencies and investigation teams was, however, a nightmare. Teams of officials and sleuths from the fire department, the Directorate of Occupational Health and Safety, the labour department and the police department thronged us endlessly to assess the cause of the blast. One theory was that there were landmines in the metal scrap we had acquired from the British Army barracks, which blew up when they were melted in the furnace. Another theory said that we were negligent in screening the scrap and failed to identify the hazardous material, hence the blast. A third possible angle of outside agencies with mala fide intentions to hamper our progress was also probed. Many other theories and possible causes were investigated as well. This went on for several weeks. In the end, unable to draw a plausible conclusion, the matter was laid to rest and we were given a clean chit. Though I knew we were clean at heart and never at fault, I could not take the memory of this incident out of my mind. Some days, I went without food and water and many a night I spent without closing my eyes for even a fraction of a second. Even today, I get goose bumps when I recall that fateful night.

News of the tragedy spread like wild fire across the globe, as it was covered by major media houses. It was all over on the net. Dealing with the international press and media was the worst experience of my life. Every second day, I would either get a call from overseas reporters or a local newspaper journalist found his way to my office. At times, I even got calls in the middle of the night***. Though we resumed our operations within a month of the tragedy, the trauma and traces of the accident took a long time to return to normal, but finally the heat cooled down.

Some painful things can teach us lessons that we didn't think we needed to know. Though employee safety had always been our top priority, this incident was an eye-opener. We began screening each and every scrap item at least thrice, before it landed in the

---

****Some links are **Daily Nation** reports:*

25 September 2007 (http://allafrica.com/stories/200709251305.html)

26 September 2007 (http://allafrica.com/stories/200709260139.html)

This found its place in the Explosion News on 19 October 2007:

http://www.infopig.com/keywords/Explosion/10-19-2007-165232.html

furnace. Whether a small battery cell, or a worn metal tank, every type of scrap went through a microscopic lens. Though this incident has left a permanent scar within me and I have been unable to forgive myself to this day for the terrible mishap, it has enhanced my commitment to my employees and my unfailing faith in the Almighty, who gave me the strength and the courage to face the ordeal. Shortly after this incident, Kenya faced general elections in December 2007, after which there was chaos across the nation and the entire economy came to a grinding halt. Most of the industries temporarily downed their shutters and their workers went on strike, demanding higher wages and better working facilities. I am again proud to share that all our Devki units kept functioning throughout the turbulence and none of them had to be shut down for any reason. We have always ensured that our workers get paid the best wages, and on time. We set an example for Kenyan industries and managed to involve the Ministry about our concern for Employee Welfare.

• CHAPTER 30 •

SUCCESS AND JEALOUSY

Climbing up the rungs of the ladder of success, I realised that nothing succeeds like success. It leads to opportunities for further and greater successes, but it also breeds envy, resentment and jealousy among family and friends. You will find very few people in this world who are sincerely delighted and happy at your success; most of them envy you. Success makes them hate you just because you have either risen higher than them or they simply cannot reconcile with the fact that you have risen higher much beyond their expectations. Unaware of all the struggles and pain you take to succeed in life, some people try to expose what is wrong with you because they cannot stand what is right about you. Many a time I wish if people accepted one's success gleefully, it would be wonderful to enjoy success without seeing envy in the eyes of those around us. I have been no exception to this human thought and experienced a near to fatal incident; thought of sharing this incident with you all before heading further.

In 1978, when I first left the Indian shores as a teenage priest, not a single soul, not even my parents had ever imagined in their wildest dreams where my journey would take me. At that time, we were broke, my father was struggling to make both ends meet and barely able to keep our family afloat. All around us were aware of our family's financial condition. Knowing me to be mischievous, naughty and hyper-active, those close of our family prayed that I would mend my ways for good. They never dreamt of who or what I would eventually become. Within a couple of years of my stepping in the world of business through my first venture, Steel Centre, we fared well and good times slowly filled our life. I supported my family back home in India, so that all of us could lead a better life. My parents moved from Mathak to Morbi; my younger brother, Bhavesh, pursued his Engineering studies in Bangalore; and my sister, Sangeeta, got married. After years of struggle, I had managed to bring a smile on my parents' face; they were proud of my achievements and able to hold their heads high in society. While some of my friends and family genuinely felt happy for us; many could not digest our success. It was then this incident occurred.

About three years after our marriage, for the first time Neeta and I travelled together to my home town in Morbi, India. It was the first time that many of our friends and family were meeting Neeta; joy, happiness and a festive mood filled the air. Proud of my achievements, my parents took me to meet all our near and dear family members, their faces full of pride and happiness. I was also keen to meet everyone as I wanted to rebuild all relationships, burying all differences once and for all. We were all happily oblivious of the fact that jealousy was boiling beneath many a smiling face.

One evening, to mark our visit to Morbi, one of our close acquaintances organised a social gathering and hosted a dinner party in our honour. It was a memorable evening; we had a good time meeting many old and new faces, all eager to know about life in Kenya, our business, our success and our married life. The celebration continued till late into the night. Though our house was nearby, we decided to spend the night at the host's place. To enjoy the cool summer breeze, we rested on the terrace. Around 11:00 pm, I felt uneasy and started vomiting, experiencing severe pain. Something was seriously wrong and I barely managed to wake Neeta, before falling unconscious. Panic stricken, Neeta tried to wake up friends and relatives resting with me on the terrace, but all in vain. Distraught, she ran down to our house nearby, woke up Bhavesh and requested him to get our family doctor. Incidentally, our family doctor was at a movie theatre. Bhavesh rushed to the cinema hall and got him.

When the doctor arrived, my body had turned pale green. On examining me, he said that I had been poisoned and immediately began treatment. We were shocked to hear this. Though we returned home after I regained consciousness, none of us slept that night. For the next couple of days, I was kept under medical observation. Later, the Doctor reconfirmed that a poisonous chemical had been added to my drink, and had I not received timely medical attention, I would have died. I soon recovered and returned to Nairobi; and for once, I regretted visiting my home town! It did not stop at this, however. Some malicious people from my home town even wrote letters to the Kenyan authorities, alleging that I was involved in illegal activities like smuggling and selling illicit liquor. I have preserved copies of this letter even to this date. Others tried to brainwash and divide our family, but all in vain.

Recalling this incident gives me goose bumps. I fail to comprehend how jealousy can make a person stoop so low that one can even think of murder? I am still trying to find an answer to the question. This incident has scared me for life, leading me to make the decision of permanently settling down in Kenya. It was this incident that made Kenya my 'Karma-Bhoomi' (place of action, as against place of birth). I was so hurt by the incident that

I renounced all rights to my father's property in India in favour of my brother, Bhavesh. I also decided to relocate my parents and Bhavesh to Kenya for good. My sister, Sangeeta, is happily married and continues to reside in India.

Every incident leaves us richer in experience. This incident reminded me of Oprah Winfrey's beautiful lines, 'Lots of people want to ride with you in the limo; but what you want is someone who will take the bus with you when the limo breaks down.' At a very young age, I realised that friends and family were only there for the good times. In your bad times, only those who really care about you keep standing by your side. Whatever I am today, is mainly due to the support of my close friends in Kenya, and of various temple managements. My real friends have stood by me like a rock through thick and thin. And it was the temple managements in India and Kenya who gave me the opportunity to step out of India, meet people from all walks of life and become the human being that I am today.

• CHAPTER 31 •

OUR FIRST MAJOR DIVERSIFICATION: MAISHA MABATI MILLS LIMITED

'Thinking' has always been my strongest forte. I constantly think a lot about our business, its growth, expansion and diversification. Early mornings always work the best, however, and it's when I have often found solutions to many problems. It has been slightly more than a decade of our stepping into the world of steel through Devki Steel Mills Limited. Over the last few years, I have been seriously thinking of either forward or backward integrating of our business into the steel industry. Additionally, with Kenya being my *Karma-Bhoomi*, I have long nurtured a dream of creating an affordable market for all Kenyans to build a roof over their heads. Right from my Gikomba days, where we had our Steel Centre outlet, the sight of the homeless sleeping outside our shop left a deep impression on me.

With the Lord's guidance and blessings, I dream of leaving behind a legacy of a construction sector that takes care of every Kenyan's housing problem.

That was how my idea of setting up a 'Roofing Sheet Mill' took birth.

In 2007, with the idea of manufacturing galvanised roofing sheet, we incorporated a new entity, 'Maisha Mabati Mills Limited'. After Devki Steel, this was our first major entity. In Swahili, 'Maisha' stands for 'life' and 'Mabati' means 'roofing sheet'. The rationale behind this name was to provide Kenyans with 'mabati for life'. Till date, there are two key players who have dominated this market in Kenya. Our challenge with our well-established competitors began right from our company name, Maisha Mabati Mills Ltd. It did not go down very well with one of the manufacturers. It was their contention that the term '*mabati*' very closely resembled their own name. They dragged us to the legal corridors; filed a petition in the Kenyan Court to obtain an injunction to stop us from going ahead with our plan. To make matters more difficult, they also filed a complaint with the Registrar of Companies to impede us from using the name, and even took it up this the Registrar of Products. Far from being deterred, we were ready to battle it out. My logic was very simple, the term '*mabati*' is a Kenyan word for 'roofing sheet' and not somebody else's is 'proprietorship'. After a year-long, hard fought legal battle, we successfully defended our right to use the name. This experience made me into a good lawyer!

Finally, we began working on setting up the mill at our Ruiru plant; and by the end of 2008, we commissioned it and began manufacturing roofing sheets under the brand name, 'Maisha Mabati'. I was overjoyed when we began our production of zinc-coated roofing sheets. My joy was short-lived, however, when I realised that though we had stepped into competition, the roofing sheets of Alu Zinc [metal coating of aluminium (55%), zinc (43.4%) and Silicium] that our competitors produced were of far superior quality. With our lower-grade product, there was no way we could forge ahead. I resorted to my strong capacity for ideation again, and planned to install a modernised plant, so that not only could we withstand the competition, but also deliver better quality sheets at affordable prices. I invested a lot of my time, energy and resources in market and product research, weighing various investment options. It took me a while to decide, before deciding to set up a modern Alu Zinc line. The next step of my concept took me all the way to Japan, where we finalised a cold-rolling mill from Nippon Steel. Then we invested US$ 80 million in a cutting edge Alu Zinc line, and finalised the deal on a turnkey basis, with the Australian firm, Bronx International Pty Ltd.

For the next twelve to eighteen months, the engineering and technical team of Bronx International managed the entire project—right from site inspection, design and layout of the mill, ensuring timely delivery, on-site installation, conducting trial runs, training personnel—took us through the entire process till we began our commercial production. Finally, on 10 March 2010, our new Alu Zinc line kicked off. We felt blessed when His Excellency, the then President of Kenya, Hon: Mwai Kibaki, official declared the mill as open. This day too will go as a red letter day in my journey through life.

Maisha Mabati Mill officially declared open on 10 March 2010 by His Excellency Hon. Mwai Kibaki, the then President of Kenya

With this, we had crossed another milestone in our journey. Maisha Mabati was not only the most modern plant in Africa, but also the third largest roofing mill in the entire continent. With a monthly production capacity of 15,000 tonnes of small gauge, this was also the fastest mill in Africa. By now, our workforce had exceeded 3,000. At one point during this phase, we were the largest employer for a single steel plant in Kenya. In a short term, we managed to capture 60 per cent of the Kenyan and East African market for galvanised Alu Zinc roofing sheets.

Maisha Mabati Mills's products

Work in process at Maisha Mabati Mills

Today, in just over twenty years of my steel manufacturing journey, our total production had grown from a meagre 300 MT per month to almost 20,000 MT per month. For a young priest who had boarded his flight from Mumbai to Nairobi in 1981, with only dreams in his heart and a great vision in his mind, this achievement was far, far beyond anyone's expectations.

I have always believed that if a simple and hard working man like me can achieve his dreams, then anyone can!

I always knew that I would go ahead and do what I needed to do, to succeed in life.

• CHAPTER 32 •

THE BIGGEST MILESTONE: NATIONAL CEMENT COMPANY LIMITED

My dreams have always been big, and my vision farsighted. By now, we were a well-established player in the steel industry and were looked upon by the East and Central African markets as a favoured supplier for all steel products and roofing sheets. My vision for our business was much bigger than this, however, and I wanted to be a one-stop manufacturer for all conceivable hardware products. I continued my focus on expansion and growth. Over the years, I realised that though generating profits was the prime motive of any business or corporate firm, it should not be the sole basis for any enterprise. I also perceived that profit making and social responsibility go hand in hand. A wise Gujarati saying that goes like this, 'સ્વાર્થ સાથે પરમાર્થ [Think of others, while you think of yourself].' had found a very special place in my heart; and through my business, I always wanted to make a difference to the community, the nation and to the entire humanity. With this twin objective in mind, we started working on the idea of setting up a cement plant in Kenya.

In 2008, in line with my vision and commitment to supply building and construction material at affordable costs to the wananchi, enabling all Kenyans to build their own homes, we incorporated the National Cement Company Limited. This was our Group's third major diversification and initiative. It was to operate and manufacture Portland cement (made from limestone and clay that hardens under water). For nearly a year after our registration, we did an extensive feasibility study and detailed market survey. After a lot of homework and number crunching, I was satisfied that it would be ideal for us to start with a single grinding mill. I took a calculated risk and we finalised a site at Lukeyna, about 34 km from Nairobi, on the Nairobi–Mombasa Highway. It was a calculated risk, because we were taking on at least two major cement giants of the East African market. To study the project viability and in an effort to approach banks for funding our proposed project, I sat with my finance team to prepare a viable business plan and financial projections.

At the time, the price of a bag of cement hovered between Ksh. 670-700. Keeping in mind our social responsibility, I wanted my team to come up with a five-year financial plan. The plan to be designed in such a way that cement prices decreased gradually, to reach a sustainable selling price of Ksh. 550 per bag by the end of the fifth year. I primarily wanted to increase the volumes to a level where we could maintain our profit levels, while selling at affordable prices for all Kenyans who wanted to build their dream houses. This did not go well with my team, who were shocked at this.

They argued that it was common sense that bankers or financial institutions would expect the projections to reflect gradual increase in prices, improved cash flows and increased profitability. They persuaded me to change my stance. I stood firm by my vision. Even during our ground breaking ceremony in 2010, officiated by His

Excellency, Mwai Kibaki, the then President of Kenya, I shared my vision of providing Kenyans with affordable building material so that they could all build a roof over their heads. We finalised the financial projections accordingly and tabled our request for financial support to the Standard Chartered Bank, Citibank, Barclays Bank and to KCB. I must admit that our chartered accountants were much smarter than me, and our proposal was out rightly rejected by three major banks. Only KCB, who was well aware of my business instincts by now, agreed to discuss the project further. They were apprehensive of the fact that two cement giants had a very strong market presence and that there was no way we could withstand such competition. I too remained firm on my stand and decided to go ahead with our plans, with or without financial support. Eventually, KCB agreed to part-finance our project, which paved the way ahead for us[1].

In 2011, we installed the grinding mill with a manufacturing capacity to of 1,000 tonnes per day or 350,000 tonnes per annum of Portland cement. Thus began our commercial production under the brand name, 'Simba Cement'. On 15 June 2011, the plant was official thrown open by His Excellency, Hon Mwai Kibaki, the then President of Kenya. Sensing the growing demand for Simba Cement, in 2013, we expanded the grinding capacity by five times; but our demand continued to outweigh our production. In 2016, hence, we expanded our grinding capacity to 2 million tonnes per annum, which we still maintain to this day. Today, we command more than 20% share of the domestic market, while exporting to neighbouring countries. Our workforce has crossed 3,700 today. Within five years of beginning our production, I fulfilled my promise of supplying cement to the wananchi at affordable prices. True to my word, we managed to bring down our prices to

---

[1] *Watch me commit to reduce cement prices after we began production: https://www.youtube.com/watch?v=UtoCsLuww*

Ksh. 520 per bag (as against my initial estimate of Ksh. 550 per bag). Truth prevailed.[2]

Former Kenyan President His Excellency Mwai Kibaki signing the visitor's book after officially opening the NCCL plant, watched by then Kenyan Prime Minister Hon. Raila Odinga and then Kenya Vice President Hon. Kalonzo Musyoka

Former Kenyan President His Excellency Hon: Mwai Kibaki cutting Ribbon on the opening of the NCCL plant

---

[2] *Watch opening ceremony of our National Cement Company: https://www.youtube.com/watch?v=2hltYHvJGoM; https://www.youtube.com/watch?v=66eGDCGNxck; and https://www.youtube.com/watch?v=JlnVdrpH0Wk*

I dream big and my business appetite is insatiable; I always look for opportunities to grow and forge ahead.

We mainly depended on imports of clinkers for our cement plant. As a part of our backward integration exercise as well as to utilise available local resources and to minimise our dependency on the international market for our core raw material, I thought of constructing a clinker manufacturing plant as well. The investment was expected to exceed US$ 200 million, which was going to be the biggest and most ambitious project undertaken by our Group so far. In the last three decades, I had moved into a league of my own. We had hired a team of expert international consultants, and following months of discussions, deliberations and R&D trips, we managed to put our entire business plan on paper. It was a marathon exercise.

This was just the beginning. Finding the right partners to understand our perception and financially support us was going to be our biggest challenge. Our search for an ideal financial partner led us to the International Finance Corporation (IFC), a part of the World Bank Group that encourages private sector development in developing markets with investments and related services. I explained our twin ideologies of not only making profits, but also contributing to the growth of the community in particular and to the economy in general. This blended well with IFC's global socio-economic objectives, and their team came down to Kenya. We had detailed discussions to understand not only our perception, but the project viability as well.

For three good years, IFC carried out studies, understood our business profile and finally agreed to shake hands with us. They agreed to fund our dream venture and eventually to place a member on the Board of National Cement. Today, ours is the only African company with a Board Member from IFC. We now had the distinction of being partnered by the World Bank Group through IFC. This has undoubtedly been the biggest tie-up that we have ever made so far.

View of the National Cement Company Limited's plant at Lukeyna, Kenya

Testing in progress at National Cement's Lukenya Plant

Packed Cement Bags roll out of the machine ready for dispatch

Arial view of NCCL's clinker plant at Emali

Having grown up in a Hindu Brahmin family and starting out my work life as a priest, I am a firm believer in the law of Karma. I firmly believe that 'what goes around, comes around', and that we constantly create consequences through our own thoughts and actions in life – whether for good or for bad. This is exactly what happened to me when we were hunting for the perfect site for our clinker plant in Kenya, rich with limestone deposits. We found it in Emali, which is around 150 km from Nairobi on the Mombasa–Nairobi Highway. It so happened that in the late 1980s, when we were still in Gikomba, there was a drought in this area. Many herds of cattle had died of hunger and thirst. On Sundays and other holidays, Neeta and I used to drive down to this very Emali region, with fodder and water to feed the cows. For hours together, we used to stand out here in the open and enjoy feeding the poor animals. Now years later, this was exactly where our clinker plant was to be set up. It was as if the Almighty had blessed us for the good deeds Neeta and I had done years ago. I also realised that the Lord was showing me the way to continue doing my good work for the region.

Life is full of surprises; it springs one on you when you least expect it. Something unexpected happened a few years back when we were expanding National Cement's capacity at the Lukeyna plant and were about to set up our Emali clinker plant. One fine morning, I was in a meeting when I received a phone call from Nigeria. Normally I avoid phone calls amid serious discussions, but heeding my instinct, I picked up this one. Believe me, it was a business offer from Africa's richest man, Aliko Dangote. The Nigerian Cement King wanted to buy us out!

For the uninitiated, Aliko Dangote, GCON, is a Nigerian billionaire and owner of the Dangote Group. The Group has business interests in commodities across West, Central, as well as East Africa to a certain extent. He was ranked by Forbes magazine as the sixty-seventh richest person in the world and the richest in Africa.

Coming back to my story, my answer was a straight 'no'. I had my reasons for not accepting Dangote's offer. Business is in every Gujarati's veins and there was no way I could accept any offer to sell my business. Moreover, mine is a family business and I carry a strong belief that it should run in our family for generations to come. Finally, the IFC coming on board meant a lot to us. They not only provided us with substantial financial support, but also brought their global expertise in infrastructure management. Their expertise would also be useful for achieving my grand vision of expanding across the continent. Most importantly, IFC's vision of supporting under-developed and developing economies to enable them to grow, blended perfectly with my dream of helping Kenyans with their dream homes.

Dangote did not give up at the first instance; however, he persisted and even changed his offer from buying us fully to acquiring a majority stake in our Group. The answer still remained 'no'. He gave up, when we finally inked the deal with the IFC. Sometimes when I am alone, lost in my thoughts, I find it amusing that the richest man in Africa had knocked on my door. The door of someone who had begun his life with nothing but big dreams and blessings! As I said, life is full of surprises, expect one yourself round the corner...

After three-and-half years of hard work, we commissioned our clinker plant at Emali in the first quarter of 2017. With an investment in excess of US $ 240 million, the plant will have a capacity of 1 million tonnes per annum, to facilitate the production of 1.5 million tonnes of cement per annum. Finally, in the first week of June 2017, we commenced commercial production at this plant. With this plant, our human resource strength exceeded 4,000 and is expected to further rise to 4,500 in the near future when we begin operating the plant in full blast.

It has been the biggest milestone of my life. For someone, who could not even afford to hire a pick-up van driver when we started Steel Centre in 1986, this is a colossal feat. This has been beyond my expectations.

• CHAPTER 33 •

OTHER BUSINESS VENTURES

My journey and dream of expansion and diversification took me beyond the boundaries of Kenya. Steel, building material and cement have been my strong business areas; but this journey took me beyond those. Today I have come to believe that I was not born for one corner, country or region; and that the entire world is my native land. Therefore, along with focusing on my core businesses in Kenya, I have begun to look beyond these boundaries.

To further their political careers, many well-known statesmen, country heads and great leaders have consulted me as an astrologer. Using my knowledge of astrology and palmistry, I have successfully guided them in their path and helped them forge ahead with their political careers. One such trip in 2001, took me to the Democratic Republic of Congo (DRC), where I had the pleasure of meeting and offering my guidance to His Excellency, the Hon. Joseph Kabila Kabange, the President of DRC. During our discussions, he told me that his country was open to foreign investments and would support us in case we planned to expand our business in the Congo.

Appreciating his ideas, in 2001, we set up our first venture beyond Kenya, with the Congo Steel Mills SPRL, a steel rolling mill in Lubumbashi, DRC. The plant successfully commenced its operations in 2005. Though it has an installed monthly manufacturing capacity of 3,000 tonnes of steel, taking into consideration the country's demand, we have restricted our monthly output to 1,000 tonnes. With a workforce of around 400 Congolese and twenty expatriates, this plant operates in full swing even to this date.

Constuction work-in-progress at the Congo Steel Mills SPRL

Copper mining is a core economic activity in the DRC. The Katanga or Shaba copper belt is about 70 km (43 miles) wide and 250 km (160 miles) long between Lubumbashi and Kolwezi. There are seventy-two economic deposits of copper, cobalt and four large mining centres along this belt. Taken together, the DRC and Zambian copper belts are the second largest global reserves of copper, about one-third the size of the Chilean reserve. A few years ago, we embarked on our first project beyond our core infrastructure business and set up a small copper smelting plant in the DRC. Employing around 165 Congolese and four expatriates, we operated this plant successfully for some time. Very soon, the current flowed against us. Global prices for copper crashed, rendering it difficult to sell the output. Sourcing copper-ore became a challenge too. Most importantly, however, the DRC, being a landlocked country, has no port to ship products, resulting in high transportation costs, leading to higher pricing for the final product. After running the show for a few years, we closed down the unit about five years back.

National Cement has stood tall against mighty giants in the Kenyan cement industry. With a market share of 20%, 'Simba Cement' has today become a household name. To have our presence felt in the East African region, in 2013, we incorporated the National Cement Company Uganda Limited, in Uganda. Our grinding mill plant, which is in advanced stages of completion, is based in the Tororo district of Uganda, in Nyakesi Village on the Tororo–Mbale Highway. Tororo enjoys better access to limestone, the main ingredient for cement manufacturing. With an annual production capacity of 700,000 metric tonnes, operations at this plant have commenced in May 2018. With this, our annual production capacity across all our cement plants would exceed 2.5 million metric tonnes. We have plans to increase our capacity to 4.0 million tonnes by 2018, and expect to become the largest cement unit in Africa, in terms of production capacity under one roof.

In Kenya, cement is commonly sold in polypropylene or polypropene (PP) bags and very rarely shipped in bulk. Right from the start, we packaged Simba Cement in PP bags sourced from outside suppliers. To facilitate product integration, as well as to commercially supply PP bags, we decided to set up our own company to manufacture them. That was how Maisha Packaging

Company Limited was born in 2013. The plant is located within National Cement's premises at Lukeyna. We installed fully automatic Starlinger (Austria) machinery, which are the best worldwide, to manufacture high quality WPP AC*star cement bags (block bottom bags). They are ideal for automated filling and packing of cement and act as better substitutes for paper bags. These brick-shaped, PP woven sacks are produced without adhesives by heat-welding the coating on the fabric. Employing a workforce between 100 and 150, we commenced production here from 2014.

We made inroads into Ethiopia as well. In 2008, together with Bhavesh, we incorporated the steel rolling mill, Habesha Steel Mills PLC at Dukem. The industrial town of Dukem is about 39 km from the capital, Addis Ababa. A few years later when I realised that I had enough and more on my plate, I handed over the company's reins to Bhavesh and his family. His son, Kishan, runs the show in Addis Ababa, while Bhavesh has settled down in Kisumu, managing his hardware trading business.

Recently, we diversified into another core area—generation of electricity. In 2014, Devki Energy Company Limited came into existence to provide assured electricity supply to the National Cement Company's clinker plant in Emali. It's a 15 megawatt unit and the first company to generate coal-based electricity in Kenya and East Africa. Through this venture, we intend to promote the utilisation of Kenya's domestic coal resources in the long run. For ease in control and operations, in 2016, we merged the company with National Cement Company Limited.

In 2008, the Kenyan Government set up the Geothermal Development Company (GDC). A fully government-owned entity in Kenya's energy sector. The GDC was formed in 2008 as a Special Purpose Vehicle (SPV) to accelerate the development of geothermal resources in the country. The GDC is tasked with developing steam fields and selling geothermal steam for electricity generation to KenGen as well as to private investors. Geothermal steam is an environment-friendly and abundant raw material used for generating electricity. The GDC awarded tenders to three firms in Kenya, with exclusive rights to set up a stream plant under a build-own-operate (BOO) model. Sosian Menengai Geothermal Power Limited was one of the three companies that won a tender to build a 35 megawatt geothermal power plant in the Menangai–Nakuru County. We have made an investment in this project and the GDC is in the process of completing all the legal documentation and formalities in this respect. This project will take off once we get a green signal and clearance from them.[3]

A few years back, I widened my horizon and stepped into the aviation sector. It was like a dream come true, which I will share as we move ahead. In the forty years of my business journey, beginning from Gikomba, I have come a long way.

Standing at the threshold of my business empire, today I wholeheartedly believe that all 'possible' limitations can only be defined by moving beyond them—into the impossible!

---

[3] *http://afrika54news.com/2017/03/01/kenya-cement-tycoon-buys-moi-out-of-sh8bn-menengai-power-plant-firm/*

• CHAPTER 34 •

FLYING HIGH: A DREAM COMES TRUE

At twelve, when I dreamt of flying and owning a helicopter, I was thought to be insane. People around me laughed and I was greeted with mockery wherever I went. They were right in their own way, for it was a little boy's dream. A little boy, who did not own a pair of proper shoes for his feet; or a decent pair of clothing for his back; a boy, who studied in a boarding school on a free scholarship, and who could not even afford to buy a second-hand bicycle. But I have already shared these childhood aspirations and hardships with you. What I would now like to tell you is that you, too, can fulfil any dream and achieve everything you desire, but only if you believe in yourself.

Remember what America's first lady from the 1940s, Eleanor Roosevelt, once said, 'Believe in yourself; you gain strength, courage and confidence by every experience in which you stop to look fear in the face. You must do that which you think you cannot do. The future belongs to those who believe in the beauty of their dreams.'

Put all that sweat, hard work and determination to achieve your dreams. Have the courage to face all adversities; and never give up on your dreams even if it means standing alone. Only and only then will your dreams come true.

Let me share another little anecdote with you.

By now, I had achieved all that I desired, had fulfilled all my dreams, whether personal or professional. The one thing that had eluded me so far was my dream of flying in the sky in my own helicopter! In 2013, I was sitting with my family and discussing education. At that time, Devang had just graduated from Brunel University in London and our daughter, Tulsi, was pursuing her graduation from the same UK University. Both argued that education today is more challenging than what it was in our times, and to graduate in any specialisation is a task by itself, especially for someone like me who had studied only up to high school back in 1978! I did not concur with their views and counter argued that age is no bar for anyone to achieve anything if he is determined enough. I also told them that I would prove this very soon. That very moment, a burning desire to become a pilot was ignited within me.

At fifty-two, the challenge of graduating as a private pilot was an uphill task for me. The stakes were high; it had to do with human lives and the slightest error could mean a life and death situation! I was determined to face this challenge and spent the next few weeks researching about courses for becoming a private pilot. I felt like a high school boy, who had completed his studies and was on the threshold of joining a University for higher studies! From the comfort of my office, I contacted institutions across the globe and finally by the end of 2013, I registered myself with the German Aviation Institute. It was a two-year course, with eleven papers to complete. Each subject had at least ten different textbooks for reference. I had to study all by myself, unlike a classroom environment. Most importantly, the minimum marks required to qualify each paper was 70%. It was not easy to focus on my studies while managing our business empire, which by now had grown sizeably. Nevertheless, I was determined to fight out the battle. For the next seven months or so, I burnt the midnight oil. After months of strenuous efforts, I took the plunge and decided to appear for the examination. With that, I stepped into an examination hall after a gap of thirty-six years. I was the sole examinee above fifty years, while the rest were youngsters of less than half my age!

The examination was conducted at a centre in the Jomo Kenyatta International Airport of Nairobi. It was an online test and each paper had forty-six questions that had to be answered in one-and-a-half hours. I was confident in a few subjects and hesitant about others. However, I mustered the courage and appeared for all eleven subjects. In my first attempt, I cleared nine of them and very soon re-appeared for the other two papers and cleared them too! In most of the papers, I secured over 85%, and in a couple of them I score above 97%. On 7 October 2014, the German Aviation Institute granted me a Private Pilot's License (PPL). I had done it!

That evening, I presented the PPL certificate to my children. I had proved that nothing is impossible in this world for a willing heart and a determined mind.

A dream accomplished: Flying my own chopper

This achievement meant that my dream was almost fulfilled. By now, I was bubbling with excitement and could hardly wait to start flying my own chopper! To pursue this dream, we incorporated our aviation company, Northwood Agencies Limited. This would not only fulfil my dream of flying, but would also enable easy and fast access to distant and difficult sites. We decided to commercially charter our helicopters to government agencies, ministers, political leaders, private sector corporate firms and to tourists. We started out with two helicopters in 2014, and by November 2016, added a third chopper to our fleet.

In 2014, after we received two of our helicopters, we offered prayers to invoke the Lord's blessings. In Athi River, we run an orphanage where more than seventy children are taken care of. These children were among the first to accompany me in my maiden helicopter ride! Turn by turn, I ensured that all the children got an opportunity to ride up into the clouds with me.

The children at the orphanage run by us were the first to accompany me in my maiden helicopter ride

I could see myself among these small children, reminding me of my dream of riding a chopper forty-four years ago. I blinked back tears of joy and my happiness knew no bounds that day! I was thankful to God who had made this dream possible.

I would like to share my thoughts on dreams with the youth of today. Remember to believe in yourself and don't give up your dreams. The future belongs to those who believe in the beauty of their dreams!

• CHAPTER 35 •

BUSINESS, POLITICS AND ASTROLOGY

It is a common belief that business and politics go hand-in-hand. The success of an individual businessman, business conglomerate or international corporate group, is always linked or associated with political leaders, ruling parties or with governments in general. Today, after having achieved reasonable success in the four decades of my experience as an entrepreneur and industrialist, everywhere I go, questions on my business growth and politics are always posed to me. 'Guru, are you successful today because of your close ties with all the presidents of Kenya and other African nations?' Or, 'Guru, is it your allegiance with political parties that has seen you grow from strength to strength?' Or even, 'Guru, is it the influence of political parties and leaders because of which your business has thrived so much?' The list is endless; once I was even asked in a media interview whether I was interested in joining politics in the near future and contest the presidential elections!

I feel saddened and hurt when one's success in general is attributed to one's close proximity to political heads or the success of an industrial house or business conglomerate is ascribed to their closeness with a country's government. The world conveniently forgets all the efforts, struggle, hard work, sacrifices and failures that one has endured on the way to success and accredits one's entire success to political connections! In this connection, I would like to share an anecdote with you.

The study of palmistry, astrology and predicting the future based on these studies is part of a Brahmin's life in India. I was born in a Gujarati Brahmin family and all these studies were part of our family's hereditary practise. My first serious attempt of studying these subjects came when I started out as a young priest in the Swaminarayan Temple at Bhuj in India. Devotees in Bhuj and later in Nakuru, Kenya, began consulting me to resolve their challenges in life. With time and experience, I furthered my knowledge in preparation of horoscopes and predications based on astrology. Over time, my confidence level increased. As a twenty-two-year-old priest, I became popular as an astrologer when more than 90 per cent of my predictions turned out to be true.

In 1983, while in Nakuru, it was by sheer coincidence that I met the then Kenyan President, His Excellency, The Hon. Daniel Arap Moi. It was during this first meeting that I first shared my interests in palmistry and astrology with His Excellency. This had interested him, and eager to know more about astrology, he had extended an open invitation to me to visit the State House in Nairobi, and that's how our relationship began. Over the years, through my practical experience, my knowledge became powerful and I soon became a political advisor. Both retired Kenyan Presidents, Hon. Moi and Hon. Kibaki, consulted me during their political careers, both before and during their Presidency tenures. Thanks to my proximity to President Moi, I had the privilege of being associated with many great leaders. I have successfully advised presidents of other African nations and heads of some

European nations as well. But I have never taken undue advantage of my personal relationship with prominent political leaders and never transacted any business with any politician or political party. Personal benefit or gain was never the motive of these consultations. In fact, the motive behind these interactions was for the benefit of the nation or the economy as a whole, but never for the benefit of individuals.

We have always invited our country heads or political leaders to bless us and inaugurate all our plants and units. The objective behind this was to share with national dignitaries how we can contribute towards the economy's growth and progress; but never for gaining any political mileage or personal benefits. I have always believed in helping generously, but have zero tolerance for corruption. Though it is a general belief that corruption to a minimal extent is healthy for an economy's growth, I personally feel that it is cancerous, if it becomes uncontrollable. Hence we do not encourage bribery or corruption at all in our Group. It has been my policy right from our inception never to have any business connection with any politician, political party or government agency.

We do not bid for any government tenders, as a matter of policy. We put this policy in place because I believe that my staff or even I, may be forced to entertain corruption. Though indirectly, through our distributors or distribution channels, we supply to various government agencies, but we have never dealt with them directly. In the future too, to ensure that none of our staff is compromised, we will not encourage direct dealings with government agencies. Since we do not encourage corruption, it becomes imperative for us to seek the blessings and guidance of political leaders for our expansion and development.

Time and again, I have established that Kenya is my Karma-Bhoomi. I have always gone out of my way to ensure the overall economic growth, peace and prosperity of this nation. I have maintained cordial and harmonious relationships with all important political heads. I played a pivotal role in maintaining peace and order in the Kenyan political scenario before the December 2007 elections. The then President, the Hon. Mwai Kibaki, was in the race for a second term, and so was the Hon. Stephen Kalonzo Musyoka, the leader of the Wiper Democratic Movement Party.

As a leading industrialist and responsible citizen of Kenya, I felt it was my responsibility to ensure that peace prevailed. I approached the then President, the Hon. Mwai Kibaki, and expressed my desire to call a meeting to discuss Kenya's current scenario, save the nation, and discuss the country's growth and stability. He welcomed my idea. I arranged for a dinner meeting at my residence and invited the President, a very close friend of mine, and the Hon. Stephen Kalonzo Musyoka, leader of the opposition party the Wiper Democratic Movement Party. They willingly accepted my invitation. Over dinner, the President, his advisor and strategist, Mr. Stanley Murage, and the Hon. Stephen Kalonzo Musyoka, discussed about various strategies. During the meeting, both leaders sat down and chalked out a plan for peace and growth in the country. Efforts were made to request the Hon. Stephen Kalonzo Musyoka, to back out of the Presidential race, but he was firm on his candidature. Unfortunately, after the elections, violence broke out in Kenya and the economy came to a grinding halt.

A few weeks after the elections, to ensure that peace and harmony prevailed in Kenya, the Hon. Stephen Kalonzo Musyoka, accepted the position of Vice President and deputy to the President, the Hon. Mwai Kibaki. The economy began moving forward again. In course of time, peace prevailed and Kenya progressed further. I organized this peace meeting, for the sake of the betterment of the Kenyan people and for the country's progress. The Almighty gave me the strength to do this and at the end of the day, I was successful in my efforts[4].

In conclusion, I would like to reiterate what Ratan Tata, the ex-chairman of India's renowned business house, the Tata Group of Companies, once said, 'I will certainly not join politics. I would like to be remembered as a clean businessman who has not partaken in any twists and turns beneath the surface, and one who has been reasonably successful.'

---

[4] *Article in The Daily Nation on 19 December 2016: http://www.nation.co.ke/news/politics/Secret-Kibaki-deal-that-offered-Kalonzo-vice-president-post/1064-3490366-format-xhtml-kxqujt/index.html*

• CHAPTER 36 •

OUR CONTRIBUTIONS TO THE KENYAN ECONOMY

Yes, like every entrepreneur and industrialist, steady progress in our revenues and gradual growth in our bottom line have been the key motivators in my journey. But more importantly, the economic growth of my Karma-Bhoomi, Kenya, hand in hand with our business growth, has been my guiding force for further progress. It is this land, which embraced me as a young teenage boy, when I first came here with big dreams and empty pockets! It is this nation that has given me love, support and shaped me into what I am today. Therefore, the key to my success has been our direct and indirect contributions to the growth of the Kenyan economy throughout our journey.

Over the years, we have made a substantial contribution to the national exchequer, with tax payments through our various business entities. I was overwhelmed when the Kenyan Government felicitated me as one of the highest tax payers in the country in 2013. It was a proud moment, which gave me the satisfaction that I had made a small contribution to the nation's progress. In 2016, our Group was the highest contributor to the Kenya Value

Added Tax (VAT), for which the Kenyan Government, felicitated us through the Kenya Revenue Authority (KRA). Recently, in 2017, I was declared as one of the Top 12 billionaire taxpayers by the KRA.

Smiles all around: Proud to receive the Highest Tax Payers 2016 award by Kenya Revenue Authority (KRA) at the hands of His Excellency President of Kenya Hon. Uhuru Kenyatta, while KRA's Commisioner General John Njiraini watches.

KENYA REVENUE AUTHORITY

Certificate

This certificate is awarded to

Maisha Mabati Mills Limited

As a Distinguished Taxpayer in the year 2013
in the Category:

Authorized Economic Operator (AEO)

Presented by:
H.E. the president Hon. Uhuru Kenyatta CGH

KENYA VISION 2030

Commissioner General

Certificate of Distinguished Tax Payer Award for 2013 granted by Kenya Revenue Authority (KRA) to our company Maisha Mabati Mills Ltd

Receiving the Kenya Revenue Authority's Highest Tax Payers Award 2013, at the hands of His Excellency President of Kenya Hon. Uhuru Kenyatta

Generating employment in under-developed economies like ours is always a challenge. In 1986, when we began our journey from Gikomba, though I had very big dreams, it was only Neeta and I working together. That was when we could not afford a single employee. In 1994, we started off with a workforce of about seventy-two, when we first stepped into manufacturing with Devki Steel Mills. We have come a long way since then. In the twenty-three years of our business journey, we have expanded, diversified, acquired, integrated and grown our employee strength to more than 4,000 as of today. I am proud to share that nearly 98 per cent of our employees are Kenyans. Apart from the families of our direct employees, there are millions of others who have indirectly benefitted from our economic growth. Through our corporate social responsibility (CSR) programmes, local communities around our manufacturing facilities have benefitted as well.

Kenya's economic performance heavily relies on exports and imports, both of which determine the balance of trade. Fluctuations in the foreign exchange rate have always had its effect on the balance of trade. Since Kenya is a net importer, fluctuations in foreign exchange rates hamper the economy's progress. In the infrastructure and building materials industry, in which we operate, billets and clinker, the two most important raw materials for steel and cement manufacturing are imported. By setting up our induction furnace for manufacturing billets from scrap and investing in a clinker plant, we have reduced Kenya's dependency on imports to a large extent, which will save the nation not less than US$ 100 million per annum in terms of foreign exchange savings, which for an economy like ours, makes a significant difference.

Kenya, like all underdeveloped economies, faces the challenge of providing basic amenities to its citizens. It is a challenge even for individual entrepreneurs or industrial houses to fulfil these needs in-toto. We endeavour to contribute however best we can in these critical segments. Our Group supplies free electricity to the schools and local communities in the vicinity of our 15 megawatt thermal power plant in Emali. In addition, for the past twenty-five years, we have been supplying free water to all communities and villages around our manufacturing locations and plants. Moreover, we promote education and run schools in Athi River, Emali and Ruiru, where our plants are located. We invest in the construction of school buildings, incurring revenue costs, including the salary and medical facilities for the teachers and provide one free meal per day to the students. We also have a system of monitoring the progress of the students, and in deserving cases, sponsor their university education. Currently, more than 300 students across universities in Kenya are pursuing their education through our sponsorship programmes. We have even provided gainful employment to many of these sponsored students after their graduation. Apart from this, there are many children of our existing and longstanding employees, who have studied and graduated through our sponsorship programmes before being absorbed by us.

With the passage of time, I have noted that the key to life is not accumulation. It is definitely what we contribute to our community.

• CHAPTER 37 •

MY BUSINESS VISION: THE WAY FORWARD

Vision is the art of seeing what is invisible to others. From the time I first set up Steel Centre in Gikomba, I realised that if I wanted to achieve my business goals and dreams, then my vision had to be of enormous scale. As a hardware trader, I was familiar with the pains and needs of the trade. Every trader desires to supply his clientele with the best quality products in time, every time. This is possible only if you have a reliable supplier or you manufacture what you trade. At that time, there were hardly any steel and hardware manufacturers or suppliers in Kenya. I saw that for our business to expand, sooner or later, we would have to manufacture the products we traded. With this vision in mind, and well ahead of the times, I thought of venturing into the manufacturing sector.

When we set up our first manufacturing facility, Devki Steel Mills Limited, my vision was to manufacture all those products that hardware traders dealt with. I was aware that this was a very ambitious dream and that managing finance and other resources would be a great challenge. But it was this vision that saw us grow from strength to strength, increasing the range of products we manufactured. Today, almost two decades after we stepped into manufacturing, I am proud to have become a one-stop shop for manufacturing all products required by the infrastructure industry. Today, there is no steel manufacturer in Kenya, who produces steel from raw material that is entirely sourced from the domestic market.

For our raw materials, we are largely dependent on imports. It was my vision to work on a plan to commission an integrated steel plant in East Africa that will produce and provide steel from raw materials sourced from within the region. Through this effort, not only will there be substantial savings in Foreign Exchange to the region, but will also help East Africa build its infrastructure at relatively lower costs. Of course, this dream would be possible only with the support of the governments of all East African countries. For only national governments can insist on reducing imports; avoid dumping and supporting local industries. To achieve this vision, we are working closely with the respective governments for quite some time now and waiting for it to become a reality.

When I began my journey as a manufacturer, apart from the normal objective of generating profits, I had a noble motive in mind of supplying quality building material to the wananchi. I wanted to supply the necessary materials in adequate quantities and at affordable prices, so that every Kenyan can have a roof over his head. Now that we manufacture the entire range of infrastructure products, our aim is to improve our efficiency and productivity. This will increase our business volumes and revenues, and assist in bringing down the cost so that we achieve the twin purpose of generating higher profits while supplying the common Kenyan man with higher quantities at affordable prices. You can call it charity or CSR, but our aim is to support the less fortunate members of society to build their own homes.

Continuous expansion and growth have always been my perceptions. Currently, we have a market share of 40–50 per cent for all our building material products across East Africa. Though my vision is to gain a strong foothold in Africa, we will continue to focus initially on the East African markets. In Kenya, we want to spread our presence beyond the seven counties that we are currently present in. As on date, four major projects for setting up manufacturing facilities for infrastructure products are in the pipeline in Kenya. Each one has a timeline of two years to take off. Additionally, our cement plant at Tororo in Uganda has commenced production in May 2018. Moreover, to have a strong regional presence, we want to expand to other countries in the region by creating manufacturing facilities at the consumers' doorsteps. Through these initiatives, it is my vision to firstly increase our current employee strength to 10,000 in the next five years. Secondly, by 2020, I plan to achieve a market share of more than 65 per cent in the East African region for all our building material /infrastructure products. Furthermore, it is my dream to become the largest cement manufacturer in the region.

Currently, our cement production stands at 1.2 million tonnes, which is slated to grow to 3.5 million tonnes (including the production in our Ugandan plant), which will be more than 60–65 per cent of today's market for cement in Kenya. Most importantly, through our regional expansion, we want to deliver the highest quality customer care service. By setting up manufacturing facilities at the consumers' doorsteps, we want to increase their confidence in our products, by offering better quality products, timely deliveries, speedy resolution of grievances and standing by them through thick and thin. Through this, we want our existing brand to not only become the first choice of the final consumer, but also a household name in the entire region.

Recently, we diversified into the geo-thermal power sector. We have been awarded a tender by the GDC to build a geo-thermal power plant in the Menangai Region of the Rift Valley. Once all the formalities are completed, we intend to commence operations.

We have plans to list our company's shares on the Nairobi Stock Exchange as well as on other exchanges in the region. I want to accomplish this task once we have perfect corporate governance in place and once we have completed building our capacities. I have a much bigger intention than merely raising capital through this proposed listing. For funding, we can always approach commercial banks or global financial institutions. The objective of our proposed listing is to share a portion of our success and profits with Kenyans and other shareholders. It is my desire that the investors should earn a better rate of return, on a long-term basis, than the one they currently earn on bank deposits. I repeat that Kenya is my Karma Bhoomi. It is my biggest dream that every Kenyan should share the fruits of my success and have a decent capital appreciation on his investments in our shares.

I want to give Kenyana a chance to own a part of what is innately their company

Last but not the least, it is my aim to continue to be a respectable citizen of Kenya throughout my life; to be an honourable tax payer and contribute directly to our economy's growth. During the last four years, the Kenyan Government has felicitated me and our Group for our contributions to the national exchequer. I am proud to share with you, once again, that in 2013, the Kenyan Government felicitated me as one of the top taxpayers in the country. In 2017, the KRA recognised our Group as the highest contributor to VAT in Kenya. The same year, the KRA also declared me to be one of the top twelve billionaire taxpayers in the country.

In life, we are limited by our vision rather than our abilities. Our dreams hold the key to our future. Remember: 'Not all dreamers are winners, but all winners are dreamers.'

PART V

CHARITY AND PHILANTHROPY

• CHAPTER 38 •

GIVING BACK TO SOCIETY

Each one of us is God's unique creation, born with qualities that are distinct to us, including generosity and kindness. However, I also feel that time, circumstances and the hardships that we experience during our lifetime also determine the way each one of us thinks and acts. By nature, I have always been ready to extend a helping hand to anyone in need and have loved to make a positive difference in their lives. However, poverty, pain and struggle, together with a couple of heart-touching incidents that I experienced, totally changed my outlook towards supporting the needy.

At a very young age, I had decided that whenever God blessed me financially, I would not only raise the standard of our living, but more importantly, raise the standard of my giving.

I was born in a small village and though my Dadaji's family was rich, prosperous and well to do, our life changed 180 degrees after my father separated from my grandfather's family. It was then that I first experienced poverty, deprivation and what it meant to be poor. Having spent many nights without food, I can feel the pain of a poor man, especially when you don't have a single morsel to eat! Days together we filled our bellies with

Karthi beans, making me realise the importance of food. Food was scarce and we got it by 'chance' and never by 'choice'. For many years, my pockets were empty, without a single penny in them, which made me understand the worth of money and what it meant to survive without it. This is why, I always think twice before spending on myself and have inculcated this trait in my children too. I always tell them, 'Think twice before you spend a single penny on yourself, but never think twice if you want to spend a million dollars on helping others.'

At times, my philosophy of 'thinking before spending' lands me in funny situations! There is a very famous Indian restaurant in Nairobi that we often patronise. After eating, I normally leave a small tip for the waiters. One day, as I was about to leave, a smiling waiter asked me, 'Sir, why is that you always leave a very small change as a tip, whereas your son offers us a very handsome one?' Patting his back, I replied, 'He is the son of a rich man, but I am a poor man's son, so I have to think before I spend!' Similarly, my habit of keeping very little money in my wallet also creates embarrassing situations for me. Often, when I feel like having a 'paan' (traditional Indian betel leaf wrap chewed as a digestive, stimulant or mouth freshener) after meals, I visit my favourite paan shop at Westlands in Nairobi. If I find close friends or acquaintances at the shop, I automatically offer them paans, out of habit, without realising how much money I have in my pockets. More often than not, when I open my wallet to pay the shopkeeper, I invariably find that I don't have enough money on me!

My childhood experiences with poverty and paucity of money have today become my guiding force for going out of my way to support the needy. The two Rajkot and Wankaner incidents that had occurred years ago had left a permanent impression on me. At Rajkot, my father and I were ill-treated by a shopkeeper because we did not have money to eat in a decent restaurant. This incident had affected me so much that today I have made sure that anyone visiting our office, factories or home is always welcome at our table. This incident, in a way, was responsible for changing my outlook and forming a strong foundation for our Group's CSR programmes. All in all, I believe that whenever I extend my helping hand to any needy person out there in the world, then I am helping someone like me, who had nothing in this world!

I am blessed to have Neeta as my co-traveller in life. She has stood by me like a pillar of strength through all my challenges. She is the driving force not only behind my business decisions, but also of all my philanthropic pursuits. Her personal involvement in our Group's CSR programmes and her philosophy of 'help people even when you know that they cannot help you back', keeps me motivated.

Born in a Brahmin family and starting my career as a priest, I have always been guided spiritually through life. Driven by this spiritual outlook, I believe that I am a guardian of wealth earned through my business success. Supplementing this thought, I feel that if I am a mere custodian or protector of this wealth, then it is my obligation to utilise it for social benefit and not for my family's benefit alone. I also believe that all of us on earth have equal rights to consume food that is available to all of us. If I have plenty of food on my plate and my neighbour is starving, I deem it my moral responsibility to share my food with him. I will be failing in my duties to the Creator if I don't do so. The main motto behind my philanthropic activities is to give without expecting anything in return. The Lord has given me in abundance, much more than I need, and he takes care of my family, while I take care of the people around me. I utilise 50 per cent of my personal earnings on charity. This is over and above the community development programmes undertaken by our Group. Personally, Neeta and I assist people in building their homes, with food, medical support and clothing, as well as with financial support to the deserving for higher education.

Giving back to the society is something that comes from my heart. I feel that I am more blessed for my ability to give rather than to receive. I don't think I will ever stop giving. Philanthropy has become such an integral part of our lives that the legacy will continue even after I am gone.

• CHAPTER 39 •

CORPORATE SOCIAL RESPONSIBILITY

As the Devki Group of Companies, we take our CSR very seriously and contribute substantially to the Kenyan economy. Through our wide range of programmes focusing on food and nutrition, water, power, medical aid, shelter and clothing, we play a vital role in the growth of both the local community and our employees.

Our employees are our best resource. Starting with seven employees in 1986, today we have grown to a very 'big family' of more than 4,000. I call it a 'big family', because each one of them is like a family member who is equally responsible for our success. Through financial assistance and scholarships, we encourage our employees to pursue higher education and graduate in various disciplines. We also support their families with education opportunities. Many of our existing employees' children also work with us in key positions. Socially, we have also encouraged marriages among our employees, and hence it has become one 'big family' today. They are my top priority, and we have ensured that they are paid higher than industry standards and always on time. I am proud to share that we have set an example to the Kenyan industry and the concerned Ministry about our employee welfare programmes.

As a child, I spent many lonely years, studying in boarding schools and staying away from my family, thus understanding the pains of an 'orphan'. In the early 1990s, when we acquired the land in Athi River for our plant, Neeta and I often visited the site to inspect the development. We came across many children, mostly orphans, struggling through life without proper food, clothing or shelter. It was pitiable to see them begging, seeking alms, stealing and some of them looking at us with expectations. Moved by this sight, we decided to set up an 'orphanage' in Athi River. We managed to secure a disputed community land and though we could not construct a permanent structure on it, we built a temporary structure and started an orphanage to shelter these homeless children. At any given point in time, there are more than seventy children residing here. It's more than twenty years now that we have been successfully managing the place. We take care of all their basic needs like food and nutrition, shelter, clothing, medical care and education. We provide them with books and teachers so that they continue their education. Many of the children staying here are HIV positive patients, but we take care of their needs as well.

Service to mankind is service to God: Serving children at our Athi River orphanage

Though I am not a highly qualified person, I know that education is the most powerful weapon that we can use to change the world. The brave young Pakistani girl and Noble Peace Prize winner, Malala Yousafzai, once said, 'Let us pick up our books and pencils; they are our most powerful weapon.' With this thought in mind, we took our first initiative in the education sector by building the Devki Primary School at Ruiru, very close to our Corporate Headquarters. We operate the school, right from constructing the building to providing reading material, stationery supplies and teaching staff. More than 300 students, including the children of our employees, take the benefit of this education facility. Recently, we commissioned our clinker plant at Emali, which is predominantly a Masai region. We adopted the Devki Emukuntan School, which is situated very close to our plant, and invested in the construction of school buildings, incurring revenue costs including salary and medical facilities for the teachers and providing one free meal per day to the students. This school, which had less than fifty students when we took it over three years ago, today proudly educates more than 200 students. Incidentally, Emali is the same area that Neeta and I used to visit on Sundays and holidays to feed the starving cattle with fodder and water during the terrible drought of the 1980s.

Drinking water base for cattle provided by our Group, constructed near our Emali plant to enable free and continious drinking water to Masai cattle.

Flanked by Mrs. Cherie Blair, CBE QC, wife of former British Prime Minister Tony Blair, trustee of Loomba Foundation and The Lord Raj Loomba CBE, Founder Chairman of the Loomba Foundation, at my residence in Nairobi.

Attending the cermony to celebrate completion of fencing of Devki Emukutan Primary School, near our Clinker plant, Emali, Kenya, on 23 March 2017

Remembering my childhood days and enjoying with the school children at Devki Emukutan Primary School

With the Police Officer's team after handing over the Administrative Police Post to them, proudly built by us

We also monitor the progress of the students in our schools and in deserving cases; sponsor their higher education as well. Presently, more than 300 students across universities in Kenya are pursuing their education through our sponsorship programmes. We have even provided gainful employment to many of these sponsored students after their graduation.

We have initiated other CSR programmes as well. Firstly, medical facilities are a big challenge in Kenya; they are both expensive and largely unavailable. We support cancer and HIV infected patients, both financially and medically. At all our manufacturing locations, we have in-house doctors, where all our employees are consulted and provided medicines free of charges. Notably, we have also extended these medical facilities, free of charge, to the local community as well. Moreover, at Emaili, we have installed a bore well and a water tank, where the Masai cattle quench their thirst every day. We have also been supplying free water to all communities and villages around all our manufacturing locations and plants. Importantly, we also provide free electricity to the school and local communities in the vicinity of our 15 MW thermal power plant in Emali.

Women in Kenya are economically dependent on men. They have deprived of many rights that men are entitled to; hence they become extremely vulnerable on their husband's demise. 'Widows' carry a social stigma, often blamed for their husband's deaths; while others are disowned by their in-laws and in most cases, looked down upon by society. In short, a woman's life becomes miserable on their husband's death. Individually, Neeta and I have been striving hard to financially support widows, but I had a vision of pursuing this imitative in a much wider spectrum.

This dream of mine came true when I was introduced by a common friend to Lord Raj Loomba in London a few years back.

He is a philanthropist, a successful industrialist and a Member of the House of Lords. Well known for his charity and philanthropic activities, he is the founder chairman of The Loomba Foundation, established two decades ago in the United Kingdom. In recognition of his contribution to charity, in 2008, Lord Loomba was appointed as a Commander of the Order of the British Empire (CBE). He received this award from Prince Charles at a ceremony at Buckingham Palace. Loomba Foundation aims at improving the lives of widows and their families around the world.

This is achieved by implementing poverty-reduction strategies and providing educational opportunities to widows and their children, thus giving back to these families the fundamental rights to secure their own future. This Foundation wanted to promote the welfare of widows in Africa, that's how we joined hands and came together. I felt honoured when I was appointed a Trustee of the Foundation for Africa, which has celebrities like Mrs. Cherie Blair, wife of the former British Prime Minister, Tony Blair, and Richard Branson, Founder and Chairman of Virgin Atlantic Airlines. Through Loomba Foundation's Africa's efforts, we are focusing on changing the lives of widows in Kenya by making them self-reliant and independent. We assist them financially to set up kiosks, through which they can trade in essential commodities, earn a livelihood and take care of their families. In case of younger widows, especially those who are able to learn, we provide them with sewing machines to make them self-reliant and financially independent. In Kenya, women-folk in villages have to travel quite a distance to fetch water. In many regions, to overcome this hassle, we have set up bore wells near the communities, so that the women can easily fetch water. So far more than 430 widows across Kenya, especially from the poverty-stricken regions of Kajiado County and Masai Land, have benefitted through our Foundation. Though I have cherished all my philanthropic pursuits, this one gave me immense pleasure.

Along with our Group's CSR programmes, I am associated with a couple of charitable, religious and social organisations that promote human welfare. For a long time, I have been on the Board of Trustees for The International Society for Krishna Consciousness (ISKCON) in Kenya. This global foundation was founded in 1996 by A.C. Bhaktivedanta Swami Prabhupada to promote spirituality, religious culture, education and philanthropy. Under ISKCON's umbrella in Kenya, we undertake various philanthropic and community developmental programmes, in which I am actively involved, especially the daily affairs of the ISKCON temple in Nairobi. One pursuit in which I played a pivotal role was the 'fund-raising cycling activity', that we undertook about sixteen years back.

It was a 300 km cycling expedition from Nyanuki in the Laikipia County to Nairobi. Through this initiative, we raised around Ksh. 20 million (around US$ 200,000), which was a sizeable amount in those days. These funds were contributed to our 'Food for Life (FFL)' programme. The FFL is ISKCON's most important programme. It is the world's largest vegetarian food distribution programme serving millions of free meals daily, with projects in over sixty countries. With roots in the Vaishnava culture of charity and the distribution of food to all, the project is a modern day revival of the ancient culture of hospitality and a belief in the equality of all beings. In Kenya, as part of the FFL, we serve hot meals every afternoon to more than 3,000 children from various slums across the country. I am also on the Board of Trustees for the Down Syndrome Society of Kenya. This Society is part of the Down Syndrome International (DSI), a UK-based international charitable organisation, comprising a membership of individuals and organisations from all over the world, committed to improving the quality of life for people with Down syndrome and promoting their inherent right to be accepted and included as valued and equal members of their communities.

On 7 June 2018, the United States International University (USIU), Africa, officially launched the 'Narendra Raval-Guru Entrepreneurship & Social Innovation Program (ESI)'. Under the one-year structured programme, students aspiring to be future entrepreneurs will be trained. I will be one of the faculty members of the programme. The Devki Group of Companies will entirely sponsor deserving and merited candidates, who lack the financial resources to attend the program.

I believe that the act of 'giving' is part of life and not a project. A project ceases once a goal is achieved; but 'giving' and 'sharing' are continuous and eternal, which I will continue throughout my life. I have inculcated this quality among my children as well, so that it will continue even after I am gone. I also encourage all successful entrepreneurs, industrialists and all the rich and wealthy of the world to be kind, generous and adopt this act of 'giving' in their lives.

• CHAPTER 40 •

BHUJ EARTHQUAKE

Kenya has made me what I am today; it showed me who I am and taught me to stand on my own feet. If today there is a smile on my face, it is because of this country. I owe my growth, success and every happiness to this wonderful land and its loving people. India is my birth country and where I began my life's journey. Though it reminds me of my struggle, pains and poverty, India will also always have a special place in my heart and in my life. Whenever trouble brews or a natural calamity strikes my mother land, especially Gujarat, I get very emotional and consider it my moral obligation to help, support and do whatever best I can for people in their hour of need. Once such incident that shook me up badly, and where I personally tried to contribute was the massive earthquake that hit Bhuj in 2001.

Friday, 26 January 2001, will go down in India's history as a Black Friday. While the entire nation was in a festive mood, celebrating India's fifty-second Republic Day, disaster struck Bhuj. At 08.46 am, one of the worst earthquakes in the world's history, measuring around 7.7 on the Richter scale, rocked the region. The epicentre was about 9mm south–southwest of the village of Chobari in Bhacau Taluka of the Kutch District in Gujarat. The entire region in and around Bhuj was devastated, leaving more than 20,000 dead, 170,000 injured and rendering 400,000 people homeless. More than that, it left the whole nation shell-shocked and in mourning.

That day here in Nairobi, I had just woken up, when news of this tragedy began trickling in. At first my ears could not believe what I had just heard, but was dumbfounded when reality dawned on me. Unable to control my emotions, I broke down for I had deep ties with the town. This was the very place from where I had began my priest's life. There was a massive loss of human lives and property, even our own family home in Morbi was razed to the ground. I was not as financially strong as I am today, but felt that in this hour of need, when the whole world united to support India, it was my duty to contribute whatever best I could. I took the first available flight and reached Ahmedabad in Gujarat. Though I wanted to help, I was unsure of where to begin. So I met my childhood friend, Naranbhai Vadgama, and expressed my desire to do something for the community. Everything was in a mess and we had a tough time reaching Morbi.

While driving from Morbi to Rajkot, we passed through Nasitpar. With a population of not more 2,200, it is a small village at Tankara Taluk in Rajkot District of Gujarat. I was traumatised by what I saw there. Excepting a temple and a couple of dwellings, the entire village was razed to the ground. It was a pitiable sight; with debris lying everywhere, panic-sticken people looking for their families, crying womenfolk, hungry, thirsty and helpless children wailing. This village was cut off from the rest of the world and I decided that if at all I wanted to help, I would do it here in Nasitpar. Without adequate resources and without thinking twice, I made up mind to re-build the entire village, on my own. With folded hands, I looked up for the Lord's blessings, asking for the strength to accomplish this task.

Naranbhai Vadgama and I consulted the villagers and I decided to fund the construction of houses for them. Since I was based in Kenya, I requested my friend, Naranbhai Vadgama, to handle this project on my behalf, which he executed to perfection. We were in constant touch with each other; and he updated me on the progress as I kept remitting funds to him to continue the venture. With Naranbhai's supervision and with support from Narendra Zala, another friend from Morbi, we built twenty-five houses in a record time of four months. Each house contained two rooms, a kitchen, a bathroom, a washroom and a small veranda in the front. Before the end of six months, we handed over the possession of these homes. Considering the substantial loss of life and damages to property, I knew that my contribution was too small, just a drop in the ocean; but every drop matters in the creation of the ocean. This humanitarian initiative gave me immense satisfaction and solace that I was able to contribute something to my land of birth, when it really mattered!

મોરબી નજીકના નસીતપર ગામે કેન્યા સ્થિત દાતા નરેન્દ્રભાઈ રાવલ દ્વારા ભૂકંપગ્રસ્તને બાંધી આપવામાં આવેલા મકાનોની તસવીરો. ઈન્સેટ તસવીર નરેન્દ્રભાઈ રાવલની છે.

મોરબીના નસીતપર ગામે કેન્યા સ્થિત દાતા દ્વારા ભૂકંપગ્રસ્તો માટે ૨૨ મકાનોનું નિર્માણ

રાજકોટ તા. ૧૪: મૂળ મોરબી હાલ નૈરોબી કેન્યામાં દેવકી સ્ટીલ નામની ફેકટરીના માલિક શ્રી નરેન્દ્રભાઈ રમેશચંદ્ર રાવલે ભૂકંપગ્રસ્તો માટે ૨૨ જેટલા મકાનો બનાવવાનો વ્યકિતગત સંકલ્પ કર્યો હતો. જે પૈકી ૧૨ જેટલા મકાનો મોરબીના નસીતપર ગામે બાંધવામાં આવ્યા છે. અને તેનો અર્પણવિધિ તાજેતરમાં કરાયો હતો. બાકી રહેલા મકાનોનું નિર્માણ કાર્ય હાલ ચાલુ છે.

મકાન બાંધી આપવાનું સેવા કાર્ય કરનાર નરેન્દ્રભાઈ રાવલે જણાવ્યું હતું કે, વિનાશક ભૂકંપમાં હજારો લોકોએ જાન અને માલની ખુવારી સહન કરી છે. આ દુઃખની વેળાએ અનેક સંસ્થાઓ અને દાતાઓ આગળ આવ્યા છે, ત્યારે મેં પણ માનવધર્મ બજાવવાં ૨ ૨ મકાનો બાંધી આપવાનો નિર્ણય કર્યો હતો. આ મકાનોમાં બે રૂમ, રસોડું, ઓસરીનું બાંધકામ કરાયું છે.

આ સેવાં કાર્યમાં મોરબીના નરેન્દ્રસિંહ ઝાલા તથા અમદાવાદના નારણભાઈ મિસ્ત્રીએ સહયોગ આપ્યો હતો.

Article that appeared in a Gujarati Daily Newspaper highlight our relief contribution to the Bhuj Earthquake victims at Nasitpar Village.

• CHAPTER 41 •

AWARDS AND ACCOLADES

Over the years, through my continued social services, I have realised that what we get by supporting and helping others is not as important as what we become by achieving these goals. I have always served mankind and supported local communities without expecting anything in return. My experience says that if you are helping someone and expecting something in return, you are doing business and not kindness. However, appreciation or recognition, little or big, will definitely motivate one to keep going. The awards and appreciations that I received during the last few years have kept the flame of service alive in my heart and encouraged me to contribute more. I will always be thankful to the Almighty who has bestowed the honour of serving mankind upon me.

I have shared with you earlier that it is Kenya that has made me what I am today and my contribution to this nation will always continue. I felt blessed when the Kenyan Government awarded me the Elder of the Order of the Burning Spear (EBS), which is the highest award conferred to an individual not associated with any political party or to any government agency. Orders, decorations, and medals of Kenya are awarded by the President of Kenya 'in recognition of outstanding or distinguished services rendered to the nation in various capacities and responsibilities'. Awards are made by the President upon the advice of a National Honours and Awards Committee in the President's office.

Individuals are nominated for awards by district committees, government ministries, religious organisations, non-governmental organisations, individuals and others. I received this award at the hands of the then President of Kenya, His Excellency, the Hon. Mwai Kibaki, on 12 December, Kenya's Independence Day (Jamuri Day) celebrations, during his second term between 2007 and 2012. This was in appreciation of my outstanding and distinguished services rendered to the nation in various capacities and responsibilities plus our contributions to the Kenyan economy through our CSR programmes, and more importantly, the vital role I played in peace-broking after violence erupted in Kenya post the 2007 elections.

For more than a decade now, we have been promoting the welfare of widows and their families, through the Loomba Foundation. In 2012, the British Government honoured me with an award for promoting the welfare of widows in Kenya. I was to receive this award at the hands of the British Prime Minister, David Cameroon. However, due to his prior commitments, he could not attend the award ceremony. On 23 June 2012, at a function held at the British Prime Minister's official residence at 10, Downing Street, London, I had the honour of receiving this prestigious award from the hands of the then British Deputy Prime Minster, the Rt. Hon., Nick Clegg MP. This award meant a lot to me because it was coming from the same country that had refused me an entry visa three-and-half decades ago!

Flanked by British Deputy Prime Minister Rt. Hon. Nick Clegg MP and The Lord Raj Loomba CBE, receiving an award in recognition of my support for widows in Kenya at No. 10 Downing Street in London on 23 June 2012

Lions Clubs International (LCI) is an international secular, non-political service organisation founded by Melvin Jones in 1917. With more than 45,000 local clubs and membership in excess of 1.4 million, it serves in over 200 countries around the world. Headquartered in Oak Brook, Illinois, USA, the organisation aims to meet the needs of communities on a local and global scale. Worldwide, the Lions Clubs recognises outstanding individuals by bestowing on them the Melvin Jones Fellowship Award that is named after its founder, Melvin Jones. This is the highest form of recognition and embodies humanitarian ideas consistent with the nature and purpose of Lionism. In recognition of my services to mankind, I was bestowed this award by the Lions Club of Nakuru in August 2012. This honour has a special place in my heart, for I received this in Nakuru. It was the people of Nakuru who had lovingly given me the title of Guru.

Receiving the Mlevin Jones Fellowship Award from Lions Club of Nakuru, Kenya in August 2012

I have fond memories of my association with Lions International. In 2015, at its annual event of SOL Gold Awards, Lions Club in Mumbai felicitated me with the 'Guru of Entrepreneurs' award for my contribution to the business world. For a person who began his life's journey as a businessman, this meant a lot, especially since I received it in my country of birth—India.

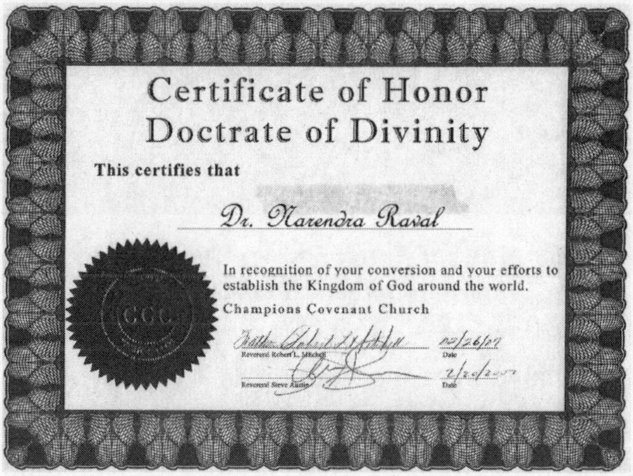

Certificate of Honor
Doctrate of Divinity

This certifies that

Dr. Narendra Raval

In recognition of your conversion and your efforts to establish the Kingdom of God around the world.

Champions Covenant Church

Reverend Robert L. Mitchell — Date

Reverend Steve Austin — Date

Champions Convenant Church, USA, felicitated me with Doctorate of Divinity in recognistion of my services to establish the Kingdom of God around the world.

Receiving the 'Guru of Entrepreneurs' Award from Lions Club International in Mumbai in 2015

These awards have kept me going, but I would like to reiterate that I am working for humanity and not for any applause. Starting from a humble background, I have endured the pains and hardship of poverty. It is my endeavour to give back my best to society till my last breath and beyond.

Proud Moments: Receiving the 'Pride of India' Award from Feelings Multimedia. Ltd, India, at the hands of its Founder and Chairman Mr. Atulbhai Shah and Mr. P.P. Vrajraj Kumarji

PART VI

FAMILY

• CHAPTER 42 •

MY FAMILY

Family is where life begins and love never ends. It has been my lifeline and means the whole world to me. With my family by my side, I have never felt that I am alone. They are always behind me, desiring the best for me and I know they will always be there for me when I need someone to talk to or a helping hand. As a child, my parents and family formed the first relationship. I enjoyed their love and that of my siblings. When I first came to Kenya as a priest, the entire Swaminarayan temple committee with its devotees and fraternity accepted me as one of their own. Even when I returned to Kenya the second time around, the emotional and moral support that I got from all those who treated me as one of their own family, helped me in weathering storms and overcoming my loneliness. Finally, after meeting and marrying Neeta in 1985 and rearing our own family, I have never looked back in life. I am what I am today because of the love, affection, care and support of my family.

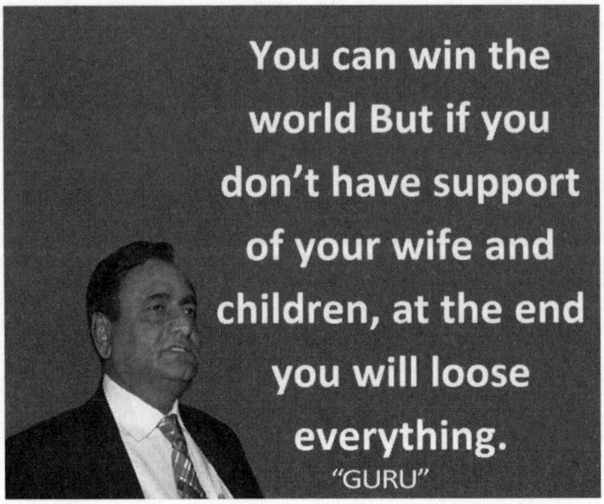

I was fortunate to have Neeta as my fellow traveller in life. After our marriage, we settled down in Kenya. My parents and family were in India; and since I was the eldest in the family, I did not have any older sibling with whom I could share my woes. Though I did have some distant relatives and a few friends, there was really nobody close enough with whom I could communicate, share my frustrations and dreams. It was Neeta, who held my hand, became my friend and offered me a shoulder to cry on. We are more friends than husband and wife. Right from the day we got married, I have shared everything with her, personal or business related. I am an early riser and finish my morning walk before the world awakes! Neeta and I then sit down with our morning tea, talk and discuss things. I have shared all my dreams and visions with her; she has supported me in my decisions and has been equally instrumental in our growth. She is a good friend, loving wife and a caring parent. My life would be incomplete without her.

Neeta and I value our relationship and family bonding much more than the material happiness of this world. We are fortunate to have been blessed with three children—Devang, Tulsi, Devrath—a very loving daughter-in-law, Prakurti, who is more of a daughter to us; and our two little darling grandchildren—Aaryan and Ananya. We have instilled family values in our children, so that they can lead a simple life and survive under all circumstances. The best part of my day is the time that I spend with my family at the dinner table, fostering a bond of unity and togetherness. I have always tutored my children, including my daughter-in-law, to be a good and responsible human being. I have never pressurised them with any strict regulations, nor restricted them from doing anything they wanted to do. As a parent, I am happy that they are mature and responsible enough to understand what is good for them and what is not.

My family: Neeta and I flanked by my son Devang, daughter-in-law Prakurti, granddaughter Ananya with my younger son Devrath, daughter Tulsi and grandson Aaryan in the front

My world begins and ends with my family. In the end, I feel that, 'You can win the world, but if you don't have the support of your wife and children, you lose everything.'

• CHAPTER 43 •

GURU IS GOD'S BLESSING TO ME

It's amazing how we can fall in love with someone we didn't even notice the first time we met them. That's how Guru and my story began. Ours was not 'love at first sight'. When I first met him in May 1985, at the Golden Candle Hotel in Nairobi, I did not have any such feelings for him. Introduced by my uncle, ours was a very brief meeting. I even used to meet him at our home in Thika, when he used to visit our family during his sales visits. Even till such time my feelings remained unchanged. During our first meeting, we had exchanged our telephone numbers. Then he started calling me, and I used to call him back, and that's how our friendship developed. It was my uncle, who first brought up the subject of our relationship and asked my feelings for him. I told him that I liked Guru and that we were good friends, but I also shared that we were too young to decide anything as yet. Gradually, the frequency of our meetings increased; we started opening up to each other and I started liking him more; in a way, I started loving him. Guru was a very easy person to talk to and I could speak about anything and everything with him. He reciprocated his feelings too and that's how our love began.

As we came close to each other, Guru suggested that we join our paths together and get married. I confided our intentions of getting married to my parents; it was then that my mother questioned me in Gujarati, 'તમે કેન્યામાં જન્મે છે અને ઉછેર કરી છે ગુરુ ભારતથી છે, જો ભવિષ્યમાં, તેત્યાં પાછા જવાનું નક્કી કરે, તો શું તમે ભારત ને સ્થાનાં તરિત કરી શકશો [You are born and bred in Kenya. Guru is from India. If in the future, he decides to go back there, will you be able to relocate to India?]' Even Guru had the same concerns; and he asked me if I' d be able to live in a small village like Mathak. It was a matter of my life, so both Guru and my mother advised me not to decide anything in a hurry. They say love is blind and I was deeply in love with Guru. As long as I could marry and share my life with him, I was willing to go anywhere in the world with him.

My parents are very understanding; and my happiness was their only concern. They never asked about Guru's earnings, but only wondered whether he would be able to take care of me and keep me happy. He assured them that he would always keep me happy and never allow a single tear to drop from my eyes. At his assurance, my parents consented to our marriage. Guru then spoke to his parents; and sent our horoscopes to his father. His father confirmed that the horoscopes were in order and both his parents happily consented as well. On 14 July 1985, we got engaged. Guru has kept the promise that he made to my parents. Even after thirty-two years of our marriage, our family's happiness, especially mine, is his top priority. After our engagement, we started going out together. His visits to Thika increased. We enjoyed watching movies at the Fox Drive-in Cinema in Thika with his friends. Finally, on 8 December 1985, we were married at Thika.

Life after marriage was not a bed of roses; we had our own set of challenges and struggles. Guru's parents, who had come for our wedding, returned to India after staying with us for some time. The real challenge began within a few months of our marriage, after Delta Hardware, where Guru was employed, shut down its business. He became jobless; even the car that we drove, belonged to his employers and had to be returned. Suddenly, life changed for us. We had very meagre savings that soon dwindled! We did not have enough money to even buy daily groceries at one go. One day we managed with bread, the next day on vegetables and the third day on milk. Most of the time, we spent indoors, watching television. These were the days when video cassette recorders (VCRs) were in vogue; and we used to borrow movie cassettes from our landlord, Rameshbhai and entertain ourselves. We never informed my parents about our plight, but honestly, this was one of the most difficult periods of our married life. It was his caring nature, understanding and love that kept us going.

My soulmate, best friend and wife, Neeta

With love and togetherness, we can face any challenges that life presents us. I realised this truth when we started our own hardware business, Steel Centre. For weeks together, both of us wandered around looking for a place to start our business to suit our pocket.

Ultimately, we finalised a shop in Gikomba. When we commenced our business, we had only one pick-up van for both business and personal use. Guru used to start his day early by 7.00 am, travelling by public transport, while I used to finish my household chores, drive the pick-up with our lunch boxes. Guru and I worked hand-in-hand. While he managed the shop, I used to drive the pick-up and deliver goods to the clients' shops.

Times when Guru travelled, I managed the business alone. In those days, riots were common in Gikomba and managing a shop alone was not a child's play. But the people around always helped and protected me from any danger. The memories of those times come to me, whenever I happen to visit Gikomba today. We were young and energetic in those days and often worked till late nights, sometimes beyond 8.00 or 9.00 pm. Returning home, I used to cook Guru's favourite meal,'Khichdi' (mishmash of rice and lentils), which he liked to eat every day! We never knew when our day ended; and this went one for about five years. Undoubtedly, it was sheer hard work; but we valued each and every moment of the struggle because we were together. We supplemented and supported each other, more as friends than as life partners.

As a husband, he is a gem of a person; the kind of man every woman would love to have in her life. Though we wanted to have children, I could not conceive for five good years. I was a worried soul; in the Indian culture of the 1980s, a woman unable to convince was looked down upon, it was a social stigma. Guru stood by me during this dilemma and encouraged me to seek the best medical consultation and hospitals in London. At that time, Cromwell Hospital was one of the best centres for IVF treatment, yet expensive, costing around GBP 10,000, which was our entire life's savings at that time. Without a second thought, he agreed and I successfully underwent the treatment in London. A year later, our first son, Devang, was born. Our dream of having a daughter was fulfilled when Tulsi came into our lives in 1998. The Doctor had advised me that conceiving would always be a challenge. As a family, we were happy with Devang and Tulsi; but God had other plans. In 2004, once when Guru had travelled to Congo, I experienced some uneasiness. I called him up and shared this with him. He jokingly suggested that I take a pregnancy test. Believe it or not, I tested positive for pregnancy! It was a miracle. Guru supported me during my pregnancy in 2005 and our 'miracle boy', Devrath, was born and our family was complete.

As a son, he has been a pillar for both mine and his families. For ten years before our marriage, I was residing with my parents and family in Thika. We had a hand-to-mouth life with barely any savings, as my father's earnings were little. After our marriage, he has taken care of my parents, while my two brothers work with him. As for my younger brother, Kaushik, we have brought him up like a son. Guru has also been the backbone of his family. While serving as a priest in Nairobi, he supported his brother Bhavesh's engineering education and his sister, Sangeeta's marriage through his savings. On completing his education, when Bhavesh joined us in Kenya, he taught him all the tricks of the hardware business. Bhavesh's marriage too was a result of Guru's efforts; right from finding his bride till taking care of all his wedding expenses. Later, when Bhavesh expressed his interest in working on his own, he assisted him by setting up a hardware business and his house in Kisumu. Today, Bhavesh has settled down well in life and is successfully managing his own hardware business. A few years back, Guru went a step further and commissioned a steel rolling mill in Addis Abba, which Bhavesh's son, Kishan is managing successfully. He has been instrumental in bringing up both our families. It gives me a great sense of happiness when I see both our parents and families smiling because of him!

As a businessman and entrepreneur, he is a blend of exceptional leadership skills. If there is any person in this world who can vouch for his business acumen, it's me, for I have been a witness to his exponential growth from being a small hardware trader in Gikomba to a steel tycoon in Africa. He is bold, courageous, fearless, a risk taker; a man with big dreams and visions. Coming from a non-business background, I had absolutely no business experience whatsoever. So initially, when he shared his big ideas and plans, I was concerned about his risk-taking capabilities and business decisions. Gradually, as we progressed and succeeded, I realised his vision and accepted his decisions, and to a certain extent, became a risk-taker myself. Initially, it was our dream to own a house, have a couple of cars and lead a decent life.

I never imagined that we would reach where we are today. It is only because of his vision, sheer hard work and persistence that we have achieved this milestone in our life. One important secret of our success, I must admit, is our joint decision making. Guru has always consulted in before taking any step or making a decision. For more than three decades, it has been his everyday practise to spend time with me in the evenings, share his business plans and what he intended to do next. Together, we weigh the pros and cons, only then does he decide the way forward. I had faith in his decisions and have always supported him. It is God's grace that whichever business he has ventured in so far, success has always followed him. There is no decision that he takes without consulting me, be it personal or professional. That's how our love and bonding has been all these years.

Guru has been more of a friend than a husband to me. He is my God's greatest blessings. It was our life's most beautiful moment, when we decided to share our hearts and lives together. Our marriage was the most wonderful thing to have happened to us.

Neeta Narendra Raval

• CHAPTER 44 •

NEXT TO GOD, THY PARENTS

What I am today is because of my parents…

Both my parents are very supportive of all of us, especially of me because of the medical challenges that I faced during my younger days. We are fortunate to have a father like mine; we mean a lot to him. He is so sensitive when it comes to our sickness, that he leaves the entire business world aside, just to be with us. As a child, I underwent a painful surgery of my legs in Chennai, India, and he sacrificed his business interests for me. He shut down all the operations for three months, just to be with me. His presence worked wonders for me. The best moments that I have cherished with him are of those when he used to sit and enjoy coffee and Kit Kat with me.

The education phase is the most challenging one for any student and it was so for me as well. Both my parents have morally supported me. My mother ensured that I got admission in the best of universities. There came a time in my educational career when I had decided to give up; it was my father who encouraged me to continue and not to give up. My father guides us in each and everything we do; he spends quality time with us every day. He has been instrumental in assisting me through all phases in my life; he is understanding, caring and an excellent parent. What I am today is because of them; both my parents are my real God.

Devang Narendra Raval
(Eldest Son)

My elder son Devang and daughter-in-law Prakurti with our grandchildren Aaryan and Ananya

My 'Mom' and 'Dad' mean more than my own parents…

Before marriage, every girl desires getting into a family that will love and care for her more than her own parents. I am blessed with this dream becoming a reality. Ours was a traditionally arranged marriage; I met Devang and Mom for the first time in Ahmadabad, India. In our first meeting, Mom made me feel comfortable and at ease. I knew that I had found the right home for the rest of my life when Devang and I got married three years ago.

I was born and bred in India, totally unaware of the life and culture in Kenya. When I first arrived here after our marriage, I had lots of questions—what would the lifestyle be like? Would I get Indian food? Would there be Indians around? The list was endless. Though Mom and Dad accepted me as their daughter from the day I stepped into this family, I was worried about adjusting to the life here. In the first year of our marriage, I felt like returning to India! Every day both Mom and Dad used to sit and counsel me. It was during this tenure that I came close to both of them. My every demand finds a positive response from them. It was their love, care and affection that made me forget my worries forever! Dad is so friendly that I converse with him more than I used to with my own father; Mom is a very modern and understanding lady, unlike a traditional Indian mother. She is so friendly, accommodative and supportive that I feel very close to her. Honestly, I am closer and spend more time with her than with my husband, Devang!

I am privileged to be a part of this family; both Mom and Dad are more than my own parents.

Prakurti Devang Raval
(Daughter-in-law)

The best gift my Dad has given us is his 'time'...

Both my parents are close to all of us. The best part of our life is the family get-together that we have every day when my Dad returns from his office and starts having fun with us, totally forgetting his business. He has taught us to stay united as a family.

We have all our meals together, especially over weekends when the entire family enjoys time together. Family unity and bonding is the most important lesson that he has taught us. He always shares with us that 'the family that prays and dines together, stays together'.

My daughter Tulsi

My Dad is a busy person; despite his hectic business schedule, he always takes out time for us. The biggest contribution that he has made to our family, the biggest gift he has given us is his time. Caring and loving as he is, we appreciate his efforts to make time for us. We are all blessed to have such wonderful parents.

Tulsi Narendra Raval
(Daughter)

My parents are the most important people in this world to me...

God has blessed me with two unbelievably loving, caring, attentive and devoted parents, who are always there for all of us. My Dad always says 'yes' to everything I ask for. He never says 'no'. My parents are the most important people in the world to me.

My younger son Devrath

Devrath Narendra Raval

(Youngest Son)

CONCLUSION

MY LEGACY

I have come a long way in life—a journey that I started from India as a seventeen-year-old Brahmin priest, culminated in East Africa's industrial world of steel, cement, infrastructure and aviation. These four decades of my journey that I began with big dreams and empty pockets, have neither been a bed of roses nor a mid-summer night's dream. God has filled my life with all the colours *He* could possibly fill it life with—poverty, starvation, struggle, frustration, failure, loneliness, love, smiles, tears, jealousy and, finally, success. Today, at the peak of my successful business career, after I found myself in *Forbes Africa's Who's Who List*, people attribute my success to good fortune. Very few, however, acknowledge the hardwork, pain and struggle that I had endured as a twenty-five-year-old when I started my career as a hardware trader from Gikomba, where no Asian had ever dared to enter in the 1980s, and many think twice before doing so even today!

Education is the key to a successful career and eventually to a good life. Lives of successful professionals like doctors, engineers, accountants and bankers, bear testimony to the fact that education leads to a good career. Yet there are millions of youth like me, who struggle with their education, and aspire to become businessmen, entrepreneurs and industrialists, and succeed in their lives.

As I head to the closing pages of my life's story, I would like to share the secret of my success and leave behind my legacy for today's youth, especially those of you who want to venture out on your own, start your own business or manufacturing industry, script your own destiny and succeed in life. Here's my piece of advice to you for becoming a successful entrepreneur…

Nothing is impossible in this world for a willing heart and determined mind. The limitation is in our minds. If someone like me—with so little formal education, but a lot of common sense and determination—can become a steel tycoon with more than 4,000 employees in his fold, then anyone can achieve whatever he truly desires. I am reminded of the achievements of the thirty-year-old sportswoman from India, Arunima Sinha. She was a national level volleyball player who was pushed from a running train by miscreants in 2011, while resisting their assault. As a result, one of her legs had to be amputated below the knee. Her aim was to climb the highest peaks of all the continents and plant the Indian national flag on each summit. In the hospital, when she found herself still alive after her amputation, she reasoned that God must have kept her alive for a reason. So she resolved to achieve her dream of climbing all the highest peaks around the world. As I write, she has already scaled the five peaks of Everest in Asia, Kilimanjaro in Africa, Elbrus in Europe, Kosciuszko in Australia and Aconcagua in Argentina. If a differently-abled individual can achieve such a colossal feat, what stops you from realising your dreams of becoming all that you wish to become? Nothing is impossible in this world!

Moreover, when you pursue your education in an institution, all that you probably gain is a theoretical knowledge of life. When you qualify in your examinations, you still have no practical experience of how a business is run or managed. So I suggest, before jumping into your own business, work in a business house or industry, so that you can gain an insight into the business. If you venture out on your own without obtaining any practical training or experience, chances of failure are bright. During your training or internship, always keep the vision of setting up your own venture in mind. Ensure that you learn all the tricks of the trade at your work, so that when you eventually start out on your own, you are better placed to make the right decisions.

Remember, entrepreneurs or corporate leaders are not the only ones who set up their own businesses. Many of us have the ability to run an enterprise, but lack the capital or resources to venture out on our own. This does not mean that such people are not entrepreneurs. Take up an employment, utilise your skills in fields like production, marketing or finance, thus benefitting both the organisation you work for as well as yourself! You can earn handsomely too.

Have a 'dream' or a 'vision', whether you are a 'working entrepreneur' or you run your own business, and stay focused on it. It does not matter where you begin from, you might even start as a clerk, as long as you stay focused on your vision. I started my career as a priest, yet ventured into business. Never lose focus on your vision and strive hard to accomplish your goals.

Keep your focus on money. Think practically and understand the importance of money and its worth in your lives. This is the modern age, where people view what you have rather than what you are. If you don't have money, people will never recognise you. The incident at Rajkot, where we were chased away by a shopkeeper because we did not have money to dine in a restaurant, left a permanent impression in my mind. Today, even forty-five years after this incident, my focus on earning has not diluted. While earning money, I have taken care of thousands of others, to ensure that they do not experience the same suffering that I experienced that day. By saying this, I am not over emphasising the importance of money; but I believe that being born in a poor family or as a poor person is a matter of our destiny, which we have no control on, but if we die poor, then it is our mistake and not the Creator's fault. So while studying or working in a business, stay competitive and focused, lest you get thrown out by competition.

My advice to entrepreneurs aspiring to step into manufacturing or an industry…

Though I started my career as a hardware trader, I carved out a niche for myself when we leapt into manufacturing. The traits that one requires to be a trader or an industrialist are more or less the same, but there are certain peculiar qualities or factors associated with any particular industry that I have experienced and would like to share with you.

Stress often sets in, if we undertake any project that we don't like or care about. Always undertake a project that you love or are passionate about, be it your maiden venture or the tenth one! Once you decide on your project, don't do it just for the sake of doing it. Immerse yourself fully into the entire gamut of the industry, right from the initial paper work and sourcing of raw materials to the production, marketing, sales and credit collection. In short, get into the entire business cycle. Then and only then you will be successful and nobody will be able to take you for a ride. If you do not do this, you will be limiting your chances of growth and success.

Asses the nature of your project before venturing into it; avoid projects that have challenges from the inception, which are likely to land you in troubled waters! Never take up projects that have litigation issues or are likely to face environmental problems. Similarly, if you perceive one as high risk or expect public resistance or volatility, never step into it. If you venture into such a project despite knowing the risks, chances of your failure are high, leading to loss of your hard-earned resources permanently.

The world of accounting has given us a vital concept of conservatism. The convention of conservatism, also known as the doctrine of prudence in accounting is a policy of anticipating possible future losses but not future gains. This policy tends to understate rather than overstate net assets and net income, and therefore lead companies to play safe. It's through my experience, I advise you as new entrants or as existing industrialists to be cautious in your planning and projections if you want to grow and succeed. While submitting your figures to your bankers or financial institutions, ensure that you adopt this principle of conservatism and that you can achieve them. This is the first step of securing your future finances and meeting your financial obligation in time.

Once you commence manufacturing, ensure that the product meets the industry standards or are superior. Customer service holds the key to your continuity, so offer nothing but the best service to your customers. More importantly, make sure that your obligations to your bankers, financial institutions and suppliers are met on or before they fall due. These three factors are vital to your continuity, growth and success.

If your project, industry or trading business is sizeable, then hire professionals into your team; don't depend on quacks and avoid the 'Yes Bosses'. Hire the ones who are well qualified, experienced, with high integrity and honesty, fearless and courageous, so that they can present you with the true picture, instead of cooking information to please you. At times, even the most courageous employees break down under pressure. To avoid such situations, ensure that communication lines are free flowing and open right from the lowest rung to the top. Even if yours is a big organisation, develop close ties with your staff right from the grassroots level, for the right information at all times, which will help in improving your business or industry.

Once you have established yourself, don't rest on your laurels. Focus on growth, expansion, betterment, quality or process improvisation through automisation and cost reduction. This is a competitive world with no room for complacency. If complacency sets in, you will either be left behind or left out. However, while planning for growth and expansion, ensure that you take care of your existing business as well.

Most importantly, monitor your progress microscopically; ensure a firm grip on your finances. The moment you find that your business is not faring well or that your financials are not healthy, start taking precautionary measures immediately without waiting for things to go from bad to worse. Take steps to cease all your recurring expenses, begin repaying your loans and borrowings. This will aid in reducing your overheads and minimising your losses. If your venture doesn't fare well at any point in time, don't prolong your decision to close down operations. Remember, the longer you take to decide, the bigger will be your pile of losses!

While embarking on a project, ensure that you have a continuous process of research and development in place. If at any stage you perceive that the project is not feasible, or that you've erred in your assessments, initiate immediate action to cease all activities; and limit your losses and do not continue investing in it any more. Quick decision making based on your study is the key. In 2011, as part of our backward integration process as well as to utilise our available local resources and to minimise our dependency on the international market for the supply of core raw materials, I decided to construct a clinker manufacturing plant in Emali, Kenya. The project was expected to cost us around US$ 225 million. We commenced work on the project, incurring more than US$ 50 million in civil works, when warning bells began to ring. Our site engineers informed me that there were no deposits of limestone near our plant site, which is the key ingredient for clinkers. My heart sank! I weighed my options, took an immediate decision to stop the project. I decided that the burden of losing US$ 50 million was better than losing US$ 225 million!

We stopped work on the project, cancelled all civil contracts and released all site workers. About 7-8 months later, one of our senior employees, Mr. Swamy, who was instrumental in installing our first grinding mill, approached me with a second opinion on the project. I interact with him on a daily basis, and so trusting his experience and instincts, I decided to reconsider it. We held detailed deliberations and brainstorming sessions before we agreed to hire professional consultants to undertake a research on our behalf. We retained the services of a firm from southern India, Vasudha Laboratories, at an investment of around US$ 100,000. Much to my relief, their research confirmed that there was adequate limestone in the region and we could resume work on our clinker plant. Once I was assured of this, we resumed our work. We then approached the World Bank's International Finance Corporation (IFC) and other banks for funding our project. The IFC said that they would only consider funding us if we got our data on the limestone reserves tested by Holtech, a reputed global consultancy firm. We agreed and appointed Holtech for the same. While they began their research, we resumed work on our project. After a wait of more than 7-8 months, and incurring more than US$ 400,000, we presented a detailed report to the IFC confirming that there were adequate limestone reserves in the region and that the project was good to go. Though we had approvals from other commercial banks, we decided to stay with the IFC for this project. We successfully completed the plant and in June 2017, commenced production for the best quality clinker!

What I am trying to drive home here is that there is no substitute for research and development when you commence a project; and if it is not viable, don't continue further investments and suffer more losses.

My advice to entrepreneurs aspiring to become traders…

Beginning my career as a hardware trader and becoming the biggest one in less than five years, I have a fair grasp of the trading business. The factors that I have shared above also hold good for traders. However, trading has some salient features that I would like to share with you.

As a new entrepreneur, you are a fresh starter and unaware of how a business is managed. No pain, effort or experience is ever wasted. This holds good for any business. So once you start any business and manage it for one or two years, you will have gained a reasonable understanding of the tricks of the trade. Then you can consider venturing into a business that suits your vision, experience and style.

Commence business with your own capital or resources, howsoever small it may be. Manage your business with your own funds and experience for a year at least, till you are confident and capable of taking risks. Then borrow moderately, but never over borrow. For example, if you start with you own capital of around US$ 10,000 and then at the end of the first year, you can assess your performance and can borrow up to US$ 20,000–40,000. Many aspiring youngsters feel that it is easy to start a business with borrowed funds, so that tomorrow if they fail, nothing is at stake or they have nothing to lose. My experience says that if you depend heavily on borrowing, then in a falling market, prospects of your business collapsing are highest! This axiom applies to industries as well.

Many years back I came across a very meaningful board displayed at a retailer's shop. It read, 'We believe in God and rest in cash'. Initially when you begin, apply this rule to your business as well. If you want to offer a credit facility, then offer it those with good credibility and standing in the business. Never offer credit facilities to strangers. Before deciding to allow a credit facility to anyone, perform a profile or background check and undertake a reasonable 'know your customer' (KYC) exercise. A little precaution and care before allowing a credit can save lots of stress, energy, efforts and resources later on. Nevertheless, if you do want to help beginners by offering them credit, fix a credit limit considering that there may be delays in receiving your funds or even the risk of not receiving them at all.

My advice commonly applicable to entrepreneurs aspiring to become traders or industrialists

Experience says that whenever you are presented with an opportunity to expand or grow, or to increase your revenues, and if you have resources like time, capital, knowledge and experience at your disposal, then grab them with both hands. Opportunities never knock on your door twice. There is a famous saying in Gujarati, લક્ષ્મી જયેર ચંદો કરેવા અવે તારે મોડો ધોવા ના જાવેય '(When fortune knocks on your door, you welcome it and don't turn your back.)' This has been one of the most important factors in my success. Whenever opportunities have come my way, I have always accepted them with both hands; I have weighed their pros and cons and implemented them without wasting any time.

BUSINESS LESSON LEARNT

It is said, 'Vision is the art of seeing what is invisible to others'. This holds true in business as well. Focus clearly on the profit that you expect from your venture, even if others are unable to do so. Let me share an interesting and intriguing lesson that I learnt way back in 1981, when I lived in Morbi, Gujarat. Exactly opposite to our house, there was a small charcoal trader with a small yard for retailing coal. The trader followed a fixed daily routine. A truck would deliver around 100 bags of coal every morning at his open yard, where he and his son (who was of my age) would sit on two small stones and sell the charcoal in small quantities to customers, weighing the coal in buckets. Generally, before sunset they would have sold their entire merchandise. Every afternoon, between 2:00–4:00 PM, when the trader went out for lunch, his son managed the business. At times during this lunch break, keen on understanding the business, I would sit in the yard with the trader's son, watching him go about his work. Having a sharp business mind, I noticed that they sold coal at Rs 40 per kg, which was exactly their cost price, and wondered how it was possible to trade without profit. After observing this for two weeks, one afternoon, I questioned the trader. He smiled and said, 'Son, come back this evening when we wind up, and you will have your answer.' Around 5:30 PM that evening, curious to know the answer, I reached their coal yard. I saw that at day's end, a truck arrived again; but this time to collect the empty coal bags, and the trader was offered Rs 2 per bag. In total, Rs 200 for his 100 bags. That was when it dawned on me that Rs 200 was their profit. I had my answer! What I want to drive home here is that, have a clear vision of the profits that you want to make, even though it may not be visible to others.

Like in life, business is also a mixed bag of ups and downs, good and turbulent times. It is during the downturns that we have to be exceptionally brave and courageous, otherwise they can prove disastrous for our existing business. Many times in my career, adverse circumstances have challenged me, but I have bravely weathered all storms. Let me share a recent incident from a couple of months back, to illustrate my point.

For the past twelve years, we have been operating a steel rolling mill in the Democratic Republic of Congo (DRC) with the blessings of their country's President. We made this investment because there were no major steel mills in the Katanga region and because it would immensely benefit the nation with steel at relatively cheaper prices for building their infrastructure economically. In the last four or five years, other steel mills have begun operations too. No doubt we have braved many minor ups and downs, but recently we faced a major challenge. A couple of months back, a 30 km railway line was vandalised in the country and it was believed that the stolen line was sold as a scrap to the steel mills in the region. To investigate the matter and bring the culprits to book, all the steel mills in the region, including ours, were ordered to shut down their operations, under the President's directive. I was upset by this step, as our Group policy is never to buy such vandalised material and nor to encourage other steel mills to do so. In all our plants, we have a thorough system to ensure that we do not receive such stolen material.

We always support a country's development; and would never generate revenues by destroying a nation's infrastructure. Though I share a very personal and cordial relationship with the DRC's President, I did not approach him for any favours in this regard. Instead, we formally communicated our Group's business principles and ethics with the concerned authorities. We shut down our operations, released all of our 500 employees, including expatriates, and supported the Government in carrying out their investigation. In was only recently in July 2017, that they concluded their investigation, gave us a clean chit and we resumed our operations once more.

The investigations had revealed that the stolen railway line had been smuggled out of the country and sold in Zambia, where it had already been melted down. Over the years, we had written to the Government multiple times, requesting for a permanent ban on exports of iron and steel scrap from the Congo. The fact is that scrap is sold at around US$ 150 per tonne in Congo, while it fetches around US$ 300 per tonne in neighbouring countries, thus encouraging vandalism and smuggling. This was one of the lowest points in my career as an industrialist. What I want to advice you is that whenever you pass through such low times in your business career, be a brave fighter and battle it till the end. If you are not at fault, it is your right to challenge an unfair situation; and if you have wronged, then too, be bold and brave enough to own up to such a responsibility.

These practical guidelines for succeeding as a trader or an industrialist are all based on my personal experiences in the world of commerce and industry, and not drawn from any management textbook. I leave you with my legacy of success, trusting that whatever I have achieved so far, wherever I have reached today, will inspire you to make the change that you want to see in yourself; and will motivate you to chase your dreams and succeed in life.

My life's journey continues, there is still much more to be done and achieved; the destination it still a distance away. Like Robert Frost put it so beautifully:

The woods are lovely, dark and deep,
But I have promises to keep,
And miles to go before I sleep,
And miles to go before I sleep.